The Decolonization of Knowledge

In 2015, students at the University of Cape Town used the slogan #RhodesMustFall to demand that a monument of Cecil John Rhodes, the empire builder of British South Africa, be removed from the university campus. Soon students at Oxford University called for the removal of a statue of Rhodes from Oriel College. The radical idea of decolonization that was at the forefront of these student protests continues to be a key element in South African educational institutions as well as those in Europe and North America. This book explores the uptake of decolonization in the institutional curriculum, given the political demands for decolonization on South African campuses, and the generally positive reception of the idea by university leaders. Based on interviews with more than 200 academic teachers at 10 universities, this is an innovative account of how institutions have engaged with, subverted, and transformed the decolonization movement since #RhodesMustFall.

JONATHAN D. JANSEN is Distinguished Professor of Education at Stellenbosch University and President of the Academy of Science of South Africa. He is a curriculum theorist, and his research is concerned with the politics of knowledge. His recent publications include *Fault Lines: A Primer on Race, Science and Society* (2020), *Learning under Lockdown: Voices of South Africa's Children* (2020), and *Learning Lessons* (2021).

CYRILL A. WALTERS is a Research Fellow in Higher Education at Stellenbosch University. She also teaches on the MBA programme at Stellenbosch University Business School. She is currently engaged in projects examining decolonization within South African universities, the intersection of race and gender in higher education, and complexity theories in leadership.

The Decolonization of Knowledge

Radical Ideas and the Shaping of Institutions in South Africa and Beyond

JONATHAN D. JANSEN
Stellenbosch University

CYRILL A. WALTERS
Stellenbosch University

CAMBRIDGE
UNIVERSITY PRESS

CAMBRIDGE
UNIVERSITY PRESS

University Printing House, Cambridge CB2 8BS, United Kingdom

One Liberty Plaza, 20th Floor, New York, NY 10006, USA

477 Williamstown Road, Port Melbourne, VIC 3207, Australia

314–321, 3rd Floor, Plot 3, Splendor Forum, Jasola District Centre,
New Delhi – 110025, India

103 Penang Road, #05–06/07, Visioncrest Commercial, Singapore 238467

Cambridge University Press is part of the University of Cambridge.

It furthers the University's mission by disseminating knowledge in the pursuit of
education, learning, and research at the highest international levels of excellence.

www.cambridge.org
Information on this title: www.cambridge.org/9781316514184
DOI: 10.1017/9781009082723

First published 2022

A catalogue record for this publication is available from the British Library.

Library of Congress Cataloging-in-Publication Data
Names: Jansen, Jonathan D., author. | Walters, Cyrill, author.
Title: The decolonization of knowledge : radical ideas and the shaping of institutions in
    South Africa and beyond / Jonathan D. Jansen, Cyrill A. Walters.
Description: Cambridge, United Kingdom ; New York, NY : Cambridge University Press,
    2022. | Includes bibliographical references and index.
Identifiers: LCCN 2021056972 (print) | LCCN 2021056973 (ebook) | ISBN 9781316514184
    (hardback) | ISBN 9781009077934 (paperback) | ISBN 9781009082723 (epub)
Subjects: LCSH: Rhodes, Cecil, 1853-1902–Public opinion. | University of Cape Town. |
    Education, Higher–Social aspects–South Africa. | Decolonization–South Africa. | Curriculum
    change–South Africa. | Racism in higher education–South Africa. | Student movements–South
    Africa. | BISAC: POLITICAL SCIENCE / American Government / General
Classification: LCC LC191.98.S59 J36 2022 (print) | LCC LC191.98.S59 (ebook) | DDC
    378.68–dc23/eng/20220217
LC record available at https://lccn.loc.gov/2021056972
LC ebook record available at https://lccn.loc.gov/2021056973

ISBN 978-1-316-51418-4 Hardback
ISBN 978-1-009-07793-4 Paperback

Contents

Figures

Acknowledgements

This book would not have been possible without the generous contributions of time, expertise, and insights from more than 200 academics across the 10 universities who were interviewed for this study. An additional word of gratitude must go to the ten scholars who provided additional time and documentation for use in developing the case studies of decolonization-in-practice in the humanities/social sciences and engineering/natural sciences. A special word of thanks to our academic editor, William Daniels, for his extraordinary knowledge, expertise, and patience in editing various versions of the manuscript. We owe continued gratitude to Sarie Wilbers, the education librarian at Stellenbosch University, for bringing together hard-to-find bibliographic resources, and to Graeme Mehl for technical and design support on various aspects of the writing.

1 | Introduction

The Decolonization of Knowledge – Radical Ideas and the Settled Curriculum

1.1 Introduction

How does a radical idea make its way through an institution? This is the novel question at the heart of this study of curriculum change at a historic moment in one country, when a profoundly radical idea came to command the attention of twenty-six public institutions of higher education. That radical idea was decolonization, which bannered student protests in South African universities in 2015–2016. The national protest movement had two banners, in fact: one focused on decolonization, and the other on free higher education. At some point in the struggle, those two ideas came together in a rousing student slogan demanding "a free, decolonized education."

The focus of this study is on the element of decolonization, so visibly expressed in the public removal of the prominent bronze statue of the imperial figure Cecil John Rhodes on the campus of the University of Cape Town (UCT); other scholarly texts from this period have attended to the question of free higher education (Booysen 2016; Habib 2019).

While the press for decolonization in South Africa was a broad one – demanding changes to institutional cultures (seen as too exclusive), complexions (seen as too white), and curriculum (seen as too European) – this inquiry further limits itself to the third element: the decolonization of (curricular) knowledge. It also takes on the decolonization of knowledge as an institutional problem, rather than as a study of the curriculum on its own terms, such as, for example, changes to the physics or sociology curricula.

1.2 The Backdrop to the Charge of a Colonized Curriculum

South Africa's educational institutions are products of colonial rule, segregation, and apartheid. The elite English schools in South Africa were once regarded as "nurseries of imperial patriotism" (Lambert 2004, 67; see also Jansen and Kriger 2020, 106–109). Mahmood Mamdani (2019, 16) offers the timely reminder that "the institutional form of the modern African university did not derive from precolonial institutions; the inspiration was the colonial modern."

Over the centuries, Dutch and English colonial regimes changed hands as settlers became natives through the years of segregation (from 1910) and the coming to power of the apartheid government (from 1948). And yet, to this day colonialism casts a long shadow over all educational institutions – expressed most durably in things such as the pre-eminence of the English language in teaching and learning – despite nominal commitments to a multilingualism that recognizes the neglected indigenous languages of South Africa.

Therefore, when student activists trained their eyes on the prominent statue of Cecil John Rhodes on the lower flights of the Jameson steps at the University of Cape Town, it was that visible symbolism of colonial power that attracted political attention. Yet those same student leaders recognized that the downing of the Rhodes statue was simply the start of a decolonization imperative that needed to shift focus to the invisible and more troubling legacies of the past, such as institutional cultures and the problem of knowledge.

The curriculum in its simplest definition is a codification of knowledge that is assigned value and legitimacy through well-established institutional processes, such as the external accreditation of professional bodies and the internal validation of academic senates. Whether it is the anatomy curriculum in the medical sciences or the anthropology curriculum in the social sciences, that codified knowledge has a history and a legacy expression in the present (Jansen and Walters 2020a).

The fingerprints of colonial epistemologies (or theories of knowledge) remain visible in matters ranging from the resilience of racial science in disciplinary curricula to Eurocentric accounts of knowledge in virtually every field of inquiry (Jablonski 2020; Saini 2020). It was perhaps inevitable that at some point there would be a robust political response to the knowledge problem in South Africa, and that came through in the demands of protesting students in 2015 to decolonize the curriculum.

Not that the emergence of the decolonization moment in South Africa happened in isolation from worldwide currents of discontent with legacy knowledge from the colonial period. Almost from the start of #RhodesMustFall in 2015, the movement in South Africa inspired students at the University of Oxford to call for the removal of another Rhodes statue, but they were rebuffed at the time. Five years later, in the wake of a worldwide movement inspired by the horrific police killing of a Black man in the United States, George Floyd, Oriel College (Oxford) indicated that it would remove the memorial of the British imperialist from the façade of its Rhodes Building.

The murder of Floyd further re-energized the Black Lives Matter movement, bringing down Confederate statues in the American South, the statues of slaveholders Edward Colston in Bristol and Robert Milligan in London, as well as statues of the rapacious King Leopold II in Belgium.

International protests, however, went beyond the removal of colonial-era monuments. For example, students at British universities called for the study of more inclusive texts that represented authors and literatures outside of the dominant West. A student movement at University College London made popular the slogan, "why is my curriculum white?" (Peters 2018), and a University of Exeter lecturer explained that "while decolonising the curriculum can mean different things, it includes a fundamental reconsideration of who is teaching, what the subject matter is and how it's being taught" (Muldoon 2019).

For the University of Victoria, in Canada, decolonization is concerned with "the effect of colonization on higher education and liberating the curriculum and wider university culture from selective narratives" (James 2020). In countries such as New Zealand and Australia, the case for decolonization was made in relation to the marginalization of the knowledges of First Peoples, such as Aborigines or Maoris, on the curriculum (Moeke-Pickering 2010; Harvey and Russell-Mundine 2019) .

In the wake of student protests around the world, decolonization would come to constitute a thematic focus for academic articles, for example, "Decolonising Curricula and Pedagogy in Higher Education" (Morreira et al. 2020) and to occupy special sections of established journals, such as "Dance and Decolonisation in Africa" (Kabir and Djebbari 2019) in the *Journal of African Cultural Studies* – quite apart from journals dedicated wholly to the subject, such as *Decolonization: Indigeneity, Education & Society*.

By the end of the second decade of the century, decolonization was firmly on the social and educational agendas in several countries around the world, casting a critical light on schools and universities as both the problem (for reproducing colonial epistemologies) and the solution (by transforming inherited knowledge systems).

The purpose of this book, however, is less about making the case for the decolonization of the curriculum and more about tracing the course of this radical idea as it made its way through higher education institutions. In fact, one of the key weaknesses of the expansive literature on decolonization is its exhortatory excesses, while there are relatively few systematic studies of how such a radical idea is received, encountered, and transformed within the daily churn of institutional life. In short, what actually happens to decolonization when it marches onto campuses and demands changes to the institutional curriculum?

1.3 Approach

Our broad approach to the study of decolonization is anchored in an intellectual tradition that can be described as *the politics of knowledge*. The starting point for this approach is that knowledge – its origins, nature, purposes, and consequences – is never neutral. Knowledge does not emerge from thin air; it is actively produced through social processes that involve human actors. Those who produce knowledge are those with the social power to lend legitimacy to knowledge, whether it is the scientist in a laboratory, the scholar in the library, or the software engineer in a technology company.

Even a cursory review of history will reveal that some people's knowledge matters more than others'. The knowledge of indigenous communities with strong oral traditions matters much less than the knowledge of the scientist in a prominent university. Those are not natural outcomes of the status of knowledge; those hierarchies of knowledge are produced and legitimated through visible and invisible social processes. The scientist typically generates knowledge through significant funding in well-resourced laboratories and highly skilled research teams; that knowledge is reviewed by peers, published in journals, and its significant findings are translated into policy directives (e.g., housing mandates) or concrete products (e.g., vaccines). By contrast, the traditional healer in a marginal community has little access to resources or the authority to transform local knowledge into powerful benefits for her community – let alone to export that indigenous knowledge across national borders for purposes of global consumption.

In recent history, Western countries colonized poor countries, from Africa to Asia and Latin America, and extracted material resources that were processed in the rich nations and returned to the developing world as products for purchase. Some argue that such economic transactions were mirrored in intellectual transactions, in which ideas and resources from southern nations (e.g., plant species, indigenous artworks) came to populate the large botanical gardens of the richer countries (Schiebinger and Swan 2007), as well as their national museums and galleries (Chick and Brown 2019). Southern scholars have therefore argued that even though colonial rule as a political and historical event might have ended, postcolonial influences are still felt in the unequal distribution of ideas, resources, and expertise between the global north and the global south. Decolonial scholars from Latin America, for example, have argued that these forms of "epistemic injustice" continue to be reflected in whose knowledge gets vindicated in the curriculum and how such knowledge (pedagogy) is transmitted in the classroom. Ann Stoler (2016), for example, speaks of "the imperial durabilities of our times."

It is not simply that knowledge is unequally produced between the rich former colonial powers and the poor former colonies. It is also the fact that indigenous knowledge is marginalized, ignored, and even suppressed. When archaeologists from the North enter communities to study ancient ruins or distant cultures, they bring with them particular frames of understanding and methods of operation that privilege their own prior knowledge, rather than the knowledge of indigenous communities (see Chapter 7). When colonial authorities impressed French or English or Portuguese on the curriculum of a diverse group of African schools (and universities), they ensured that *to this day* knowledge is mostly produced, engaged, and understood through the languages of empire. A succession of nationalist initiatives (or promises) to change the knowledge of intellectual exchange and transaction have failed dismally – a reality reflected in the library holdings on university campuses and prescribed texts in primary and secondary education.

It is not, however, as if there has been no knowledge produced or texts generated by academics in the South. Nor is it the case that scholars from the North have not produced texts critical of a history of domination and subjugation with respect to the state of the curriculum (Jansen 2019). Yet the question remains: whose knowledge comes to enjoy prominence in the curriculum? It is to this question that the curriculum theorist Michael Apple offers insight through what he calls "the selective tradition" in curriculum studies.

What does this mean? That when the universe of knowledge is available for teaching and learning, there are social processes that actively select for privileged knowledge at the expense of marginalized knowledge. While the decision makers might rationalize their selections in relation to practical concerns, such as the limited time available in a crowded curriculum or the shortage of resources for a more expansive curriculum, the reality is that students are much more likely to learn about the knowledge of the powerful than of the marginalized. To take one example only, long after the end of colonial rule, students in the colonies were more likely to learn of European conflicts (such as World Wars I and II) from the perspective of the Europeans and in the language of the Europeans than the other way round. This is no accident of history; it is a product of selection bias and the unequal distribution of knowledge and power.

What this means is that knowledge of the marginalized is not only "selected out," but that *particular* images of subordinate groups are "selected in." A number of recent studies have demonstrated how stereotypical, and even racist, images of despised groups still appear in university curricula, as well as in published research (Jansen 2019; Jansen and Walters 2020b; Saini 2020). Depictions of "Coloured" women as lacking in cognitive function, or of slave-yielding regions of Africa as less intelligent, or of Roma as unhygienic, or of Blacks as having lower IQs are by no means distant knowledge; they find expression in contemporary research and the curriculum.

One reason such offensive knowledge comes to light is because what once passed as common sense is now more commonly resisted. Journals retract racist articles; curricula are withdrawn. It is this contestation that reveals the politics of knowledge not simply as something imposed, but as the subject of struggle on campuses and in communities.

Such a broader view of the curriculum implies that learning is not only a private contractual agreement governing teaching and learning within a classroom, but a public representation of memorial knowledge, as in the case of treasured statues and monuments. In *Public Art and/as Curriculum*, Brenda Schmahmann (2019, 198) raises the important question of what to do with such monumental curricula, so to speak. In other words, is there another way of dealing with these public memorials for purposes of radical teaching, since "they have the potential to become part of a new and vital curriculum rather than seem to be remnants of the past that hamper transformation"?

When protesting students demanded a decolonized curriculum, it was therefore a criticism lodged within a politics of knowledge that recognized the lingering intellectual legacies of colonial and apartheid education, reflected in what is taught (knowledge content), how it is taught (knowledge hierarchies), and, for some, by whom it is taught (knowledge authorities). But how is such a colonial curriculum to be changed? Simply demanding change is not the same thing as achieving it, especially in institutions that are more than 100 years old. To understand the prospects for change, and to predict the possibility of change, this book introduces a set of concepts deployed in the analysis of the curriculum.

1.4 Key Concepts in the Study

We start with the notion of *the institutional curriculum*. It is common to think of the curriculum as composed of school subjects or, in the case of universities, as the subject matter of the disciplines, such as music or chemistry. It is relatively easy to change the disciplinary curriculum, and universities around the world do that on a regular or scheduled basis. Content is revised, readings are updated, and new assessment methods might be applied. But these often cyclical changes to a course of study seldom alter in fundamental ways the "what" (curriculum) and "how" (pedagogy) of teaching, because of something we call the institutional curriculum.

The institutional curriculum is made up of the laws, regulations, procedures, and assumptions that govern what is taught in universities. It is what marks the outer borders of change and the inner content of that change. To use extreme examples first, any university that proposes to replace the traditional medical school curriculum with an indigenous health curriculum proposed by community practitioners will suffer immediate and severe consequences; that is because what counts as acceptable medical knowledge is sanctioned by tradition and regulation, and inscribed in policy and practice. Medical professors are themselves products of traditional medical schools. Like all academics, they are socialized into their understanding of acceptable knowledge through the process of peer review in learned journals, through networks of professional communities, and through membership in honorific societies.

As a result, when medical knowledge changes, the change is often incremental, due to a discovery here or there, but it does not fundamentally alter the understanding of what counts as legitimate medical knowledge. There are, of course, echoes here of the work of the philosopher of science Thomas Kuhn ([1962] 2012), who argued that scientific knowledge does not change easily or evolve gradually but is governed by a paradigm (or scientific worldview) that remains constant over a long period of time. In this stable paradigm, scientists agree on what are relevant problems and how to solve them until a scientific revolution occurs. At that point, a new paradigm offers a better explanation for what is observed and becomes incommensurate with the old paradigm that can no longer explain certain anomalies – a paradigm shift then happens.

The institutional curriculum therefore governs what counts as knowledge across the university. Institutions themselves set up a series of hoops through which a new curriculum proposal must pass in order to win internal approvals for change. As explained in much more detail in later chapters, the academic department, the faculty, the senate, and the university clearance office scrutinize curriculum proposals before they are sent for external approvals. Assuming the new curriculum clears all these internal processes, it then passes for approval through government, statutory bodies, and professional regulators.

While each of these internal and external authorities applies a dizzying array of specific criteria with which a new curriculum must comply, what they actually do in the bigger scheme of things is to ensure that any radical deviation from established knowledge is contained within institutional norms and procedures. This means that a radical departure from the institutional curriculum – as might be demanded through the decolonization of the curriculum – will encounter major difficulties when it comes to the question of acceptable or legitimate knowledge of, say, physics or sociology. As we will demonstrate, it is the failure to account for the institutional curriculum that explains the very limited prospects for radical change in universities, where long-established knowledge agreements are embedded in relations with powerful actors and processes in the name of compliance.

This "embeddedness" is what we call *the settled curriculum*. The double meaning is meant to be descriptive of the state of the resident curriculum as both bedded down, or comfortably ensconced within institutional life, on the one hand, and also reflective of its settler colonial origins on the other hand. Therefore to *un*-settle *the curriculum in place*, or the settled curriculum, is to disrupt a way of knowing and doing that is held as intimate knowledge and is cozily familiar. As we will later show (in Chapter 3, for example), the threat to the disruption of settled knowledge is experienced by academics not only as intellectually strange but also as emotionally disorienting. In response, academics quite literally make up their own meanings for decolonization that fit more comfortably within their own emotional, intellectual, and, ultimately, political comfort zones.

Sheltered in place, the *curriculum*, so conceived, is embedded in the context and cultures of particular kinds of institutions. Universities in South Africa have different social, political, and intellectual traditions that give expression to the curriculum in different ways. The historically Black University of the Western Cape (UWC) represents in institutional accounts of itself a radical anti-apartheid struggle history; this reflects in their ways of doing things (highly consultative with the people "on the ground") and in tales of a heroic past that make their way into the public curriculum (Lalu and Murray 2012).

The more liberal universities, such as UCT and WITS, on the other hand, express their Englishness and, at least formally, their openness to progressive ideas, in their ways of doing things (highly critical in their institutional postures) and in curriculum practice (Curriculum Change Working Group 2018). And the traditional Afrikaans universities, such as Stellenbosch, project an institutional robustness in their management and administrative systems that stress compliance with curriculum regulations and that with extraordinary dexterity can mimic commitments to curriculum change while sheltering in place (Le Grange et al. 2020).

And yet, despite the different ways in which the three institutional types give expression to the claims of a decolonized curriculum, they all inhabit a common set of constraints when it comes to unsettling the institutional curriculum. In all cases, the curriculum is governed by external regulations that set the ceiling on radical change. All these institutions employ academic teachers, who work to conserve the foundations of their disciplines and, especially in the natural sciences, actively resist any attempts to radically change the curriculum in place. They all host radical curriculum enclaves, which remain on the margins of institutional life, with their origins in the pre-2015 (i.e., Rhodes Must Fall) moment. And in all three cases, the institutional attention to radical curriculum change gradually dissipated as protests died out and other imperatives (such as Fourth Industrial Revolution and online learning) started to take centre stage, in terms of curriculum policy and delivery.

This brings us to another key concept in this study: *radical curriculum change*. We argue that decolonization, for many activists, was a quest for radical changes to the inherited curriculum, not simply accommodation within it (see Modiri 2020). We take the normative position that radical curriculum change addresses issues of power, equity, justice, access, privilege, equality, and representation. Radical curriculum change therefore means taking on racism, sexism, and classism in the content and delivery of the curriculum. It does not simply mean good pedagogy, or the remediation of learning deficits, or the uses of indigenous examples in teaching; these might be important interventions, but our position in this book is that those lighter conceptions of change gave academics a way out of dealing with more fundamental concerns about the resident curriculum – questions about the origins, ownership, claims, and consequences of inherited knowledge.

If the politics of knowledge illuminates how power operates within the institutional curriculum, the sociology of knowledge demonstrates how institutions work to maintain the status quo.

1.5 Notes on Theory

The study brings into dialogue insights from curriculum theory and institutional theory in order to understand the uptake of decolonization within the ten institutions studied. Curriculum theory sheds light on curriculum change and constancy over time. There is a voluminous literature that seeks to explain the complexities of curriculum change from different perspectives (Georgiades 1980; Apple and Christian-Smith 1991; Jippes et al. 2015; Hall et al. 2021). Most of this literature accounts for the difficulties of curriculum change from technical (e.g., the lack of key elements, such as stakeholder buy-in); cultural (e.g., the misalignment of the new curriculum with the context of implementation); or political (e.g., the power of the state or publishers in determining textbook contents) perspectives. While much of this literature deals with schools, there are broad insights that apply to higher education institutions as well. In sum, within this change literature little attention is given to the institutional analysis of curriculum.

Institutional theories, and in particular a variant known as neo-institutional theory, call attention to the internal workings of different kinds of institutions, including schools and universities. One particular area of interest for this study is the way institutionalization happens, that is, how institutions deal with radical ideas (e.g., incorporation or rejection) that do not fit in or conform to the dominant knowledge arrangements that define what we call the institutional curriculum. In this sense, institutionalists have an interest in "the latitude and the limits that we confront if we attempted to change the existing institutional order" (Meyer and Rowan 2006, 4). How do embedded actors in institutions make sense of, or give meaning to, new ideas? What are the rules and procedures that keep existing knowledge in place, and intruder knowledge out? And why is it so difficult for radical ideas such as decolonization to find a foothold within institutional life?

In this literature on (neo)institutional theory, research on educational content has largely been limited to cross-national studies of *curriculum convergence* (Nordin and Sundberg 2016; Johansson and Striethold 2019), rather than the micropolitics of knowledge within institutions. As a major review on the use of institutional theory in higher education found, curriculum issues such as

course design, academic work, knowledge and research, particularly at the levels of individual, course/programme and department/centre are more rarely approached through institutional theory. (Cai and Mehari 2015, 15)

Until now, there has been very little research that brings into conversation what we know about curriculum change and what we have learned about institutional change. This study therefore tracks the path followed by a radical curriculum idea (decolonization) through institutional life, drawing on, but also extending, insights from theory in both areas of inquiry (see Chapters 3 and 8).

1.6 Notes on Methodology

1.6.1 Sampling

This research is concerned with the uptake of decolonization in ten out of twenty-six public universities in South Africa. The ten universities were sampled on the basis that the most intense student protests and demands for decolonization were heard on these campuses; these are also the institutions that responded to the student call with elaborate measures, such as special senate committees, to drive the process of change.

Perhaps understandably, the felt need for decolonization was less emphatically expressed at the historically Black universities, in part because the major agitations among disadvantaged institutions were material rather than ideological, concerned with the bread-and-butter issues better represented by the #FeesMustFall movement. These universities, too, at least in their student enrolments and cultures, were more distinctively Black than institutions such as the University of Cape Town. As Leslie Bank (2019) found in his landmark study of universities in the "African motor city" of East London,

The struggle of the poorer and middle-class black students at the historically black universities focused on access to, and the cost of, higher education … There was less focus on the intellectual orientation of their universities and curricula and the composition of their management structures, which were, in most cases, almost entirely black anyway.

Put somewhat differently, the symbolism of European culture and identity was less visibly on display in these younger apartheid institutions. As a student leader at UWC, the only Black university in our sample, put it, "We have no statues to throw down." This is not, of course, to suggest that the lingering effects of colonialism and apartheid were not also resident in the curriculum of the Black universities, only that it was less visible and less felt in a context where financial hardship overwhelmed and defined the experiences of poorer Black students at these institutions.

Still, our main concern as researchers was to study institutions with an active register of complaint and response, contained in expansive documentation, with respect to the decolonization of the curriculum. The universities chosen were, therefore:

Nelson Mandela University[1]
The University of Cape Town
The University of the Witwatersrand
Rhodes University
Stellenbosch University
The University of the Western Cape
Durban University of Technology[2]
The University of KwaZulu Natal[3]
The University of Johannesburg[4]
The University of Pretoria

1.6.2 Methods

The research strategy consisted of one or more rounds of interviews with more than 200 academics involved in the curriculum change processes of each university. We interviewed senior members of the executive management teams of universities, especially those charged with responsibility for leading the institutional responses to the demands for decolonization; this often included the Deputy Vice-Chancellor (DVC) for academic affairs.

The investigation combined individual interviews and focus groups, with the format determined by staff availability, position (e.g., Senior DVC), and the preferences of schools or departments. Where large numbers of staff in a particular field presented themselves for an interview (e.g., more than twenty health sciences academics at Wits), the sessions allowed for rich discussions and for diverse perspectives to emerge across the larger group. Every interview, in either format, was transcribed for analysis.

---

[1] Nelson Mandela University was formed through a merger of the white University of Port Elizabeth, the white Port Elizabeth Technikon, and the black urban campus called Vista University (2005).

[2] The Durban University of Technology is the product of a merger between the white Natal Technikon and the ML Sultan Technikon, the latter designated in the apartheid years for Indian South Africans (2002).

[3] The University of KwaZulu-Natal was formed from the white University of Natal and the University of Durban Westville, which was originally created for Indians (2004).

[4] The University of Johannesburg was a merger of the white Rand Afrikaans University, the white Technikon Witwatersrand, and the black campuses of Vista in Soweto and the East Rand (2005).

We interviewed academics at each university who were deemed by their colleagues to be actively engaged in attempts to decolonize the curriculum in their departments, schools, or faculties. Most of these academics were among the more enthusiastic respondents to the call for decolonization, although we did ask the organizers of our campus visits for permission to interview those who were sceptical of, or resistant to, any forms of radical curriculum change.

While interviewing some participants, we were pointed towards others in an ongoing process of referral sampling. We were particularly interested in those academics who were regarded as resources on decolonization within their institutions (and for other universities) and who were often called on by staff, students, and management to advise departments or to address campus gatherings in the heat of the protest movement. We returned to most campuses more than once for interviews and, after the pandemic-enforced lockdown of 2020, we conducted the remaining interviews virtually via Zoom or Teams.

In addition to our efforts to obtain a panoramic view on the decolonization of curriculum across each institution, we also sought out exemplars of radical change. We asked participants in the first set of interviews to point us in the direction of colleagues who enjoyed regard for their exemplary decolonized curricula. The curricula of these academics were then studied as reputational samples from the perspective of colleagues in their institutions. We further refined the choice of radical curriculum exemplars to give us a broad set of disciplines from the humanities and social sciences, as well as from the natural sciences and engineering.

The reputational cases of decolonized curricula selected for the humanities and social sciences were:

- Political Science or Politics (Rhodes University)
- Media Studies (University of Johannesburg)
- Visual Arts (Stellenbosch University)
- Philosophy (University of Pretoria)
- Psychology (Rhodes University)

The reputational cases sampled from the science and engineering disciplines were:

- Engineering (Wits University)
- Organic Chemistry (Stellenbosch University)

- Archaeology (University of Pretoria)
- Computer Science (Nelson Mandela University)
- Occupational Therapy (University of the Free State)[5]

The in-depth interviews with these practitioners allowed us to compose five- to seven-page case study reports (i.e., ten reports in all) on how they enacted decolonization within the curricula of their respective disciplines. The case interviews posed questions about the intellectual biographies of these academics, that is, how they came to hold such critical dispositions towards knowledge, and such clear, if not always unconditional, attachments to the decolonization project. In other words, what was it within their social lives that explained their commitment to decolonizing the curriculum?

These targeted interviews also sought to capture, in the first instance, exactly how these academic activists understood decolonization, given the varied meanings attached to this potentially radical concept among South African academics (see Chapter 4). Finally, we explored how these curriculum activists squared the radical demands of curriculum decolonization with the conserving requirements of the institutional curriculum, such as those for student evaluation and assessment.

It is important to note that the case interviews were mainly conducted with *individuals* who were transforming their own courses and curricula within their respective fields. However, in the case of the philosophy curriculum at the University of Pretoria, the incoming head had been given a mandate to decolonize philosophy in his department as a whole; therefore the interviews in this case considered the *departmental* curriculum as the unit of analysis, not simply the individual courses taught by the professor (and head of department) interviewed. And in the case of engineering at Wits, the focus was on an innovative core curriculum designed for all incoming first-year students, involving a team of academic teachers; in this case, therefore, the interviews were conducted with the two academic leaders driving the decolonization

---

[5] While the University of the Free State (UFS) was not included in the broader study because of the lack of a systematic and institution-wide response to decolonization, the case of Occupational Therapy was included because of the unusually critical perspective of the academic Tania Rausch van der Merwe towards a field like OT. Tania's attempts at changing the OT curriculum were also interesting in that she both embraced and was critical of the politics of decolonization. She later moved to take up a senior position in OT at Wits University.

initiative with the supportive Dean of Engineering as part of the interview set.

In the course of the analysis, we moved back and forth between the curriculum documentation (study guides, course outlines, prescribed readings) provided and the interviews to compose a complete and compelling account of the curriculum deliberations of the designers and teachers of these case exemplars. In most cases, the draft case reports were returned to the respondent(s) for verification before the final case studies were written up.

It was, however, the study of *institutional documentation* that provided particularly insightful renditions of the thinking of each university at the start, culmination, and conclusion of the protest movement. That is, we studied hastily produced documentation from the start of the protests (e.g., terms of reference); draft documentation at their height (e.g., conceptual documents to guide the process); commissioned reports to be delivered to management (e.g., final task team reports); and the final documents accepted for stakeholder distribution and the institutional record (e.g., the management reports lodged with senates and councils).

In this analytical process, for each of the ten universities, we carefully studied how original briefs (or terms of reference) were interpreted inside and outside of task teams' remits; how they were developed over the life of the commission; how they were received by management; and how final reports were embraced, ignored, and in some cases diluted of radical content before being released for the management record, governance compliance, and, eventually, public notice.

Read on their own, the initial, framing documents certainly indicated an earnestness of response signalled by invoking the authority of the highest academic body of a university, the senate – except in the case of UCT, curiously – to oversee the commission on decolonization, which, in turn, was populated by senior activist scholars and, of course, representatives from among the more prominent student activists.

Once the task teams handed over their commissioned reports to the senior management (in some cases, to the Vice-Chancellor, but more often, and more properly, to the Senate) for action, they were given to the academic deans for purposes of "implementation" in their respective faculties.

After the point of handover, little happened, for in most cases the decolonization report simply became part of the body of routine administrative reports that form part of the general institutional reporting on academic matters. Sometimes, the task team report was placed on the institutional website for reaction from the university community; again, little happened beyond the website announcement. In one particularly surprising case, the university authorities accepted the commissioned report, which was then completely diluted by executive managers (to the shock and surprise of the committee) and then handed to senate and council "for noting," without any discussion about the intellectual or political significance of the report or the modalities of its implementation. That was quite literally the end of the institutional response to decolonization.

In response, chairs of the so-called decolonization committees resigned, in some cases, and left their institutions with a deep sense of disillusionment about the lack of any concerted institutional action that would drive the implementation of a radical curriculum down to the level of the academic departments.

This tracking of the course of institutional documentation on decolonization – from initial mandates to the formation of special committees and the handing of their final reports, and finally to the briefs to deans – provided rich insights into our initial question: How does a radical idea, such as decolonization, make its way through an institution? But the analysis of documents also revealed for the first time precisely *how institutions work* to both embrace and throttle radical ideas for curriculum change.

As indicated, the research strategy required interviews with critical players on the inside of institutions; that is, executive managers, deans, department heads, and academics, as "institutionally embedded actors" involved with the curriculum. But the strategy also included interviews with regulatory agencies external to institutions. These agencies were the Department of Higher Education and Training (DHET), the government department that gives initial clearance and the funding agency for new curricula; the South African Qualifications Authority (SAQA), which registers approval of new programmes in terms of a National Qualifications Framework; the Council on Higher Education (CHE), which accredits the new curricula of institutions; and the professional bodies that additionally accredit the new curricula for the professions in question.

We selected three of the most prominent of the professional bodies for interviews – the South African Institute of Chartered Accountants (SAICA), the Engineering Council of South Africa (ECSA), and the Health Professions Council of South Africa (HPCSA). Most of these interviews were conducted as focus group sessions with administrators, which allowed for a rich exchange among colleagues in each regulatory authority, as well as with the researchers. In the data analysis of the interview transcripts, we compared the internal actors' data (e.g., the deans) with the external actors' data (e.g., SAICA) in order to develop more reliable accounts of the effects of regulation on the university curriculum.

It should be noted that we did not interview students, for the simple reason that this book is about the *academic* uptake of decolonization within the curricula of the ten universities. Where students were involved, especially in larger focus group meetings, it happened to be student leaders who were holding postgraduate research or junior teaching-assistant positions within academic departments. These encounters with former student leaders in the decolonization protests were particularly illuminating, since they had dual insights from the vantage points of their activist roles and their new academic positions.

The research process was generally smooth, and academics and senior managers opened their doors for interviews on what we found to be a very delicate subject on some campuses, the decolonization project. At one university, UCT, a few senior academics among the decolonization activists refused multiple attempts to secure interviews in what was clearly an orchestrated response. One of them explained that her refusal was based on the criticism by one of the authors (in his general role as a public intellectual) of the institution's Black Academic Caucus. Fortunately, the largest group of interviewees per institution nevertheless came from UCT, which more than made up for those who would not participate.

1.7 Research on Radical Curriculum Change: What We Know So Far

Most of the education literature on radical curriculum change is limited to studies on schools, such as the prolific works of Michael Apple (2000) in, for example, his book *Official Knowledge*, or a set of urgent articles by scholars such as Bryan Deever (1996) on topics like "radical theory and systemic curriculum reform." More common in higher education are online writings with an advocacy angle, such as Ruth Mather's (2015) "Teaching on a Moving Train: Curriculum Bias & Radical Curriculum Change." And it is worth noting that when curriculum publications carry in their titles the word "radical," it sometimes means *organizational* restructuring rather than the *political* repurposing of knowledge – as in "Developing the New Columbia Core Curriculum: A Case Study in Managing Radical Curriculum Change" (Galea et al. 2015).

Until now, there have been few, if any, systematic studies on the course of a radical curriculum idea through different kinds of higher education institutions. Sara Ahmed (2012, 29) comes closest to a study of the uptake of a radical idea – in this case, diversity – within institutional life. Through the exquisite use of metaphor, Ahmed explains how institutions take up, or fail to take up, the mission commitment of diversity within everyday life. Using examples from her own experiences of working with diversity, and interviews over time with diversity workers, she documents their struggles to have "diversity go through the whole system."

This study draws on some invaluable concepts from Ahmed's (2012; 2017) work, though it is different in three key respects. First, this is a study on a powerful curriculum idea (decolonization), and not simply a mission or mandate to "diversify" an institution through, for example, the hiring of more Black or women academics. This distinction is important because the curriculum itself is an institution, or an institutional commonplace, as will be shown later.

Second, this is an empirical study of ten very different institutions and how they take up the radical demand for decolonization within the curriculum. In other words, the diversity of the universities themselves becomes part of the analysis of what is possible when a radical idea courses through institutional life.

And third, this research starts with the notion that institutionalization is a problem to be studied, not simply a goal to be pursued. In other words, what do institutions do to radical ideas such as decolonization? How do they act on forceful curriculum ideas when they come through the gates of the university? When "decolonization goes through the whole system," to adapt Sara Ahmed, is where the problem starts.

1.8 The Broader Significance of This Study

The South African case offers a unique opportunity in the scholarship on curriculum change to examine close-up what happens when a radical idea (i.e., decolonization) commands, and receives, institutional attention. The source of those pressing demands for curriculum reform was not governmental authority or regulatory requirement but sustained and unprecedented student protests over an intense period of at least two years' duration.

What also makes the South African case interesting for the wider academic community is that every one of the ten institutions in this study responded with considerable energy and enthusiasm to the political demand for curriculum change; all those institutional actions (funding, task teams, conferences, performance assessments, etc.) appeared to signal a commitment to the decolonization of knowledge.

Broadly, this moment raises that enduring question in curriculum studies – did the university curriculum in fact change (and if so, how?) in response to unprecedented political demand and, on the face of it, institutional commitment? In the context of this specific study, the question could be posed this way: Five years since the very public downing of the Rhodes statue, that symbolic moment that placed decolonization on the university agenda, what has been the uptake of this radical idea within the institutional curriculum?

Specifically, as a study on the micro-politics of knowledge within institutional life, this research offers unique insights into *how* institutions receive and respond to initiatives for radical curriculum change as they work their way through the institution. By bringing together curriculum theory and institutional theory, the study makes visible the different ways in which institutions act on decolonization. In the chapters that follow, we identify and describe those institutional actions as posturing, diluting, bureaucratizing, disciplining, regulating, marginalizing, and domesticating radical curriculum change. These first-ever analyses of institutional responses to radical ideas under seemingly receptive conditions lie at the heart of the *intellectual significance* of this study.

The *practical significance* of the study follows from the scholarly analysis of the institutional treatment of radical curriculum ideas. We suggest that the pursuit of radical change must take as its starting point an institutional analysis of curriculum. Our thesis is that by understanding how institutions quarantine radical ideas, it is possible to advance more meaningful changes to the inherited curriculum that is so comfortably settled in place (see the strategies proposed in Chapter 8).

Finally, the *social significance* of this study for political movements is the demonstration of what happens when the project for radical curriculum change is driven by a compelling cause and carried by a strong moral authority but nonetheless undermines itself in pursuit of deep change. Overreliance on slogans, self-righteous posturing, ideological purity, anti-intellectualism, intolerance of dissent, and the recourse to nativist language all tripped up a promising moment in the struggle for decolonized institutions and, specifically, the decolonization of knowledge.

1.9 A Roadmap

This first chapter introduces the central question in contention: *How do radical curriculum ideas travel through institutions?* We make the case for the study, starting with the fall of the iconic statue of the imperialist Prime Minister of the Cape Colony (1890–1896), Cecil John Rhodes, on the campus of the University of Cape Town – an event of enormous symbolic importance in the press for decolonization that inspired student protests in other parts of the world, including the University of Oxford. The approach to the study is presented, and the methods of inquiry explained in some detail. The intellectual, practical, and social significance of this work on the politics of knowledge is outlined in the context of the literature on curriculum change.

Chapter 2 explains the ways in which the ten different institutions responded when decolonization first came knocking on the doors of the senior management of each university. Without exception, each institution responded quickly and enthusiastically to the demands for radical curriculum change. Nobody quite knew what decolonization meant in those early days, but the pressure was relentless, and the warning could not have been clearer: A very prominent institutional fixture was dramatically toppled at the continent's preeminent research university.

In record time, senates were convened, committees were established, task teams received terms of reference, working groups sprang into action, symposia were launched, budgets were redirected, international speakers were invited, performance appraisal systems were recalibrated, and charters were made public. What did all this mean?

We borrow from Deborah Anderson (2018) the term *institutional posturing*, which she defines as "an explanatory mechanism whereby uncertainty and indecision stemming from institutional pressure are masked by stopgap responsiveness." While Anderson's subject was private regulators in the accounting industry, the term carries considerable explanatory power for another kind of institution, the public university, under political pressure for change. Institutional posturing is a visible response to an urgent crisis that remains "noncommittal in the long term." Such posturing conveys a sense of resolve "in the nearer term, while maintaining the appearance of control and expertise," and – in the process – mitigating the potential loss of credibility with, in this case, a national uprising of a powerful student movement.

Chapter 3 presents the theoretical arguments that underpin the study. Drawing on key tenets of what has been called the new institutionalism in education, the chapter outlines the key claims and assumptions that frame the study: that universities are rule-conforming institutions; that, as institutions, universities find their stability in deeply institutionalized rules, norms, and regulations; that institutions owe their legitimacy to "institutionally situated" human actors with shared beliefs and understandings; and that under these conditions, "institutional logics" (or shared rationalizations) work to give curriculum practice its sense of normativity.

Chapter 4 delves deep into the many meanings assigned by activists and academics to the mobilizing term that bannered the protests – decolonization. What is of significance here is not the witty observation that there were as many definitions of decolonization as there were universities, but rather *what those contending conceptions allowed for* as academics sought to respond to the demand for radical curriculum change. The key meanings of decolonization distilled from interviews with 200 academics included decolonization as simply the addition of inclusive content; as Africanization; as remediation; as critical pedagogy; and as simply good teaching. Each of these conceptions of decolonization enabled and disabled particular kinds of curriculum change within the universities studied.

Chapter 5 provides insider accounts of the ways in which regulatory agencies acted to defang radical curriculum initiatives. The roles of government through the DHET and key statutory bodies, the CHE and

SAQA, are explained in relation to the complex approval processes for programmes of study.

Another layer of regulatory authority is those governing professional curricula. In this chapter, we also describe the workings of the following professional bodies: SAICA, ECSA, and the HPSCA.

The authority of regulatory agencies in influencing and constraining radical change has not enjoyed sustained empirical attention in higher education. Of particular intellectual interest is that the standards of these professions are often determined by international bodies in the West, when one of the most important strains within the decolonization moment was the call for the Africanization of curriculum knowledge. How did the conflicting imperatives of internationalization and Africanization face off in the political battles for the decolonization of curriculum, and who won?

Chapter 6 presents case studies of exemplary curricula aligned with decolonization within the *humanities and social sciences*. What explains the emergence of these radical curricula within university environments? How do its designers and teachers understand decolonization and its expression within their curricula? What is the relationship between personal biography and curriculum choices? How do these academics negotiate the teaching of radical content within the constraints of the institutional curriculum, for example, conventional evaluation standards? What is the place of such radical curriculum options inside the mainstream offerings of a department or faculty? And how do students and colleagues of progressive academics respond to such radical options?

Chapter 7 presents a similar set of curriculum exemplars associated with the decolonization of knowledge, this time drawn from engineering and the natural sciences. How do these academics respond to the claims of their colleagues that science is a value-free enterprise and that atoms, sound waves, and heartbeats are universal concepts that stand above politics? What does a politics of knowledge look like in polymer chemistry or occupational therapy, to take two of our examples? Is decolonization in these fields simply an application of scientific ideas to new contexts, or is the very idea of science-based knowledge itself up for grabs?

The final chapter, Chapter 8, draws theoretical and practical insights from the overall study for the prospects of radical curriculum change within institutions. An extensive search of the literature suggests that there are no systematic studies on the course followed by a radical curriculum idea through different kinds of institutions. In fact, the bulk of neo-institutional studies of universities have been conducted at the macro- and meso-levels of analysis (such as the voluminous work on the worldwide institutionalization of education), and few on the micro-level politics of the institutionalization of knowledge.

It is still the case that "there are certainly possibilities for more qualitative and micro-level methodologies framed by neo-institutional theory" (Wiseman, Astiz, and Baker 2014). In the context of South Africa, there are certainly no detailed studies on the processes and politics of institutionalization beyond slim, generic, and often normative accounts of what should be, rather than considered empirical research on radical knowledge and institutions (Zawada 2020).

The final chapter, therefore, offers a critical synthesis of the main findings of this novel inquiry into the path of a radical idea such as decolonization through the institutional machinery of higher education. In the process, it answers new questions about the politics and prospects for radical curriculum change in higher education institutions.

We begin with the march of decolonization onto South African university campuses in 2015, that landmark year in the history of student protests, and the institutional posturing that followed.

2 | Institutional Posturing
The Coming of Decolonization and the Scramble to Respond

2.1 Introduction

When the bronze statue of Cecil John Rhodes came down in a spectacular demonstration of student activism on the campus of the University of Cape Town, university leaders across the country made two hasty calculations: that this powerful statement on decolonization was going to spread across the twenty-six public universities, and that they needed to brace themselves with an adequate institutional response. In the weeks and months that followed, it was not only statues that were defaced, as at the University of KwaZulu-Natal (UKZN), or destroyed, as at the University of the Free State (UFS), but whole buildings that were burned to the ground at North-West University (NWU) and the University of Johannesburg (UJ) as angry demonstrations engulfed universities around the exclusionary costs of a university education and the alienating content and cultures of higher education institutions.

This chapter documents the varied ways in which institutions decided to respond to this short but intense period in the press for decolonization and explains those responses as a form of "institutional posturing," which, as we will demonstrate, was intended primarily to weather the political storm rather than deal incisively with what we call the settled curriculum. We also found that what was significant for the trajectory of curriculum change was *which* authority or structure within the university was charged with leading the institutional response.

2.2 We Have No Statues! The University of the Western Cape

The prominent statue of the imperialist figure Cecil John Rhodes provided UCT students with an ideal target for making a powerful political statement about the need for decolonization. However, a mere 17 km away lay the University of the Western Cape (UWC), a historically Black university, where the attitude was, in the words of a student leader, "We have no statues! What is there to decolonize?"

After the downing of Rhodes, even off-campus statues in public places came under attack by political party-affiliated youth who targeted war commemorations, such as Horse Memorial Statues in Uitenhage and Port Elizabeth, and Boer President Paul Kruger's statue in Pretoria's Church Square. The opportunistic acts of political imitation made statues an easy target precisely because they were so public and the attack on them so spectacular. On and off campuses, statues offered "an economy of symbols" that could be dealt with on the spot (Mbembe 2016).

But how do you decolonize a Black campus without any statues – let alone colonial ones – for playing out the politics of spectacle? For UWC, the politics shifted towards Africanization (for students) and transformation (for management) because "it didn't make sense to just talk about decolonization," as a senior academic puts it.

Still, the pressure was on at UWC to respond to no less than forty student demands from the Pan Africanist Student Movement of Azania (PASMA)-led SRC that included everything from "free sanitary towels" and "10 gigabytes per student per month" to the "renaming of buildings" and "free quality black-centered education."

The responsibility for leading the institutional response to decolonization fell to the Deputy Vice-Chancellor: Academic, a professor of law. Under her leadership, UWC created a task team that was approved by the Senate in 2016. What followed was a complex and intensive consultative process that typifies the conduct of an institution that is profoundly self-conscious about its struggle history, identity, and politics (Gerwel 1987; Lalu and Murray 2012). As one campus leader stressed, "We have a very strong community focus at UWC; it comes out in everything."

Unsurprisingly, the institutional response to decolonization was "to take a totally different path" and revisit what it called "its institutional identity." What, for example, did the university once dubbed "the intellectual home for the left" mean now, in the context of the very intense student struggles and demands of 2015–2016?

Since there was, as was said ironically, nothing to decolonize on this campus, the curriculum struggle became a muddle of concepts that included Africanization; transformation; "all things decolonization"; and even internationalization, because, as one senior academic offered, "they're not necessarily polar opposites of the curriculum." In part to clarify meanings, the university leadership initiated a series of "courageous café conversations" using the World Café (2021) methodology, as it facilitated this process. Through these conversations, UWC did what the struggle university had always done, that is, talk – this time about the intellectual identity of the university in the present and for the future. The café conversations were further extended to alumni off campus.

Back on campus, consultations continued in the faculties "from the ground up," where the issue of decolonization was raised and responded to in very different ways, depending on the faculty. A September "Academic Month" followed, during which each Thursday was dedicated to decolonization. All the inputs then went to a Senate Academic Planning Committee, where a new task team synthesized the results of the conversations and consultations, which were then sent to a large Colloquium, out of which emerged a planning document titled "Curriculum Principles for Transformation."

Once approved by Senate and taken to Council, the highest governing body of the university, some faculties were intended to "pilot" these curriculum principles in their programmes. What were some of these curriculum principles? That UWC should retain its progressive voice and its critical and non-conformist tradition; and that students should "see themselves in the curriculum," and find their experiences validated within it and come to share an African identity. The question of "intellectual identity" was stated as broadly as that – so broadly, in fact, that the leader of the project stated, "I'm not even sure all of them [the curriculum principles] speak to decolonization," in an institutional context where the claim was made "we don't have whiteness here."

In sum, the institutional response to decolonization at UWC was emphatically different from that of neighbouring UCT, where "Rhodes" fell. UWC's response was consultative and open-ended, without a commitment to decolonization as the singular, driving concept of protest. It did not "just want to jump into a decolonization language," as one campus leader explained.

The whiteness found at UCT was less obvious on this Black campus; therefore, the language of decolonization was less strident. Even the student demands that related to curriculum issues tended to emphasize "Africanization," rather than decolonization.

Importantly, the pursuit of curriculum change at UWC through the "intellectual identity" project quickly became consumed with concerns about "institutional operating procedures" (IOPs), including references to "graduate attributes," and the urgent academic development needs of disadvantaged students. At UWC, as elsewhere, student demands for the decolonization of knowledge (a political matter) became entangled with the institutional regulation of curriculum (an administrative matter).

2.3 Rhodes Must Fall: The University of Cape Town

If UWC had a tentative, exploratory, and open-ended consultative process in response to the decolonization moment, the nearby University of Cape Town (UCT) had a highly focused, combative, and politically driven institutional response to the problem of curriculum change. Unlike UWC, the charge was not led by a member of the executive management but by a group of activist academics working outside the authority of the Senate. It was a complaint made often by academics, although seldom openly, that by the authority of the Vice-Chancellor, "this work was taken out of the normal teaching and learning committee of Senate" and given to a separate task team called the Curriculum Change Working Group (CCWG).

The mandate of the CCWG was to identify curriculum innovations already in place, enable curriculum change, document the change process, raise critical issues that emerged from curriculum dialogues, and develop a proposed "framework to guide curriculum transformation."

From the start, the CCWG made no bones about its political mandate. It was Black-led, institutionally funded, and "intimately intertwined with student mobilization around curricula issues." Its language of change was strident and provocative: "Colonial lies embedded in disciplines must be exposed and disrupted," and "knowledge production must always be regarded as potentially violent towards marginalized communities."

The process "to facilitate dialogue" on curriculum change was both urgent and intense. A "participatory methodology" was followed to engage students and faculty through study circles, knowledge cafés, workshops, and reading groups. Events were staged that invited "decolonial scholars" to campus; an indaba series discussed the role of public universities in Africa; and CCWG members engaged in organized events such as the Third Space colloquia (as theorized by Homi Bhabha [1990]) of the creative arts community and the UNISA Decolonial Summer School. Out of all these events, "data" was generated to inform the work of the CCWG.

The CCWG then engaged three "sites" in intensive dialogues about their curriculum practices, where critical concerns as well as innovative practices were brought to light; those "sites" were located in the Faculty of Health Sciences; the Departments of Fine Arts and Drama, located on the campus "Formerly Known as Hiddingh" (FKA-H);[1] and the South African College of Music.

Out of all these intensive consultations on decolonization across the campuses and in the three "sites," a *Curriculum Change Framework* (Curriculum Change Working Group 2018, 5–6) was generated, with the stated purpose of serving as

an invitation for academic and research units at UCT to reflect on their own understanding of curriculum change as well as on past, current and future practices of curriculum review, innovation and broader change within the academy.

Once the *Curriculum Change Framework* (Curriculum Change Working Group 2018, 56) was produced and published on the UCT website, the work of the CCWG came to an abrupt halt. By its own admission, "During 2017, student protests at UCT no longer called for decolonization of the curriculum." The CCWG gave the cessation of curriculum hostilities a positive interpretation:

From our observations, our summation is that we were effective in ensuring that student activists were confident that the CCWG would engage with the question of the decolonising curriculum and the academy with authenticity.

A more likely reason for the end of the intense period of cross-campus engagement is that since the political momentum behind the student protests had run its course, there was no longer the same institutional pressure for radical curriculum change. Meanwhile, the work of the CCWG, done at arm's length from the usual university structures, came face-to-face with institutional reality. In fact, despite its strident

---

[1] The device FKA-H at this UCT campus was borrowed from student protestors' reference to Rhodes as "The University Currently Known As Rhodes" during the struggles for decolonization on the Eastern Cape campus.

and battle-ready language, the CCWG itself seemed to back off from its more radical posture:

In order not to discard what works and push an institution into implosion, it is important to blend the formal structures with the new emergent structures. Parallel work must be allowed. (Curriculum Change Working Group 2018, 5; emphasis added)

For one of the senior academic administrators at UCT, the game was over:

This [the CCWG Report] is by no means the curriculum policy of the university. This is not policy. This is not a framework either. It is a particular experience of a particular group of people under particular circumstances. It will be brought back into the institution and the Teaching and Learning Committee (of Senate) will take a position.

In the end, the CCWG collapsed under the weight of its own moral pretensions and political self-righteousness. The Working Group not only failed to communicate the key ideas of radical curriculum change to medical, engineering, and accounting academics but also demeaned and humiliated the professions in its core arguments, as in this damning statement:

Being a great musician or a great doctor is tantamount to being a colonial subject who aspires to white supremacist patriarchal and western (classical) ways of being rather than a reflection of local influence and ways of being.

Unsurprisingly, the uptake of decolonization in the institutional curriculum was not just slow and uneven; in many academic departments, and especially those of the professions, radical change in the form of decolonization was rejected outright. Put differently, the CCWG did not have an *institutional* theory of change when it came to the settled curriculum.

2.4 Where Statues Were Fees: The University of the Witwatersrand

If UCT in Cape Town was the epicentre of the decolonization moment, its traditional rival, Wits – the other English liberal university, in Johannesburg – was at the heart of the fees protests in 2015. But student solidarity required that these struggles be linked, with the result that the Wits student leadership was certainly not inattentive to the press for decolonization.

When decolonization did, however, come to the Wits campus, the institution was already grappling with a quality review process by the regulatory authority the Council on Higher Education (CHE); in fact, the "Quality Enhancement Project Phase 2" (QEP2) of the CHE had concentrated the minds of the Wits management on a range of matters, including the Council's "Focus Area: Curriculum."

By the time the protests arrived on campus, and in response to the regulatory review, Wits had developed a "Baseline Study on Curriculum Transformation," which documented the state of curriculum initiatives at the university.

This baseline document was published in 2017 – well after the heat of protests had subsided – and contained a rich survey of curriculum initiatives in the faculties; it was, therefore, an ideal institutional document for surveying the extent of the decolonization of curriculum across the university as a whole. The document promised to showcase "the terms of curriculum renewal" and "how to decolonize the curriculum." Surprisingly, what the institution actually showcased had much to do with the first object and very little to do with decolonization.

The commerce faculty advanced a "learner-centred approach" and "guided mastery" within its disciplines. Under "decolonization of content," the engineering faculty listed writing skills, English, and critical thinking courses. The health sciences faculty referred to "technology enhanced learning adaptations" in anatomy and physiology. One of the largest faculties celebrated "an increase in the number of take-home exams," and another claimed that, through "continuously updating the curricula," students learn relevant skills while it maintained "international standing in terms of quality and relevance."

Intermingled with this dominant understanding of what can be described as normal curriculum reform – the cyclical changes that academic disciplines routinely apply to their curricula – are scattered references to the language of decolonization. In the main, the institutional interpretations of decolonization came to mean things such as the use of cases, applications, ideas, perspectives, literatures, and examples from South Africa and the rest of the continent.

To take forward institutional and curriculum changes, Wits instituted a Transformation Implementation Committee (TIC) to report on and monitor transformation across the institution. Deans regularly reported to the TIC on their progress against eight transformation objectives, which included the transformation of curriculum. The eight objectives appear in the documents "Wits Transformation Strategy," "Priorities," and "Transform the Academy"; they are:

1. Diversifying the Wits Academy
   Internal and external sourcing process including the advancement of identified talent
2. Curriculum Reform
   A curriculum reform which includes African theorists and is both locally and globally relevant
3. Student Admissions
   Demographic and class diversity, and cosmopolitanism of students, across all programmes
4. Promote a diverse and cosmopolitan residence life experience
   Cosmopolitan residence that is representative of students from different backgrounds and race
5. Institutional culture
   Optimizing organizational design and cultural change
6. Institutional naming
   Symbolic names and or statues that are informed by both Western and indigenous traditions
7. Language
   A resource instrument to enable staff and students to develop competence in one of at least two South African languages – Nguni and Sotho
8. Insourcing the outsourced
   Process to ensure insourcing all outsourced services that involve vulnerable workers

As should be evident in this list of the eight objectives, the Wits authorities did not foreground the new concept of decolonization in its academic work, either before or after the advent of decolonization; the term certainly did not displace the primary descriptor of change – transformation.

The real work of curriculum deliberation took place in decentralized structures known as teaching and learning committees (TLCs). The TLCs of the various departments fed their work into the TLCs of their faculties, which, in turn, reported on curriculum work to the TLC of the university Senate. It was here, in the Senate, that curriculum deliberations – whether for transformation or decolonization – were considered, though always in the shadow of the regulatory requirements of the QEP2 directives of the CHE. Here too, the radical and the regulatory were intertwined in the curriculum deliberations of the university.

In this context, the institutional posture of Wits in relation to decolonization was to "track" all the curriculum activities of the departments, schools, and faculties, which were then reported by the respective deans at regular meetings of the TIC, where they were accountable to the senior executive manager in charge – a professor of chemistry who served as the DVC: Academic. The DVC in charge saw his primary role as one of overseeing and monitoring ("tracking") the changes as a manager, rather than of persuading or "converting" deans and their faculties towards a more radical curriculum change posture under the banner of decolonization.

Still, the Wits leadership encouraged and funded numerous seminars, symposia, workshops, and colloquia on decolonization during two years of intense student protests in support of the twin demand of the struggle – fees. With the monitoring posture of the senior executive, TICs regularly recorded important curricular changes that were always under discussion, but which were now "accelerated" because of the press for decolonized education.

Two such changes were the decision to offer, eventually, a common core first-year engineering course that included more examples from Africa in the curriculum. In both engineering and medical education, students were to learn an African language as the means for communication with clients and patients. It is not clear how these specific initiatives represented radical curriculum change, but they were presented as evidence of institutional responsiveness to the press for decolonization.

Within the institutional response, there were two powerful cross-currents relating to curriculum change. One was concerned with issues of regulatory compliance by, for example, the senior executive manager in charge of matters such as credits and credit hours; the other current, represented by the heads of arts and education, was concerned with the deep transformation of curriculum, pedagogy, and assessment. For the former, change is mainly managerial, such as reorganizing the curriculum to make it more convenient for students, or "a technical restructuring, rather than a pedagogical reflection," in the words of the Vice-Chancellor. For the latter, change is about the politics of knowledge. The dilemma, said the Vice-Chancellor, is that both groups:

Use the same language, so they can never understand what the tension is. Because they both use the word transformation; they both use the word decolonization. But they mean fundamentally different things by them.

In the case of Wits, nevertheless, the pressure for decolonization was much less immediate and intense than it was at UCT. Wits was immersed in the red-hot politics of the Fees Must Fall protests. This somewhat unique political space allowed two things: on the one hand, it enabled the institutional response at Wits to continue as one of regular and routine reporting on decolonization or transformation initiatives through established faculty structures. In other words, the political heat was on fees rather than decolonization.

On the other hand, this situation allowed for the flourishing of imaginative and experimental enclave initiatives that depended very much on what the individuals and departments involved understood transformation or decolonization to mean. There was, in other words, no driving political force for decolonization at the centre of the university – whether from the executive management or from a delegated authority, such as the "task teams" at other universities.

2.5 Decolonization, a Passing Compulsion: The University of Johannesburg

When decolonization came to the attention of the executive management of the University of Johannesburg (UJ), it quickly became an item on the Senate's agenda. The immediate debates reflected the national confusion. What exactly was the meaning of this relatively new term on campuses? Some thought it was another word for Africanization or simply a call for more African examples in the curriculum. Others spoke of a more diverse range of epistemologies, while the more politically attuned referred to "the who, what, and why of teaching and learning" – those commonplace questions about knowledge that were also raised at institutions like the Nelson Mandela University.

In response to the initial academic turmoil around the new term, the university leadership decided to install an ad hoc task team of Senate on the Decolonization of Knowledge and Curriculum Reform. The task team had four panels, composed of staff and students.

One of those panels, concerned with *the decolonization of knowledge*, was headed up by a senior academic who brought energy and direction to the job, "because of my work on Africa and because of my Pan-Africanist ideology." This panel saw its objective as making sense of what students meant by decolonization and how the institution could respond accordingly. But, as another senior academic administrator said of the UJ Task Team, "we didn't really know what the real goal was, but we knew we had to do something, and that we had to begin conversations."

What UJ did was what all the other universities did, which was to host seminars, workshops, and colloquia on decolonization during the intense period of student protest. A familiar list of speakers was brought in from the outside, and venues were packed to the rafters to hear them. A student group called Black Thought hosted reading groups, in which the works of anti-colonial fighters and intellectuals such as Frantz Fanon featured prominently.

Inside the academic faculties, decolonization made it onto the agendas of formally scheduled meetings, such as those of the Faculty Boards. Members of the task team attended these otherwise administrative meetings of the eight faculties to listen to and participate in deliberations on decolonization. These discussions took on more concrete form in the Teaching and Learning Committees of each faculty, where the nuts and bolts of curriculum matters were usually thrashed out.

It was, however, from the "spin-off seminars" on decolonization that tension and controversy blew up in the open. White academics, in particular, expressed hurt and bewilderment:

There was pain because some academics felt as though they had given their lives to the discipline and that they weren't colonial [simply] because they were white; they were feeling under major attack.

One academic [who] was sitting at my roundtable said to me that she's never felt so hurt ... she said part of the hurt was related to not having reflected so deeply as to what constituted a curriculum. She said, "You think about constituting a curriculum in relation to the discipline, but not necessarily in relation to the decolonization debate."

The institutional wars on curriculum were fought out in these heated seminars. Debates spilled out into the media, as advocates and critics of decolonization had their say. And then something unexpected happened in more than one of these large gatherings. After initial exchanges in English, student protestors started speaking in African languages, such as isiZulu, instantly cutting off whites and other non-speakers of indigenous languages from what was being said or discussed. They found this alarming, and it caused "heavy trauma" for some non-speakers of the African languages. The students, others argued, were making a point about cultural alienation within their university, and language was a powerful way to illustrate what they experience in their daily lives on campus, where the language of instruction and administration is English.

These vibrant and intense campus debates on decolonization soon took an unexpected turn: The university management turned the process over to the Academic Planning Department, thus immediately undercutting the political work of the decolonization task team. One task team member was blunt:

What happened with decolonization [is that] we had all of these discussions and then they shifted it to Academic Planning and then it became a technical exercise of templates, so you almost take the politics out of it and you blunt it [into a] formulaic exercise.

One instrument of academic planning is the programme review, and in this process, academics began to be asked the question, "What are the kinds of things you've done around decolonizing the curriculum?" In a short period of time, doing decolonization, or not, became a performance indicator, on which academics were assessed and which formed part of their annual performance plan. The academic planners argued that they were mainstreaming a radical idea; the academic activists retorted that management was defanging a radical initiative by taking the necessary politics out of the curriculum activism that had been led by, among others, the designated task team.

A political process around curriculum deliberation effectively became part of the routines of academic administration, with university planners producing a document called the "Charter on Decolonization." Without a blush, the Charter justified its existence by claiming that "Current efforts at decolonization in South Africa ... seek the systematic mainstreaming, promotion, production and generation of decolonized knowledge ... " The Charter itself was based on no fewer than eleven *principles* and thirteen *practices*.

The *principles*, in abbreviated and paraphrased form, are:

1. Recognizing the need for decolonizing the university
2. Promoting access to higher education
3. Promoting a culture of inclusiveness
4. Opposing the abuse of power, racism, class privilege etc.
5. Viewing decolonization as a process that includes all stakeholders
6. Understanding decolonization as an ongoing process that liberates minds and transforms universities
7. Envisioning more just and free societies
8. Envisaging a learning environment that exposes students to diversities of knowledges, methodologies, and epistemologies
9. Acknowledging and promoting African creativity, value systems, languages etc.
10. Valuing pedagogies and research from the Global South
11. Committing to being rooted in community, country, and continent

The thirteen *practices*, on the other hand, commit the university to:

1. Promoting curriculum reform
2. Reviewing curriculum on a regular basis
3. Facilitating re-curriculation at department and faculty levels
4. Ensuring feedback through academic committees
5. Demonstrating academic leadership in implementing the decolonization of the university
6. Creating safe spaces for engagement on decolonization
7. Reviewing policies and practices to ensure a decolonized and equitable environment
8. Advancing Africa-centredness
9. Collaborating with other African universities
10. Deepening South-South academic engagement
11. Embedding decolonization in institutional plans with measurable indicators
12. Using and promoting African languages
13. Providing adequate funding to support transformation.

Everything, in other words.

The university nevertheless continued with "orchestrated conversations" on decolonization, as a senior academic called it, while much of the administrative energy was now found in the Teaching and Learning Committees. In these committees, the ground was well-tilled for critical deliberations on knowledge and teaching, as a result of the leadership of the late activist academic Brenda Liebowitz before the 2015–2016 student protests. But it was clear that the drive and direction provided by the Task Team was effectively over and, surprising no one, the body was disbanded.

It was now up to the deans to take decolonization forward in line with the institution's published "Guidelines for Curriculum Transformation" (August 2016), which also included a range of traditional academic activities, such as "reviewing assessment criteria and tasks." Under the Guidelines, deans were to provide the DVC: Academic with progress reports and plans of action that included milestones and timelines in relation to decolonization and curriculum change.

Decolonization was now effectively mainstreamed, and the chances of radical change to the curriculum were muted. One of the task team leaders bemoaned the situation:

You give it to the deans who don't want to do anything with it in any case. They have it as a discussion item in their faculty boards. They are in control of how those discussions will play out. And then they just tick the box with an 'Oh, we've done that.' They then decide what happens and we go on as usual.

In the meantime, a new Vice-Chancellor was appointed, and an entirely new policy compulsion came to demand the attention of UJ academics – the Fourth Industrial Revolution (4IR).

2.6 Decolonization in a Merged Institution: Nelson Mandela University

No university had a more convoluted set of structures and processes that mark its institutional response to decolonization than the Nelson Mandela University (NMU). The momentum for the institutional response at NMU came from the Faculty of Education, which was hyperconscious of the need for change, and where an energetic new dean was generating new ideas about transformative pedagogies that were later introduced to the university as a whole.

The "curriculum renewal" in the Education Faculty started in 2009 and was characterized by a very collaborative process, involving lecturers, students, and outside facilitators. Out of this came a "curriculum framework" that used the concepts of "I" (the teacher), "Thou" (the student), and "It" (the curriculum) as parts of an enriched language of education and change. That curriculum framework was extended into what became a defining reference for the work of change in the university – "a humanizing curriculum framework." Across the university, staff talked about "a humanizing pedagogy," which was taken up in the institutional vision of NMU. This humanizing curriculum framework, in turn, reflected *on paper* the teaching philosophy of the institution.

The conception of "a humanizing pedagogy" coincided, however, with the review of teacher qualifications by the national accreditation authority, the Council on Higher Education. At the same time that academics scrambled to satisfy the technical standards for accreditation, the institution's curriculum review process posed deeper questions about the "What" (curriculum), "How" (pedagogy), and "Why" (purposes) of knowledge, including ones about the ownership of curriculum content (or "Whose knowledge?").

Shortly afterward, the education dean became the Deputy Vice-Chancellor for Academic Affairs, transferring the curriculum renewal energy of her former Faculty into the central administration. The new DVC endowed the curriculum transformation process with yet another conceptual wrinkle, this time termed "the institutional culture enlivening process."

Outside speakers were once again brought in, including African and Latin American scholars, and it was at this point (2011–2012) that decolonization and Africanization became part of the campus discourse as it grappled with curriculum change.

Inside the faculties, yet another conceptual innovation was introduced, *the grounding programme* (based on the idea that students must be *grounded* in basic understandings of themselves and their culture), which the Vice-Chancellor brought with him from his tenure in the same position at the University of Fort Hare. Now, concepts of Ubuntu and African values became part of the campus dialogues, leading to a popular module called "social consciousness for sustainable futures," which was student-led and based on seven core themes.

It was time to bring in the various faculties more directly, and a series of "Deans Retreats" were convened, with one of the themes, in 2016, being decolonization. It was at this point that the institution confronted a hard reality – that the responses varied across the faculties, which often ascribed their own meanings to the term to other faculties, for example, to science, where the dominant belief was that "science is science," and that decolonization had little to say to universal scientific laws.

Nevertheless, out of these retreats *six themes* were generated for institutional attention, including language; student voice; ways of being; changing systems; and ways of doing curriculum. These *uiteenlopende* (divergent), if not completely random, ideas were eventually crystallized in *ten curriculum statements* (on *"context"*; "transformation"; "knowledge"; "curriculum"; "innovation"; "language"; "voice"; "relationships"; "space"; and "processes"), which were produced in addition to all the earlier announcements of curriculum departures. This conceptual flourish inevitably led to a sense of curriculum exhaustion across the university.

The ten curriculum statements read as a list of seemingly random concepts, poorly articulated with each other, and vague enough to be filled with any idea of curriculum change. Curriculum, in one of the statements, was described as "more than the content of the subject," in that it takes into account "humanizing pedagogies." Knowledge, on the other hand, presumably a related concept to curriculum, "includes the principles of decoloniality, epistemological diversity and continuous review." It was, in short, a veritable soup of concepts and ideas, and it caused considerable confusion and listlessness among NMU academics.

In short, the university found itself literally weighed down by layers on layers of curriculum departures without any clear sense of curriculum arrivals. The institutional documents on curriculum change stacked up, and when its chief progenitor was asked about implementation, the response was that it was up to academics to absorb the radical idea of decolonization within their curricula.

With the institutional response to decolonization at NMU collapsing under this weight, the student protest movement ended up with little to show for its efforts to decolonize the curriculum.

2.7 The Disappearing Statues: The University of Pretoria

When decolonization knocked on the doors of the University of Pretoria, the statues there had already disappeared. "This establishment," explained a senior academic "was very clever in removing all these statues and putting them into one of the archives." What this meant was that, in the wake of the toppling of Rhodes at UCT, there was no longer any obvious monument left to play its role in the politics of student spectacle on this century-old campus. Attention shifted elsewhere.

As the clamour for decolonization started to build on campuses around the country, the University of Pretoria did what it does best – it organized a *lekgotla* (Setswana for a meeting place or assembly). And so, in March 2016, the UP management and student societies convened a lekgotla. Three streams were formed: one on *language policy* (Afrikaans, as one of the two teaching languages, was still a vexed concern for Black students ahead of a court decision on the matter than came later); a second on *institutional culture*; and a third on *curriculum transformation*.

The work of curriculum was underpinned by *four drivers* of transformation, identified as responsiveness to social context; epistemological diversity; renewal of pedagogy and classroom practices; and an institutional culture of openness and critical reflection. These four seemingly random and potentially overlapping (e.g., institutional culture was also a second *stream*) drivers were further described in hefty detail in a landmark document that emerged from the *lekgotla* under the headings Draft Curriculum Transformation Framework Document; Reimagining Curricula for a Just University in a Vibrant Democracy; and Work Stream on Curriculum Transformation at the University of Pretoria.

The first driver – responsiveness to social context – held that "a transforming curriculum is one that registers and is attuned to local and global contexts, histories, realities and problems." There followed detailed content with recognizable keywords from decolonization moments at other institutions, such as:

- Marginalized narratives
- Social justice
- Indigenous knowledge
- Subjugated knowledges
- Disadvantage within disciplines
- Common humanity
- Critical thinking
- Critical literacy
- Student life worlds

What was novel in the elaboration of this first driver was a bold, if lumpy, reference to "developing a compulsory foundational course for all first-year students in African history, thought and society, political economy and human rights."

The second driver – epistemological diversity – was described as "bringing marginalized groups, experiences, knowledges and world-views emanating from Africa and the Global South to the centre of the curriculum." The familiar keywords from the decolonization discourses included under this "driver" were:

- Hegemony of Western ideas
- Colonial and imperial hierarchies of power
- Cultural and psychological hegemonies
- Different forms of violence
- Epistemic diversity
- Pluriversality
- Excavating and recuperating African (and other) knowledges
- Epistemic racism and sexism
- Hidden histories
- Reconceptualizing knowledge
- Rethinking the structure of the disciplines

It was, without doubt, a dense and arcane language, which held little meaning for those outside of the humanities and social sciences, and, indeed, even the more traditional academics within them. But this abstruse language was not inconsistent with what was being put forward by universities such as UCT and NMU in the advocacy of decolonization.

The third driver – renewal of pedagogy and classroom practices – was described as "continuously rethinking and re-evaluating the ways in which we learn and teach," including "responsiveness to and training in new pedagogical methodologies and approaches within disciplines." This description was broad in scope and therefore open to many interpretations; further, it was free of the kind of critical and political language of the previous "driver" – in fact, its keywords suggest very traditional, even problematic, understandings (as in "student deficits") that render the curriculum problematic to begin with:

- Students' learning impediments
- Home literacies
- School literacies
- Learning beyond the lecture hall

- Support for transitions (e.g., from high school to university)
- Receptivity to new modes of delivery, e.g., technological innovations
- Skills acquisition such as literacy and numeracy

There are certainly one or two phrases in UP's lengthy exposition on transformation that suggest attention to the politics of curriculum, such as the injunction to include in "teaching and learning the affective dimension of multiple forms of oppressions, including various kinds of pain," a phrase that would certainly be hard to make practical sense of in an engineering or actuarial science classroom at any university.

The fourth driver of curriculum transformation – an institutional culture of openness and critical reflection – claims that a transforming curriculum comes with the understanding that "a hidden curriculum can be found in the spaces, symbols, narratives and embedded practices that constitute the university." These "subliminal practices" of discrimination and exclusion require action, as expressed in the following keywords and phrases:

- Openness to difference
- Transformation of academic staff
- Redefining whose voices count
- Reviewing institutional processes and traditions
- Dismantling organizational hierarchies
- Resisting corporatist and managerialist practices
- Interrogating university spaces, symbols, statues, and architectures

The fourth driver drew critical attention to everyday, invisible practices of discrimination in a traditional university that have become normalized over the decades in "the way things are done here."

In the meantime, the UP Senate approved a document titled "Reimagining Curricula for a Just University in a Vibrant Democracy" – this institutional document now served as "the official framework" to guide and inform the university's curriculum.

This curriculum transformation framework made its way from the *lekgotla* to the nine faculties of the university, and "that's where the difficulties emerged," observed the leader of the decolonization project at UP. The humanities and law faculties were easily engaged, in part because the political language of curriculum transformation was not unfamiliar to many in these academic precincts, and because some of the decolonization activists, students as well as academics, actually came from within these areas of the university. It was in the science faculties, initially, that considerable resistance to decolonization was expressed, in defence of universal claims of scientific laws and principles.

The faculties were handed "Self-reflection questions" that read more like instructions, including:

- Evaluate the current curriculum offered in your faculty in relation to the four drivers.
- List the challenges and limitations faced in your faculty in transforming the curriculum.
- Outline fully the steps you will take as faculty and departments to address curriculum transformation.
- Include an overall plan with clear timelines for curriculum transformation in which "teaching and learning committees should lead the process."

Beyond these instructions to the faculties, the university pressed ahead with its decolonization drive, and at the centre of this institutional endeavour was the lecture series "Curriculum Transformation Matters: The Decolonial Turn." The 2018 lectures are indicative of the tone and content of these public talks:

- "Decolonization, Liberation and the Politics of Knowledge Production in Africa," by Professor Abdi Samatar (University of Minnesota)
- "The Appropriation and Commodification of Decolonization in South African Universities Post-fallism," by Professor Nomalanga Mkhize (Nelson Mandela University)
- "Re-imagining the Decolonization Debates in South African Higher Education: What's Gender Got To Do With It?" by Professor Relebohile Moletsane (University of KwaZulu Natal)
- "In Search of a New Archive: Reclaiming Agency, Voice and Knowledge Production Beyond The Post-Apartheid," by Professor Pumla Gobodo-Madikizela (Stellenbosch University)

Two powerful personalities, both accomplished Black scholars, happened to be in key positions at the – in terms of staff – very white University of Pretoria at the same time; it was they who carried these institutional initiatives forward. The Vice-Rector: Academic was a prominent figure in critical studies of race and psychology, while the Dean of Humanities was a leading light in critical theory and sociology; both of these scholars had strong national and international reputations. The DVC led the curriculum transformation drive, while the Dean oversaw the generous Mellon Foundation Grant, which included a funded study (together with the HSRC) on public attitudes towards decolonization.

The critical question was whether this consolidation of the decolonization drive at the centre of the university's administrative leadership would filter down to the faculties. Both leaders were doubtful. "I cannot verify and tell you [that] has fully changed in real practice," said one; "Whether there is in fact any fundamental change in their curricula is another matter" said the other, who quickly added that "90% of the old guard are still conservative." These demographic realities hampered any chance of institution-wide curriculum change beyond the "10% who are open to the possibility of looking critically at notions of transformation and even decolonization."

By the time the Teaching and Learning Review (University of Pretoria 2018) – which carried the reports of the heads of teaching and learning in the nine faculties – was published, it was clear that decolonization had quickly been superseded by the mainstream work of the university. The almost 100-page document had a small section on one page on the decolonization lectures and "curriculum transformation through specific faculty plans and activities." The Teaching and Learning Review (2018) then launched into what UP has been known for over many years – technological innovation in the teaching and learning space, that is, e-technologies. New keywords were now highlighted throughout the document:

- Multimedia education
- Digital competencies
- Blackboard Collaborate Ultra (BCU) with millennials
- Fully online programmes
- Upscaling the use of e-technologies
- Game-based learning
- Artificial intelligence

2.8 The Verwoerd Statue Went Quietly: Stellenbosch University

When decolonization strolled onto the Stellenbosch University (SU) campus, it was a modest affair. On this predominantly white, conservative campus in the picturesque vineyard town of Stellenbosch, protests and upheaval are rare, and they are efficiently managed when they erupt. The small protesting crowd had to be fortified with students bused in from UCT, and even then, the numbers were barely around 200 protestors, one observer estimated. "It was a minority thing," said a senior academic, even though he allowed, "there was some burning on the campus, there was some marching up and down, we did see some police presence on campus."

What curriculum activism there was at this century-old university, established for white Afrikaners, was concentrated within the university's Centre for Teaching and Learning (CTL). The focus of this energetic group of scholars was on preparing new lecturers for innovative and self-reflective teaching to connect classrooms and community. For example, a lecturer in viticulture challenged students to smell and detect local aromas – rather than only traditional, European aromas – in the wine industry. That lecturer did not use the d-word, but CTL's leader claimed that such sensory evaluation training was an instance of "decolonization in the curriculum."

An annual Scholarship of Teaching and Learning (SOTL) Conference became a major gathering point for academics experimenting with new ways of teaching in their disciplines. A monthly *Auxin Padkos*[2] was convened, whose first presentation carried the title "Reimagining a Scientific Curriculum in the Current South African Higher Education Context," and warned that "science is a particularly tough customer to decolonize." Then, a Focus Interest Group (FIG) was created for more regular, informal dialogues on topics such as the decolonization of the STEM curriculum. A Critical Citizenship group was established to encourage campus-wide discussions on hot-button issues, such as the student protest movement. Out of this group came critical papers such as "Engaging with Visual Redress at Stellenbosch University: Decolonise Spaces" and "Exploring the Socio-Political History of the Arts in Stellenbosch: A Contribution to Decolonise the Art Curriculum."

When decolonization protests spread on university campuses across the country, there was a sense of frustration within the CTL community, and the academic staff it served, that "there was no direction"

---

[2] Metaphorical language, "auxin" being a plant hormone and "*padkos*" a colloquial Afrikaans word meaning food-for-the-journey.

from the senior management as to an institutional response to the moment, apart from emails about suspending lectures from time to time. In fact, there was, within these CTL-driven initiatives, "a lot of criticism of management for not having created these kinds of opportunities at the university."

Outside of the institutional forums for dealing with decolonization, ongoing activism nevertheless emerged on and around the campus. The Goedgedacht Forum published *Decolonising Higher Education: The Lived Experiences of Stellenbosch & Rhodes Pointing a Way Forward* (April 2018), an important survey of student experiences at Stellenbosch that offered a window on how some students saw decolonization. More traumatic for the institution was an earlier documentary, the so-called *Luister* [Listen] video (Contraband Cape Town 2015), which documented, through interviews, the often traumatic lived experiences of Black students at the former white, Afrikaans university.

There were also constant political murmurings about transformation on campus, something a senior manager referred to as "an energy in the air," which saw some small-scale changes here and there, without much political fuss. So, for example, in the wake of the installation of a new Vice-Chancellor in April 2015, and his public commitment to transformation, the bust of Hendrik Verwoerd, a one-time Stellenbosch professor and later the Prime Minister often described as the architect of apartheid, was quietly taken down. At the same time, opposition groups such as *Open Stellenbosch* campaigned for more changes – such as in the university's Afrikaans language policy. What could not be denied, however, was the growing movement for change on other campuses, so it was perhaps not surprising that in late November 2016, the SU Council gave a clear directive to the senior leadership of the university:

The management is requested to make a presentation to Council at a future meeting on the matter of Decolonisation of the Curriculum, the interpretation that they assign to it, what they foresee will be done about it in future, and other relevant aspects.

It was time for action, and the Vice-Rector: Academic, an engineer by profession, approached the Senate sub-committee called The Committee for Learning and Teaching on 9 February 2017. That committee decided to establish a task team to respond to the Council's directive. The Rector's Management Team (RMT) formally inaugurated The Task Team on the Decolonisation of Curriculum at its meeting of 7 March 2017.

It was as sudden and as blunt as that – but it was also curious timing, for in the same month SU published the *Transformation Plan of Stellenbosch University* (Institutional Transformation Committee March 2017) which became an overarching policy guide for the campus as a whole. In briefing the new task team, the Committee for Learning and Teaching did not refer to this institutional document, which in one of its "strategic priority and objective" statements briefly commits to

prioritize, expand and develop curriculum renewal and teaching methodologies to ensure the relevance of teaching programmes to the societal transformation needs in the contexts of Africanisation, decolonization and global relevance.

Nonetheless, the Director of CTL was appointed as convenor of the task team, onto which each faculty was invited to send a delegate. The terms of reference for the Task Team were to engage the brief of Council; make sense of the interpretation of decolonization; extend the investigation to include those processes, cultures, and identities that govern the curriculum; draw students and other partners into the decolonization debate; and

make recommendations on how the university should proceed with the Decolonization of the Curriculum and the broader feelings of alienation that underpin this call for decolonization. (Stellenbosch University 2017a)

The task team divided its work among three "sub-groups": one to deal with the meanings ("interpretations") of decolonization, another with institutional cultures ("processes, cultures and identities"), and yet another on the decolonization of curriculum ("beyond the mainstream curriculum and in-class learning activities").

The CTL had already collected rich data on the curriculum work of each of the nine faculties and moved quickly to complete its draft report in late August 2017 to serve at a meeting of Senate's Committee for Learning and Teaching (CLT). At the meeting, some of the faculties revolted during the intense debates on the report. The tone was aggressive, not inviting of discussion; "It got people's backs up," recalled the task team convenor. "The language was arcane," said some; "Science is science," said others.

The final document, *Recommendations of the Task Team for the Decolonization of the Stellenbosch University Curriculum*, was certainly strident, even radical. It was completely different in style, content, and argument from the usually sedate and apolitical institutional documents on transformation and change. Singular examples from the task team report must suffice:

The SU curricula are perceived among some "to be complicit in coloniality." The senior management is lambasted for being disengaged. There are those in the university "who still suffer from colonial oppression." The "mind space of those teaching the curriculum, should be decolonized." And the university is warned that it will pass through the epistemological equivalent of the stages of grief – now needing "to prepare for the process of Mourning, the stage of lamenting victimization."

On 28 August 2017, this radical document went to Senate, where there were already signs of trouble for the task team. Its report was hardly mentioned in that Senate meeting – the highest academic body of the university simply did not engage this crucial document on decolonization. Instead, the Rector's Management Team (RMT) prepared a diluted version for the Council, which had originally called for such a report, and, to the shock of the task team convenor, "It was a different one. It made reference to the document, but it was a whole different document ... I was not consulted."

The so-called parameters document that emerged from management had completely watered down the task team's report in a new document called *In Search of Parameters for the Imperative of the Decolonization Of Curriculum*. The task team report was an openly political analysis of decolonization with radical proposals for change, such as the bold recommendation that "Decolonization ... need[s] to be deliberately written into all future processes and practices related to Institutional Transformation."

The *Parameters* document, on the other hand, was a simple technical document that fell back on familiar institutional management language, such as graduate attributes, market differentiation, and assigned learning credits. It was a massive climb down from the task team report, and shortly thereafter the convenor resigned from her formal position at the university.

Then, as had happened in the Senate – and despite the urgent and focused brief of Council (November 2016) that management "make a presentation on … the decolonization of curriculum" – the *Parameters* document was simply tabled at the last governance meeting of the year, in November 2017, and, according to a record of that meeting, "Council had no questions, and only took note of the report." That was it.

The decolonization of curriculum was now simply a matter for faculties to consider and take forward within their authority. A letter of 5 September 2017 from the senior manager responsible for Teaching and Learning, Professor Arnold Schoonwinkel, had already set the terms of decolonization. Heads of academic and administrative units were encouraged to have discussions about the recommendations of the task team, exchange ideas, and bring students in. The Afrikaans conclusion to the senior manager's brief poignantly captures the language of political disengagement:

U hoef nie formeel te rapporteur oor u dekolonisasie gesprekke nie, maar vertrou dat dit neerslag sal vind in die prosesse en programme van u omgewing.

[You don't have to formally report on your decolonisation conversations, but (I) trust it would be reflected in the processes and programmes of your environment.][3]

That was the end of the political drive for decolonization at Stellenbosch University. In the normal curriculum review processes, it received small mention and optional status, as in this "list of [18] *possible* dimensions when considering programme renewal" (emphasis added):

(e) Decolonisation of the curriculum i.e., to ensure that a wide range of (South) African literature and case studies are included in the curriculum, to supplement learning material from Europe, the United Kingdom, and the USA.

2.9 Understanding Institutional Responses to Political Demands for Radical Curriculum Change

Our thesis about institutional posturing can now be summarized as follows: Institutions under political pressure respond with emergency

[3] The authors are grateful to the author and columnist Max du Preez for the translation from Afrikaans.

measures that signal the intention to change, but those reactions are not intended as lasting commitments to original demands. This chapter has offered a survey of such institutional postures in response to the demand for decolonization. The institutional cases have offered further insights into the workings of institutions and the prospects for radical curriculum change.

The first thing that is striking is that *institutions do respond* to student protests, especially when they sense the nationwide character of a movement. The dramatic spectacle of the toppling of the Rhodes statue on South Africa's most prestigious university campus conveyed a clear and compelling message as to what could happen on any campus as demands for "a free, decolonized education" escalated in both scope and intensity. South African universities regularly experience strikes and protests, but those are often local, cyclical, and sporadic in nature. They are also often ignored.

University leaders sensed, after Rhodes fell, that this round of student protests had the potential to disrupt and confront business-as-usual at public institutions. Unbudgeted funds were committed for task teams, followed by outside speakers and endless workshops, seminars, conferences, and colloquia. Campuses buzzed with curriculum deliberations, as institutions rushed to respond to the expanding crisis.

In the imitative politics of South Africa, statues offered the perfect opportunity for the politics of spectacle. On the one hand, a prominent statue presented an ideal target for mobilizing protest action against the institution; on the other hand, it stood for something else – the lack of deep change – whether in terms of language policy, as at SU, or an alienating white institutional culture, as at UCT, or simply relief from material hardship, as at UWC. Some institutions had read the signs of the times in good time and removed offensive sculptures before the storm, such as at SU and UP. At others, such as UFS and UCT, even progressive symbols, in the form of artworks by black artists, came under attack, simply because they were *there* in the public space (Jansen 2017). "We have no statues" – the words of a UWC student leader – is a lament about the lack of opportunity for spectacle as a way of drawing attention to other things.

It is not simply that institutions were responding; it was also that they had to be seen to be acting on the escalating demands for decolonization. In response, "task teams" of various kinds were quickly called into existence as the protests intensified on and around university campuses. Most universities created their task teams through the official structures of their institutions – typically a committee or sub-committee of the Senate, thereby lending academic gravitas to the task. For UCT, curiously, the task team was created outside of the official structures, which could only mean one thing – that the presumably "untransformed" Senate was not to be trusted to drive the decolonization of the curriculum. That said, the prospects for radical change were always going to be diminished by the placement of the academic authority for curriculum change outside these mandated bodies. In the event, UCT reined the task team (working group) and its report back into the institutional machinery of the Senate.

In this regard, the nature and content of institutional responses often reflected the leadership in charge of the decolonization of the curriculum. In the case of UP, for example, the Vice-Rector: Academic, a prominent Black critical theorist in the field of psychology, led the charge along with his Dean of Humanities, a critical theorist in gender studies and sociology; together they formed a powerful team, whose ideas were reflected in the political language of the institutional documentation on decolonization.

Similarly, the Pan-African ideology of the leader of the curriculum task team at UJ is reflected powerfully in the reports of the group, as was the case with the leader of the SU group. The politics of pedagogy, on the other hand, dominates the institutional documentation of NMU, because the leader of the decolonization of curriculum was the former education dean, and later at the helm as DVC: Academic. On the other hand, the curriculum leadership of decolonization at Wits was represented by a chemistry academic, and at UWC by a legal scholar; in these latter two cases, the institutional documentation on decolonization was decidedly less political, less pedagogical, and less strident than in the other universities.

But did it matter that the ideas of the activist leadership of decolonization framed the key institutional documents on curriculum change? The evidence suggests that the high language of the humanities, and particularly its critical-theory variants, were largely disconnected from the day-to-day curriculum work and thought of ordinary academics. While the critical language of change may have impressed activist students and allied academics, it in fact alienated many lecturing staff, who often neither understood the specialist language of humanities scholars nor found it very useful or relevant to the more scientific and technical disciplines. In fact, it will be argued in the closing chapter of this book that the strategic failure of the activists lay in their inability to speak clearly and persuasively about the decolonization of knowledge to, among others, science, engineering, and accounting academics.

It was nevertheless instructive to observe the extent to which the universities' responses to decolonization allowed for severe criticism of themselves by their newly created task teams. As their reports emerged in public, institutions were not spared. The institutional curriculum was charged with nothing less than epistemic violence, and dressed down as a remnant of colonial and apartheid epistemologies. For the activists, little had changed since the heady days of the advent of democracy in the mid-1990s; in 2015–2016, the curriculum was still white and European, unmoored from its African context. Such strident criticism of the resident curriculum was particularly acute in the case of UCT, and, perhaps more surprisingly, at Stellenbosch University. Why, the question could be asked, would more conservative universities, especially SU, bend over willingly for such an institutional lashing?

One reason is that the intense politics of the moment required institutions to absorb the criticism of staff and student protests. It would have been the worst possible managerial reaction in those pressure-filled political moments to take action against critics, or even to be defensive in the process. The institutional response in all cases was to "wait out" the student protests, and to graciously receive the task team reports. It was a low-risk strategy that worked, from the viewpoint of the institutional management of the crisis, for what happened next killed those reports, in what can only be described as different ways of dying.

For SU, the curriculum change report was completely rewritten by the senior management, defanged of all its radical pretensions, and tabled "for noting" at a year-end meeting of the same Council that originally asked for the report. For UCT, the radical curriculum change report was published on the university website along with a call for comments, and dismissed by a senior management executive as "by no means the curriculum policy of the university." For UJ, the radical document was captured in a crisp website statement entitled the *Charter on Decolonisation*, leaving the faculties with little more than *Guidelines for Curriculum Transformation*.

As task teams were disbanded, and radical curriculum change documents quietly shelved, there was another important element in the institutional posture around decolonization that was easily missed. Despite the fire and fury of the decolonization protests, and the often assertive demands for fundamental curriculum change contained in task team reports, the responsibility for further action was handed over to the academic faculties. In other words, whether or not the implementation of the radical or toned-down versions of proposals for radical curriculum change were to be taken up at all was a decision left to the discretion of the academics. Inside the faculties, it was business as usual, since the political demands for radical curriculum change from the protestors, and the institutional pressure for change from management, had gradually dissipated. On top of that, there was clear evidence in many interviews of "academic fatigue," with constant carping about decolonization in the corridors of the different universities.

This kind of voluntarism in institutional policy regarding curriculum was inevitable. South African universities, like many of their counterparts around the world, still place a significant premium on academic autonomy, when it comes to the content and methods of teaching. Despite the sharp, accusatory language flung at the settled curriculum and the radical direction proposed for change, neither student protestors nor executive managers can instruct professors on what and how to teach in a democracy, and in universities that prize autonomy as a condition of academic work. In the end, it was difficult not to notice the difference between the political bang of task team recommendations and the whimper with which the demand for radical curriculum change floundered.

This particular observation raises another important reason for the decline of decolonization on campuses. Very often, the institutional response completely misread the political moment represented by decolonization, as if it were merely an educational opportunity requiring changes to curriculum, pedagogy, and assessment. This is not to say that there were not genuine concerns about Eurocentrism and Western universality represented in the settled curriculum. That, however, was not the primary driver of the moment.

Decolonization, as this book shows, gave political traction to a broader set of social and institutional criticisms of South African society after apartheid. It was activist academics who – in their enthusiasm to demonstrate responsiveness, and, in the process, to give expression to their own particular ideologies of change – *ran ahead of* where most of the students were, in pressing for social and institutional change.

At the same time, more traditional academics also took the chance to *move away from* what students were demanding. The open-ended meanings of decolonization, in fact, meant that academics could often circumvent the more radical concerns of students (such as racialized inequalities and alienations within their universities) and recast those issues as something else – such as better scheduling of assessment tasks for travelling students, or academic development and upliftment.

The question of the contested meanings of decolonization were also reflected in the very language of institutional responses. Universities with a much more activist tradition, such as Wits, would not give up on the more familiar language of *transformation* as the driving rationale and language of choice for their change efforts. Others, such as UP, with less historical anchorage in struggle politics, completely embraced the language of *decolonization*, even if the institutional commitment, as has been shown, would dwindle very quickly as the pressure for change subsided. Transformation was certainly not jettisoned at most universities and, as the interviews revealed, all kinds of awkward conceptual connections were attempted by senior managers who remained attached to the older language of struggle, even as they were confronted with the replacement language of decolonization.

Past traditions were also reflected in *how* the institutional responses to decolonization unfolded on each campus. For UWC, a university that repeatedly reminds insiders and outsiders of its struggle history and accomplishments, the institutional response was deeply consultative. By talking to people on and off campus, and at all levels of the university, a thoroughly consultative process was followed, as part of the "awareness building" and consciousness-raising activism of another era. At SU, by contrast, the process of consultation was decidedly more top-down, driven by the authority invested in a team of activists drawn mainly from the faculties and tasked with getting the job done. Consultation was efficient and purposeful, and the authority for the final report rested in the hands of the executive management, who rewrote the task team's final document and ushered it through both Senate and Council without a single question of engagement. These very different kinds of institutional responses reflected different kinds of institutional traditions – such as the struggle politics tradition of UWC versus the (apartheid) establishment tradition of SU.

It was in the sciences that task teams encountered their most direct opposition to the language of change and the propositions of the decolonization activists. The common claims about the universal nature of science and scientific laws were not shaken by the strident language of the humanities disciplines. When some science disciplines did seek to respond to the decolonization demands, they did so in the context of the *application* of established scientific truths, rather than questioning the truth claims of science itself; in other words, the laws of science were in themselves immutable, but academic engineers were certainly open to extending the application of scientific ideas to local contexts.

Other disciplines, such as medicine, were content to "decolonize" to the extent that they would require students to learn a local African language and then present this as evidence of responsiveness to the demands for curriculum change. However, even within medical science faculties, there were fields, such as public health, where the focus of the work and the connections with the social sciences enabled a more positive response to decolonization; on the other hand, fields such as internal medicine were much more suspicious, if not dismissive of, the unsettling language of decolonization. This fissure between the humanities and the sciences was not resolved at any of the ten universities studied.

It was also striking, in the institutional responses, how the politics of decolonization as a radical initiative was constantly entangled with the moderating effects of the regulatory demands of administration and accreditation. At NMU, the decolonization drive coincided with the review of teacher education qualifications; at all of the universities, the administrative review of the LLB (law degree) came at the same time as faculty deliberations on decolonization. There is no doubt that, with one eye on administrators and accreditors, the urgent politics of decolonization found itself subdued by the administrative machinery of regulation to which institutions also had to attend.

Finally, the most salient observation about institutional responses to decolonization was the relative ease of the disablement or defanging of one of the most important political moments in the history of curriculum change in South Africa. To borrow from Deborah Anderson's (2018) concept of "institutional posturing," we contend that the behaviour of universities under enormous pressure can best be understood not only as "a cursory and transitory responsiveness," but as a strategic ploy to manage immediate political crises by signalling the intention to change without making enduring commitments to radical changes in the settled curriculum.

3 | *On the Institutionalization of Knowledge*

3.1 Introduction

When a radical idea such as decolonization comes marching onto a university campus towards the Vice-Chancellor's office, demanding the attention of the university leadership, it encounters along the way an array of familiar characters, such as professors, police, partisans, and the press. What is much less visible is a rock solid institution that, in some of our examples, has existed for more than a century. To confront an institution with the demand for change is to reckon with what scholars of organizations call "routines, procedures, conventions, roles, strategies, organizational forms, and technologies" (March and Olsen 2010) that keep things in place. In this context, what is the institutionalization of the curriculum?

By the institutionalization of curriculum, we mean the active processes by which universities recognize, accept, and embed new knowledge in their systems, structures, and procedures. Those active processes involve both the acceptance and rejection of new knowledge, as well as the reworking, or modification, of new knowledge as it becomes part of established knowledge. Through active institutional processes, such as registration, accreditation, and funding (see Chapter 5), new knowledge finds itself subjected to the routines of administration and control in a stabilized and enduring institutional curriculum (Miles, Ekholm, and Vandenberghe 1987, 251; Crossan et al. 1995, 337–360).

This chapter lays out the conceptual framework for an institutional account of radical curriculum change in universities. In the process, we lay the groundwork for a rare encounter between institutional theory (drawn from sociological studies) and curriculum theory (drawn from education studies) in an attempt to understand more clearly the problem of change.

3.2 The Institutional Analysis of Curriculum

Our approach to the *institutional analysis of curriculum* leans on the expansive literatures on institutions from different perspectives (institutionalism and the various versions of neo-institutionalism) applied to different kinds of organizations (political, economic, and educational) over time (Meyer and Rowan 1977; March and Olsen 1983; Powell and DiMaggio 1991; Meyer and Rowan 2006; Lerch et al. 2017; Nordin and Sundberg 2018).

Rather than through constant and explicit referencing to the often dense concepts, theories, and methods of institutionalism, we offer here an accessible narrative of how a radical curriculum idea, such as decolonization, winds its way through universities as complex institutions.

Throughout this chapter, the analysis is guided by some of the key claims and assumptions of neo-institutionalism, such as the fact that universities are rule-conforming institutions, responsive to concerns about accountability and legitimacy; that as institutions, universities find their stability in deeply institutionalized rules, norms, and regulations that are human constructions that become taken for granted in institutional life; that institutions owe their legitimacy to "institutionally situated" human actors with shared beliefs and understandings on which institutions are built; and that under these conditions, "compliance occurs in many circumstances because other types of behavior are inconceivable" (Meyer and Rowan 2006, 6), and "institutional logics" (or shared rationalizations) work to give curriculum practice its sense of normativity.

It is these understandings of stabilized institutions that account for our assessment of the prospects for radical knowledge within universities, focused on what we call the institutional curriculum.

3.3 How the Curriculum Is Institutionalized

Every university has rules and regulations as to how a curriculum is approved; rules and regulations for student assessment (e.g., what is a passing or failing grade); and rules and regulations as to when, where, and how often teaching takes place. Those who teach the curriculum are selected through rigorous appointment and promotions processes. There are internal and external evaluators (or moderators) who check on sampled assessment tasks. There are even rules about who those external evaluators of curriculum and assessment might be, and those standards are checked again by institutional auditors for professional degrees.

There are national and international standards that benchmark curriculum and assessment protocols. Scores of committees inside the university sit down every year to make final judgements about curricula and assessment. Internal awards are given for "best teaching," but these awards serve an additional purpose – to demonstrate what good teaching is *supposed* to be like. All of these institutional activities are tightly interlocked in institutional practices that are regularly reviewed and validated by accreditation agencies (e.g., the institutional and programme reviews of the Council on Higher Education, among other bodies) to ensure compliance with agreed standards.

To demand change of any kind, let alone radical change, is to confront this formidable monolith, *the institutional curriculum*. To press for change is to find oneself grappling with myriad rules, regulations, and routines locked up in a complex and convoluted administrative system that takes years to "process" approvals of a new curriculum. Often, the institutional failure to take up a new idea, whether radical or not, is due to what Mary Douglas (1986, 77) so artfully calls "the formulaic interlocking with normal procedures of validation."

The press for change is not, however, simply a matter of dealing with the "structures" that are a part of institutional life. To demand *radical* curriculum change is to raise the political antennae of the institutional curriculum. What is fascinating, though, is that the institutional response is seldom one of direct confrontation with the radical curriculum idea on the table.

Institutions are remarkably agile, and in this respect it is useful to think of them as organisms, which adjust to changing environmental conditions in order to survive; ecologists might call this the "institutional adaptive capacity" of organizations (Bettini, Brown, and de Haan 2015). One of the most common modes of adaptive response to radical ideas is what can be called institutional mimicry. That is, the institution takes on a resemblance to the real thing, so that it appears to be responsive to the demand for radical curriculum change.

The social sciences have grappled with this kind of behaviour; the proximate term in the sociology of organizations is isomorphic mimicry. So, for example, developing nation states gain their organizational legitimacy by developing the surface features of modernity associated with first world countries in order to gain certain benefits. Andrews (2017) and his colleagues call this kind of mimicry "a technique of successful failure."

In post-apartheid South Africa, higher education institutions find themselves under constant pressure for change (Booysen 2016; Jansen 2017; Habib 2019). For the historically white institutions, in particular, it is important to be seen as doing the right thing, not only in relation to a black majority government but to a growing number of black students, who describe themselves as alienated within former white universities. The charge often made by protesting students that "I do not see myself in the curriculum" is as damaging as the corresponding charge "I have gone through my entire degree without being taught by a black professor."

That kind of accusation stings, and one way of responding is to present the outward trappings of change without actually changing at all. The university leadership hopes that outside observers and critical insiders alike will read the signs of change and believe them to represent the substantive content of change. There is no readier institutional artefact to use for such symbolism than the curriculum.

As we have argued in other contexts, the curriculum indicates not simply the content to be taught but also a symbol to be flagged (Jansen 2002). The curriculum, like a flag, stands for something else. Like a flag waving in the breeze, the curriculum can amount to little more than a statement of intent or a signal of association. In one university in this study – the most conservative among the twenty-six public institutions – two remarkably bold headlines were carried in the national newspapers: "Decolonising Education: How One SA University Is Getting It Done" (Etheridge 2018); and, two years later, "Stellenbosch University Forges Ahead with Its Decolonisation Drive" (Mlamla 2020).

However, when we sampled seven of the major new curriculum proposals forwarded to and approved by the regulatory authorities of this same university, there was hardly a trace of any fundamental change in curricula drawn from the humanities, engineering, medicine, and the social sciences (see also Le Grange et al. 2020). The flag-waving headlines had done their job: the curriculum had been decolonized.

The reason a university does not yield readily, or at all, to demands for radical change is that the existing curriculum is much more than content to be taught; it is, genetically, the identity of the institution. In this perspective, the curriculum not only exists within an institution: It is itself a product of institutional life.[1] The curriculum is an expression, therefore, of what a university values and deems important as an institution.

To challenge the curriculum is therefore to challenge a system of embedded values, beliefs, and identities that the institution holds dear. In this respect, it is useful to think of "the curriculum as culture" (Joseph 2012), in that it reflects the significant meanings that human beings attach to curriculum in a specific place; this means that in trying to change the curriculum, account must be taken of "the belief systems that influences what is considered normal, or alternative, or simply unthinkable." Within a university, therefore, the curriculum is a set of arrangements – the institutional curriculum – that defines and sustains what is "thinkable" or acceptable as knowledge within the disciplines.

When a disruptive idea such as decolonization comes along, it therefore threatens that which is already authorized, bedded down, and sheltered in place. This is the point at which *the intruder curriculum*, or decolonization, needs to be dealt with through political ingenuity. For many of the former white institutions, this means finding ways of fending off the strange identity of the intruder curriculum, which seeks to find a home within the settled curriculum. This is a problem, for the intruder curriculum is genetically incompatible with the DNA of the settled curriculum.

To begin with, the intruder curriculum comes with a language that is unfamiliar – even foreign – to the settled environment. That is why the first response from more than 200 academics interviewed on the subject of *decolonization* was "what does this even mean?" (see Chapter 4). Learning this new language is demanding labour, intellectually, emotionally, and politically. The new language falls far outside the language of the academic socialization of the chemistry lecturer or the urban planning professor. It requires considerable effort, and even a potentially costly diversion from what academic X or Y was hired to

---

[1] It was Bill Pinar et al. (1995) who first spoke of the curriculum as "an institutionalized text" and William Schubert of "the curriculum as an institution" (Reid 1999), but neither developed the concept as a theory of change.

do in the first place. This kind of exertion is what institutions in fact avoid, for institutionalization is about regularity, stability, and routine. Institutions function to incorporate, modify, or eject radical ideas that threaten energetic reorganization or disruption (Ahmed 2012, 21, 23). Academics understandably find this demand for exertion to be exasperating, even threatening.

Perhaps one of the most threatening of such radical ideas was the *Curriculum Change Framework* (Curriculum Change Working Group 2018) of UCT. Developed as an institutional response to decolonization, the elaborate document was placed on the university's website for comment. There was a palpable sense of dread among many academics about criticizing this activist document, which was as much a radical political manifesto as it was a discussion document inviting intellectual engagement. Even liberal and left academics knew that to take on this intruder curriculum would be, as one put it, "career suicide." Weighed down by the impenetrable language and the worst excesses of high theory in the humanities, the document served another political purpose: to intimidate.

The intruder curriculum threatens the institutional order because its new language is provocative as it speaks of "epistemic injustice" or "epistemological suicide" or even "white fragility." As with intruders in your home, one of the first emotions is disorientation and, later, defilement. The intruder curriculum does not come with a language of invitation but one of confrontation. That is why the demand for decolonization, when first heard from student protestors in public encounters, is often experienced by white academics as personally hurtful and educationally harmful.

Academics were perplexed: But I thought I knew you; We were getting along so well; I taught here for many years and nobody said anything; What did I do wrong? Do I even belong here? The shouting and the screaming were intense. The intruder curriculum not only makes demands; it levies accusations. The stream of charges often does not make sense. The intruder wants something one moment and everything the next. Nothing in the institutional curriculum is sacred, whether it is the more obvious villains such as old white men in history or sociology texts or those seemingly immutable laws such as gravity and the second law of thermodynamics. Nothing is sacred, as in the celebrated case of the UCT student who stared down Newton's laws by claiming that people in her home village in rural KwaZulu-

Natal could summon lightning to smite their enemies (UCT Scientist 2016). Explain that, you resident curriculum! #ScienceMustFall became a memorable hashtag.

Institutions have learned in the past how to deal with radical ideas that come to challenge the settled curriculum. When the decolonization moment, with its curriculum demands, came to UCT, older academics allied with the students reminded all who would listen of "The Mamdani Affair," as it came to be known. This was the time in the 1990s when the Ugandan scholar Mahmood Mamdani was appointed as Head of the Centre for African Studies at UCT and dared to challenge and try to change the ways in which "Africa" was taught. His course "Problematizing Africa" was canned, and the professor suspended (Kamola 2011). The institution hit back with a force that resonates in the corridors of the University of Cape Town to this day. All of the rules, regulations, and routines that defended the settled curriculum lined up to dismiss the intruder and the intruder curriculum. It was an unusually public lesson, not only for the famed professor from the Ivy League's Columbia University, but for lesser mortals who might consider daring to challenge or disrupt what was taken for granted knowledge about Africa and development.

Institutions are seldom as ruthless as that in their defence of the settled curriculum. The more common response to all ideas – and especially radical ideas – is to put them through the bureaucratic wringer without making much of a political or public fuss. As will be demonstrated in Chapter 5, South Africa has one of the most convoluted approval processes for new curriculum ideas anywhere. An idea first has to be raised for deliberation in the academic department, where the young academic firebrand, or the new scholar from outside, already confronts a formidable problem – the senior professors hold sway. They are not going to easily allow a radical idea to be approved for presentation at the Faculty Board, in which all the departments from that faculty are represented. A radical idea does not always sit easily with settled ideas.

At the Faculty Board, difficult conservation questions will be asked of a radical curriculum, such as, Are there enough resources? Who will teach these new classes? Aren't we are already struggling to teach our existing courses with the trimmed down budgets? Where will we find classroom space? Aren't classes already overcrowded? Such important resources and technical constraints bedevil every curriculum discussion whose goal is to extend beyond what already exists. If the radical idea passes the Board, it goes to the most important academic body in the university, the Senate.

In the Senate, all the professors from all the faculties, including schools, departments, and other entities (such as research centres) gather to pronounce on the radical idea represented in the intruder curriculum. The more extensive the new proposal – for example, a core curriculum affecting all the faculties – the more intense are the debates, and the more likely the new idea will be shot down. And the more radical a curriculum idea is, the more fierce the debate in the Senate. The words "brainwashing" or "ideology" might come up, or something more polite, such as "one-sided" or "limited in perspective," as in the case of a radical idea such as decolonization.

Once a new curriculum idea passes Senate, it goes to the office of institutional planning, or "plumbing," as Sara Ahmed would have it. These are the university technicians who give the new idea an institutional once-over to see whether it is likely to scale several regulatory hurdles outside of the university. Does the new curriculum fit into the "program qualification mix" of the university? If not, the government's Department of Higher Education and Training (DHET) will send it straight back. Thus, in the context of this discussion, the radical curriculum must "fit into" what the institution already does. Then, the mechanics will go through a long checklist from the South African Qualifications Authority (SAQA) to see whether all the criteria for registration are met. For example, is this new qualification internationally comparable? and does it allow for optimal access to everyone who qualifies? Finally, there is yet another regulatory hurdle, and that is the Council for Higher Education (CHE): Does the new curriculum idea satisfy the nineteen criteria for accreditation, such as adequate staffing resources to teach the programme? But if the curriculum is for a professional degree, as in engineering, chartered accounting, or medicine, there is yet another accreditation hurdle to scale before the CHE even looks at the new idea and passes it back to the government department. If, after this process, which can take months to years, the new (or radical) idea is still alive, the government department will sign off on it, which means the programme will be funded and the university can begin preparations for teaching the new curriculum.

What is the point of all of this? The complex and convoluted process of approvals – or putting the radical idea through the wringer – is not simply an unwieldly bureaucratic process that needs to be fixed. It is an inherent part of institutional operations – to make change difficult that would threaten stability and regularity in the system. In the process of curriculum regulation, deviation is disciplined. To change the institutional curriculum therefore involves "working with the physicality of the institution: putting [decolonization][2] into the organizational flow of things" (Ahmed 2012, 28). But such regulation of new or radical ideas is much more complex than this, and the ways in which this happens are explained later in an extended analytical account of regulatory processes and their impacts on curriculum (see Chapter 5).

When faced with this mammoth institutional complex that has to be negotiated, most proponents of challenging ideas simply avoid such entanglement, and for many reasons, one of which is the urgency that often comes with a radical proposal to change the settled curriculum. *Avoidance* is what an institution banks on; it can wait out a surge of radicalism from one academic term or year to the next. The press for decolonization was intense on campuses during 2015–2016, and then, as suddenly as it came, the radical moment passed. Activists graduated, new students arrived, routines of attendance and examinations settled in, and the urgency of curriculum change was a thing of the past. "As you were," might be the curriculum equivalent of a military officer's instruction; "institutional-as-usual," is Sara Ahmed's phrase of choice.

Institutions remember. There are bullet holes in the institutional armoury, sometimes literally. Statues toppled in some places and were defaced in others (Schmahmann 2019). The smaller, but regular, protests that happen all the time on university campuses now sometimes add "decolonization" to the list of demands. It is important to demonstrate good faith, even if only in pronouncements such as "University Y Decolonizes Curriculum." Institutions do not forget, and so they might even add to the internal list of criteria for screening new curriculum ideas an item that checks for "decolonization."

This does not mean that the institutional body does not allow for a change in size and shape in response to external pressures on its epistemological frame. What are the conditions under which any such accommodation of radical curriculum ideas takes place? Throughout

---

[2] We substitute "decolonization" for Ahmed's "diversity" here to make the same point about the ways in which radical ideas are regularized through these physical, organizational processes.

this study, it was found that radical ideas were accommodated on the margins of the institution. These ideas flew in under the radar of the regulatory apparatuses on the outside, or of the vetting processes on the inside of the institution. Where a new idea fits within an existing curriculum, for example, a module within a larger programme, it is not required to pass through either internal or external review. Such a module is globular in nature, small enough not to draw attention through the numbers of students enrolled or to influence the broader qualification outcomes registered with the authorities. A module on the margins of the institutional curriculum is often optional, even within the department in which it is offered. This is what Larry Cuban (1999) calls "enclaving," which in this study simply means the ways in which radical ideas are accommodated on the margins of institutional life. When such an enclaved entity seeks to extend its influence into the broader institutional curriculum, it threatens its own existence.

Probably the most powerful way in which institutions deal with radical ideas is through the process of institutionalization, by which the radical curriculum is absorbed into the institutional curriculum in ways that "defang" its originating ideas. No recent case of institutionalization demonstrates this point more powerfully than what happened with the Cuban–South African medical school graduates. The South African government, through a cooperation agreement with the government of Cuba, sent hundreds of Black South African students (often those who failed to gain access to medical school at home) to study in the Communist country. The Cuban medical school curriculum introduced students to radical ideas, such as a reliance on primary care, as opposed to the tertiary, or hospital care, central to mainstream South African health education. However, when those students returned, their medical education was regarded as inadequate, if not inferior. They were retrained on the terms of the mainstream curriculum, and only if they passed would they be considered doctors ready to practise medicine in South Africa.

The example of what happened to Cuban-trained medical students is so transparently obvious as to take the intellectual excitement out of the critical analysis of knowledge. The radical curriculum of the Cuban medical education was not marginalized; it was absorbed into and institutionalized, so as to find acceptance as part of the institutional curriculum. "To institutionalize X," reasons Sara Ahmed (2012, 21), "is for X to become routine or ordinary, such that X becomes part of the background for those who are part of an institution." In the case of decolonization, therefore, it could be argued that "the radical idea would be institutionalized when it becomes part of what an institution is already doing, when it ceases to cause trouble" (Ahmed 2012, 27).

Sometimes, however, an institution yields to a radical curriculum idea, although under very specific conditions. When the Vice-Chancellor of the University of the Free State raised as a topic for discussion the idea of a core curriculum that would be a requirement for all first-year students, there was immediate resistance from, especially, the science faculties. The arguments were familiar and anticipated: There is hardly time to teach the demanding physics or science or biotechnology curriculum; Who is going to pay for this expensive curriculum? It has never been done before, at any institution, as a compulsory, examined core curriculum for all incoming students.

The debates continued at all levels of the institution (Jansen 2016, 105–122). Many students resisted the idea: "I came here to do urban planning, not this extra thing"; or "my parents paid for architecture, not this." These students had come to accept the institutional curriculum as given; its norms, routines, and requirements as fixed. The local Afrikaans newspaper, an eager repository for white grievance, captured and amplified those concerns of students, and now parents, citing unnamed academics inside the university (Jansen 2016, 173–200). The institution was pushing back against the threatened disruption of existing values, norms, and regularities concerning the settled curriculum. Why did the institution eventually yield?

One reason was that this historically white Afrikaans institution does yield to authority – it is a product of Afrikaner nationalism and all of its ills, one of which was a regard for authority, whether vested in the regnant political party or the academic authority of the Rector. That kind of power would have found much greater resistance in the liberal white English universities, where authority alone was not enough to advance a strong curriculum argument. It also helped that the Rector was an education specialist with the authority to recruit internal and external resources to make the core curriculum an institutional reality.

But authority is never enough. A persuasive educational argument had to be made for the benefits of a core curriculum. Further, a strategy was required to make senior professors in the different faculties part and parcel of the core curriculum modules, including ones in astronomy, history, economics, law, and philosophy. In other words, the very different faculties had to be incentivized through the financial benefits of participation and the opportunity to teach to all students the fundamentals of nanotechnology or human rights. There was one other measure that made the core curriculum acceptable – it carried a low credit value, even though it was compulsory, and every effort was made to make the teaching accessible and to optimize the learning through multiple academic support platforms. The accommodation of UFS 101, as the core was called, is exceptional as a case of radical curriculum intrusions into institutions, and even then, modifications and adjustments had to be made to secure passage of the new idea through the portals of the institution (Combrink and Oosthuizen 2020).

The fate of UFS 101 raises the question of how a radical idea comes to the attention of an institution. In the case of decolonization, the idea came to institutional attention through prolonged and often violent student protests. The bringing down of the Rhodes statue was understood to be the start of a process of decolonization, which idea was supposed to spread through the institution, including the curriculum. The spectacular demise of the heavy bronze statue in a very prominent part of the UCT campus "concentrated the mind of the institution wonderfully," as Samuel Johnson said of a man about to be hanged. The UCT Senate did something rare – by a nearly unanimous vote, it agreed to the demand to rid the institution of this most visible symbol of colonialism. The institution was about to get very busy.

But first, would a student-led protest for decolonization in fact lead to a deep and enduring change of the institutional curriculum? Until now, there have been few, if any, systematic studies on the impact of student protests and politics on the university curriculum. Virtually all the curriculum changes that take place in an institution are introduced and led by academics in the normal course of a calendar year. Such changes are, moreover, incremental in nature and very much form part of the routines of curriculum review and revision that marks everyday processes of curriculation.

For example, people in institutions routinely discuss, say, the four-yearly review of the law school curriculum, or the next accreditation cycle of the medical school curriculum. These "institutional visits" as they are aptly called, are not so much meant to examine change but to check on compliance with existing norms and standards. It is what institutions *do* – keeping the essential curriculum in place while changing gradually from one academic season to the next.

The student protest movement demanded fundamental change to what was taught, how it was taught, and even who taught the curriculum in the first place. There was nothing regular or routine about the changes demanded – the institutional curriculum itself was on the table. How would institutions respond?

The first thing universities did was to include students in curriculum workshops, seminars, and various kinds of consultations during the protest movement. It was felt that student *participation* in decision making would give legitimacy to any changes to curriculum knowledge in the disciplines. But students are not experts in epidemiology or in metacognition, so they did what students are able to do, and that was to relate their demands to their experiences – feelings of not being heard in the classroom; not being well-prepared for examinations; not seeing themselves in the curriculum. At this point, many academics responded by making out the problem to be one of relevant content (let's use African examples) and appropriate pedagogy (let's teach more empathetically). In the process, the epistemological bedrock of institutional knowledge itself was left largely undisturbed.

The democratic impulse to involve students in curriculum making is a very deeply felt need in the long history of education struggles in South Africa. *And yet, the drive for student participation in curriculum matters has never accounted for institutions.* For example, the institutional demands on student time foreclose any meaningful involvement in decisions about what and how to teach. Institutions require that students attend classes, and there are often penalties for failing to do so. Institutions make heavy demands on student time in libraries, in laboratories, and in all kinds of internship experiences that leave little room for an exacting vocation like curriculum making. Institutions set tests and examination dates for which students must prepare, or else fail a course or miss out on graduation.

In short, student participation in curriculum making has yet to take account of how institutions frame the time and space within which student work unfolds. That is why academic staff often observed that, after a few energetic meetings around decolonizing the curriculum in accounting or architecture, student participation gradually faded away. This is not because students are uninterested but because *the institution has done its work.*

What these observations suggest is that student-led curriculum change is unlikely to happen within the confines of institutions. But that does not mean that institutions do not become very busy. At all the universities where we conducted interviews, academics recalled how committees sprung up everywhere, as staff tried to pin down the implications of decolonization for their curricula. Busyness within institutions does not necessarily mean change. The appropriate metaphor for explaining this particular kind of institutional responsiveness is found in how buildings respond to earthquakes.

Countries that routinely experience earthquakes erect new buildings using shock-absorbing materials. The result is that when an earthquake hits, the building sways and absorbs the shock. In technical terms, it is said that the building and the grounds are in resonance because they share the same frequency. This analogy explains an essential feature of institutions, in that they absorb the shock of radical (curriculum) ideas such as decolonization in ways that are at once responsive and unmoved. When buildings collapse, especially in poorer countries, it means they had been built with materials that lack those shock-absorbing properties. The busyness of curriculum committees, workshops, seminars, and symposia are all ways of responding to and absorbing the radical shocks without "harming" or changing the institution itself.

The student-led protest movement for decolonization certainly demanded institutional attention at all levels, but could it keep the attention it attracted, given competing demands? If institutions are in fact "modes of attention" (Ahmed 2012, 30), in which rival demands are made for recognition, then how did decolonization actually fare? It has already been mentioned that not only are students transient communities who come and go, but that institutions work to bring them back into line – until the next wave of radical, attention-seeking ideas comes along.

At the University of Johannesburg, one of the hotbeds of radical activism during the press for decolonization, the institution responded with an unprecedented level of busyness in response to student demands. Academics received a regular checklist that asked whether they decolonized their curriculum for that week or month. There were many workshops, seminars, and mass meetings on the subject of decolonization. Lecturers were required to demonstrate that they were making progress in their curriculum changes in line with decolonization. Soon, however, the political pressure for radical change subsided, and new priorities came onto the university's agenda.

While decolonization might not have redirected institutional attention or precipitated institution-wide changes to the curriculum, it did energize and bring to light small pockets of enclaved initiatives already existing within virtually every institution. These radical initiatives were easily found within the humanities disciplines, broadly defined, and more often than not, in the liberal English universities. Sometimes, it was an anthropology department that based its entire curriculum on one or more critical schools of thought. At other times, it was a small dance programme within a school that had developed an African-centred approach to dancing and opened up their curriculum to students who did not meet the conventional admissions criteria. "Archeology is the stuff about colonization and decolonization," claimed one professor, showing off her department's new curriculum.

These radical initiatives often shared an allied language with decolonization. Academics in their enclaved spaces spoke of decoloniality and hybridity, postcolonialism and orientalism, anti-racist pedagogies and pedagogies of the oppressed, the Global North and the Global South. They also cited within their curricula familiar authorities, such as Frantz Fanon, Ngũgĩ wa Thiong'o, Chinua Achebe, Nelson Maldonado Torres, and Raewyn Connell. For these scholars, decolonization activists were at least singing from the same hymnbook.

All of these enclaved curricula shared one other thing in common. They existed on the margins of the institution, more noticed by exception than the rule. They were not always the high-status disciplines, and so common laments were "the lack of funding," and even the threat of being closed down. Institutions are good at enclavement: They accommodate a radical curriculum on the margins, but then starve it of oxygen, as any number of Gender Studies or African Studies centres attested (see Chapter 8).

Nevertheless, when the press for decolonization came along, those working with the enclaved curriculum found a welcome resonance with the protestors' demands. A common response was that "we might not have used the word decolonization, but we have been doing that for a long time." Alternatively, some of these academics claimed "there's nothing new there." That sentiment was one of both defence – we were doing the right things all along – and embrace. Decolonization was an ally in the struggle for radical curriculum reform within a larger institution that continued to encamp these initiatives.

Institutions would not, however, be outflanked by pressing ambitions for much broader change. In fact, with decolonization more than any other radical curriculum initiative, institutions played havoc with the indeterminate language of change. What does decolonization mean, after all? For some advocates, it meant replacing Western ideas and figures with African heroes and achievements. Others were more measured, calling for greater inclusion of African content without simply ejecting European ideas. A few wanted something much more radical that addressed the deeper problems of imperialism, capitalism, racism, patriarchy, and every other vestige of colonialism. There were even those who spoke of white scholars being ejected from their privileged positions at the upper end of the academic food chain, where the professorial class was still overwhelmingly non-black and male. Several advocates for decolonization spoke about a more progressive pedagogy that included students in making curriculum (as discussed earlier) and helped bridge the disadvantages of their post-apartheid schooling through more connected teaching.

Institutions thrive on conceptual fuzziness when it comes to dealing with radical ideas. In no time at all, every university was claiming to be doing decolonization, without any accountability in terms of curriculum evidence. It was here that strategic ground for radical change was lost, for if decolonization could mean anything, it also meant nothing. For example, a new online learning programme was called decolonization. Oceanography must be decolonized. An African language course called into existence was an example of decolonization.

The result was as predictable as it was strange. Journal editors from the most conservative institutions headlined special issues on themes such as the "Decolonization of X." White academics far removed from progressive debates on curriculum transformation submitted articles for journals and chapters for books with "decolonization" in the title. The *South African Journal of Education*, a mainstream conservative outlet without a single Black South African on its editorial executive team, boldly published a special issue titled "'Decolonising' Education Transformation" (Cherrington, Botha, and Keet 2018).

After all, this potentially radical term could mean anything, because of the use of indeterminate language. The agility of institutions in claiming the language of decolonization and stamping it onto a published work or teaching programme was sufficient, it seemed, to indicate alignment with radical ideas. This form of institutional response to radical ideas is known as *appropriation*.

One of the most dangerous forms of the institutional appropriation of radical ideas had to do with the version of decolonization known as Africanization. At first glance, this could be an innocent assignment of meaning among many others as decolonization activists jostled for their favoured conceptions of a radical idea. On closer examination, however, decolonization as Africanization floundered on the quicksand of racial essentialism in institutions where apartheid ideology cast a long shadow over the institutional curriculum (see Chapter 4; Kister, forthcoming). In its more progressive interpretation, Africanization gives significant recognition to African knowledge in the university in the context of a broad and inclusive Pan Africanism that threads through the curriculum.

However, in the course of the protests the face of Africanization was cast as *the racial African*, that is, those classified under apartheid as Black Africans. The heroes listed were racial Africans. The poems read were mainly those of the racial African. The knowledge recited was that of the racial African. Indigenous knowledge meant Black African. African languages did not include Cape Afrikaans. Malay slaves or San culture never featured in the drive for Africanization. In a particularly nasty scuffle to appoint a Dean of Humanities at UCT, one argument fiercely made was that a Tanzanian-born African scholar on the shortlist did not qualify because she was not *South* African. The racial African was not only prescribed by race but also by geography. In some quarters, it was *this* racial African that was envisaged in and for the decolonized curriculum.

In the process, such a narrow Africanist strain of decolonization played right into institutional hands. The crude notion that there is something in the essence of a human being that can be racially distinguished as Black or White was, in fact, the very logic of apartheid ideology. Apartheid built its institutions on grounds of this foundational idea that there were Whites, Africans, Coloureds, and "Asians," all distinguishable from each other racially, socially, and culturally. As one Black respondent at a KwaZulu Natal university asked of her colleagues, "Why is it that when I hear you speak of decolonization, I hear Zulu nationalism?"

Under apartheid, a university was designed for Indians, another for Coloureds, and a string of mainly rural institutions for Africans, further distinguished by their ethnic identities. This narrow Africanization version of decolonization was the one that found ready acceptance within the institutional curriculum, for the simple reason that "it fit right in" with the essentialist assumptions of resident knowledge. Put differently, the Africanized curriculum organized around notions of the racial African was not *institutionally* disruptive at all.

For all its professed commitments to Africanization, the institutional curriculum seldom reflected the re-centring of African content and characters in new or continuing knowledge. We asked at the end of almost every interview for this study how, five years later, the curriculum in genetics or physics or construction engineering was different from the one that existed before the start of the decolonization moment. In almost all cases, the response was, "not very different at all." Why was this the outcome?

One of the main reasons is that the institutional machinery that regulates and accredits curricular knowledge had not changed at all. That machinery did several things at once as the radical idea of decolonization arrived on campuses. The institutional curriculum absorbed, amended, appropriated, snubbed, marginalized, adapted, and mimicked the radical idea of decolonization to the point that it had very little power to disrupt the colonial and apartheid bedrock of knowledge that still underpinned the disciplines (see, for example, Thakur and Vale 2020).

One way of understanding the victory of settled knowledge as represented in the institutional curriculum is to examine what was not challenged with the decolonization movement. There were two obvious curricular candidates for decolonization in South African institutions: one was the English language and the other was assessment. Neither was disturbed.

All universities in South Africa now use English as the primary language of instruction, despite its status as a colonial language. To be sure, before and since the end of apartheid, universities were at pains to recognize the eleven official languages named in the Constitution and to advance the case for multilingualism in the conduct of university administration, teaching, and learning. Some institutions even placed name boards in their main buildings in two or three languages. English is always there with Afrikaans and isiXhosa, in the case of the Cape Town universities.

Yet in practice, the institutional regard for English remains as entrenched as it was before the decolonization moment. Ironically, at the historically white Afrikaans universities, Black students demanded the end of Afrikaans – a language that owes part of its origins to Blacks, including Malay slaves – and that all students be taught in English. After a series of legal battles, the Constitutional Court of South Africa ruled in favour of English.

There is one critical observation of relevance to be made about English and the institutional curriculum. The fall of Afrikaans and the consolidation of the primary role of English at all twenty-six public universities happened quickly because it was in line with what was already firmly in place – the dominance of English teaching, English journals, English research networks, and the organization of academic cultures of the English model of higher education. Long before the decolonization moment, Afrikaans universities had already switched much of their administration, teaching, and research towards English, because of the growing numbers of Black students on the inside and the language of the regulatory authorities on the outside. No Afrikaans university would have dared to submit their registration or accreditation documents in languages other than English.

The demise of Afrikaans therefore "fit right in" with what the distinguished Nigerian novelist Chinua Achebe decried as "the fatalistic logic of the unassailable position of English" in literature, even if his followers seldom quote the rest of his complaint: "And yet, I am unable to see a significantly different or a more emotionally comfortable resolution of that problem" (Achebe 1976). Achebe, we gauge, understood something about the processes of institutionalization.

Despite the occasional genuflection to the importance of African languages as part of the drive for decolonization (see Mayaba, Ralarala, and Angu 2018), in practice, students demanded English as their university's medium of instruction. In other words, what students demanded was already institutionally accepted as an entrenched practice in higher education institutions.

If English was one candidate for decolonization, so were the processes of examination and assessment. One of the voices supporting decolonization among academics was right to point out that:

The curriculum – and particularly its assessment system – serves to reproduce society's broader inequalities. This has received very little attention in the recent debates on decolonizing. (Shay 2016)

Shay's point is that the very act of assessment confirms inequalities built into institutional practice. By assigning an upper or lower grade, a pass or a fail, assessment in an elite university like UCT merely affirms racial and class advantage (for mainly white and middle class students) and disadvantage (for mainly Black students) – which repeatedly reflects in annually reported academic outcomes (Krige 2019).

Assessment therefore reproduces inequality as much as it might make judgements about student achievement. Clearly, then, assessment is a candidate for the radical change that decolonization demands.

Academic writing on the decolonization of assessment is not short of proposals for how to change regnant models of student evaluation. Ardavan Eizadriad (2019) presents a model of assessment that values "love, cooperation, reciprocity and sacrifice," using qualitative measures that take account of "students' thoughts, words and actions." On the South African scene, two UCT academics pose a list of "crucial questions" that lecturers could ask as they work towards decolonizing assessment – and which, for purposes of institutional analysis, are worth reciting at length:

How do your assumptions about curriculum knowledge play out in the criteria that you use to assess students? What can you do to make your assessment practices more fair and valid for all students, without inducing high levels of anxiety? What assessment methods could show what all students are capable of, drawing on their strengths and promoting their agency and creativity? How far do your teaching and assessment methods allow students to feel included without assuming assimilation? (Morreira and Luckett 2018)

The first observation about these exemplars offered for decolonization is that they are sound proposals for what most who work in assessment studies would regard as a good liberal education; they are not radical, as in disruptive at the roots. For purposes of this analysis, none of these soft approaches to student evaluation even begins to grapple with the institutional hold on assessment and its consequences.

Assessment in universities includes and excludes on the basis of an institutional machinery that passes and fails, promotes and holds back – regardless of the very different apartheid histories of Black and white families; the different kinds of schools black and white students attended; the financial struggles of working-class students compared to their middle-class and wealthy peers; emotional and other barriers to learning; and the like. That machinery produces assessment results as part of the routines and regularities of what institutions do every single day.

Assessment is deeply ingrained in institutional regulations. The standard of degrees depends on rigorous assessments measured against standards that include, in their estimation, something the curriculum regulators call international comparability. Indeed, as will be seen in the study of regulatory agencies in Chapter 5, the graduate attributes or the standards of assessment for the professions of chartered accounting, engineering, and medicine are set by international authorities. In short, institutional validation depends on rigorous systems of assessment; therefore, any challenge to the logics of evaluation in universities would fall flat. Nor do student activists regard assessment as a target of their decolonization demands, as shown by the following curious example.

One of the most intriguing events during the student protest movement at UCT vividly demonstrated the disconnection between assessment and any radical claims of decolonization. A prominent "Fallist" of the time, Busisiwe Mkhumbuzi, had failed to attend the requisite number of lectures that would qualify her to write the examination in a course on moral philosophy. In other words, she failed to obtain "duly performed" (DP) status. Some of the days absent were allowed for medical reasons. But, both before and after the incident in which she was injured, the student missed classes on a regular basis and at one stage came to the lecture, signed the register, and immediately departed – a clear ethical violation.

For a period of three years, the student's appeals, one after the other, were turned down by the institution. The student, in the meantime, vented her personal grievances against the professor and the institution on social media. The professor was supposedly racist for not allowing her to sit for the examination. The institution was "anti-Black." Since the professor held critical views on decolonization and affirmative action, this was a case of "institutionalized racism," claimed the student. When the professor defended himself against the racism charge on a departmental communication platform, the student went into overdrive: "If I kill myself today, this is the reason." After an "apology and retraction" for the unfounded claims of racism, and with the university now under a new Vice-Chancellor, the matter was belatedly resolved.

What is fascinating about this saga was the terms of the debate among student, professor, and university administration. At no point in this lengthy standoff did the student activist at any time question the institutional arrangements for her assessment. In fact, the student would argue in public messaging that she had indeed met the formal assessment criteria. The student made clear that she respected the rules and regulations governing assessment. And the student conceded that she had failed to convince the institution "to set aside the rules and regulations that she had knowingly flouted." (Myburgh 2020)

It was in the *application* of the institution's assessment arrangements to her individual case that the student raised concerns. The radical idea of decolonizing assessment was certainly not on the agenda of student protests at any time, even if the merits of doing so enjoyed attention in academic reflection (Morreira and Luckett 2018; Eizadirad 2019).

What explains the political inattention to English and assessment on the part of the decolonization movement? In relation to languages, English is still broadly accepted as the language of power that gives access to social, economic, and political status in South Africa and the world. This kind of calculation regards English as the only language that all students can access on a more or less equal basis in the learning commons. The African languages might carry emotional and social valence as neglected languages under colonialism and apartheid, but they do not give access to power in the same way that English does.

Assessment, on the other hand, was never a central component of education struggles in South Africa. The relationship between assessment and inequality was seldom raised or pursued in student activism. Its logic is accepted and never challenged. Curriculum, on the other hand, was deemed to be more straightforward, and the logic of replacement – African content over European/Western content – was a more common argument behind the decolonization protests.

Another way of reading the decolonization moment was through the lens of political calculation. To take on English and assessment is to confront a brick wall of institutional resistance. Such an attack would sap the energy of any activist movement, which would lose that struggle quite easily. Both assessment and English language education

had come to assume the status of common sense in institutional practice and were therefore impervious to change – with one possible
exception, when it came to the position of English.

The University of KwaZulu Natal was the only institution to declare
that it was going to advance the teaching of isiZulu in the university. It
was a bold move, given that registered students came from many
different language backgrounds, and the advance of this language
was happening in a province where the links between Zulu language
and ethnicity are unusually strong. What were the prospects of institutional success? According to one of the campus leaders, "We spent
about 5–8 years on the symbolic aspects of the new language policy,
and on the substantive side of things it has not translated into serious
uptake by the academics themselves."

The bold claim that the university would invest in "the intellectua-
lization of isiZulu" has been realized in part. There is now an African
language thesaurus, and tutorials are offered in isiZulu as well as
English. Despite massive resistance from both students and academics,
there is now a requirement that students should demonstrate some
level of competence in isiZulu as a condition for graduation.

Yet, it is at this point that one encounters a fundamental weakness of
decolonization as a radical idea: the problem of ethnic chauvinism and
political conservatism. Is the idea radical when it is advanced as a
cultural property or an ethnic possession? "You must learn our culture
before you can learn our language," was a common response to those
eager to learn isiZulu. "Zulu nationalism is a bloody dangerous
thing," observed one progressive academic of the ethnic turn at his
university, a sentiment heard more than once in the course of this
research.

UKZN also had to confront something common in other universities
as well – that the cause of African languages was often led by more
conservative staff, whose commitments were not to radical reinvention
but to conserving traditional culture, its language and mores. The
resultant pedagogy of the African languages was often grammar-based
and not linked to discourses of language, power, and decoloniality,
which were more commonly found in linguistics departments in the
humanities faculties. "The biggest problem," recalled a senior academic, "is that those who are teaching the language are using archaic
approaches; they simply will not get language education specialists to

teach the subject." As a result, the resistance among students grew, and enthusiasm was found to be lukewarm among academic staff.

These observations raise, of course, the question of *what* was being institutionalized and whether such a conserving approach to African languages carried the radical intent of decolonization to begin with. Even so, the bold and necessary attempts at advancing isiZulu did not mean that English was displaced by isiZulu or that significant numbers of courses at the institution were being taught in the language. While advances were made in developing isiZulu as a language, including textbook translations, it remained a small part of the overall institutional offerings, while the course could be taken over several years as many students struggled to pass. "It simply did not turn out the way we intended," said another academic.

Institutions think, as more than one scholar on the subject has observed (Douglas 1986; O'Neill et al. 2017). A radical idea that comes into the learning commons threatens the established norms and values that underpin the curriculum. When disruptive ideas are not advanced by leadership at the institutional level – as in the case of isiZulu and UFS 101 – they are easily squashed. Such leadership action is not arbitrary; it is a calculation that must take account of the institutional balance of forces in the battle over curriculum, or radical change will simply not happen.

One puzzle that confronts any scholar of this particular episode (2015–2016) in South Africa's long history of student protests is why institutions did not do more in taking up radical demands for decolonization. After all, this protest movement at universities was different from others that had come before: it was intense, it was violent, it was costly (an estimated R800m in infrastructure damage was caused), and it was relentless over a period of two years. On the question of fees, the system buckled under unprecedented political pressure by yielding to a zero-percent fee increase in 2016–2017 and free higher education for all students below a threshold income of R300,000 per family. In part, this can be explained by the nature of the subject; as one academic pointed out, "Statues fall, fees fall but curricula don't fall" (Shay 2016). However, a deeper explanation resides in the nature of the protests themselves.

South African protest movements are performances. The public act said to have inaugurated the decolonization moment was the moment when a student leader hurled human excrement at the statue of Cecil John Rhodes, with media photographers in planned attendance. A naked woman lay on campus with a cardboard covering that reads "NOTHING TO SEE JUST ANOTHER DEATH OF A BLACK STUDENT AT UCT. KEEP MOVING" (Senne 2017). (The point, of course, *was* to be seen). At another moment, two naked students lay on the road blocking access to the same university's Lower Campus (GroundUp 2017b).

"Does my naked body embarrass you?" asked a writer in *Cosmopolitan* magazine, photographs of elegantly dressed women, its main business, appearing alongside a story of naked protesting bodies on campuses.

Lectures were disrupted by (mainly) men jumping and dancing on classroom desks with long whips. Students broke into an off-campus venue, dancing on tables and taunting the Right Reverend Archbishop Emeritus, who was chairing the Council meeting of UCT. It was a well-planned political spectacle that became emblematic of the humiliation of university leaders, as when students at Wits kept their Vice-Chancellor confined to the ground in the main concourse of the university.

In South Africa, it is not enough merely to protest. The politics of spectacle demand what are by now ritualized performances, such as the burning of tires, the incineration of university property, and the building of shacks on campuses. No march is unaccompanied by singing, dancing, and insulting the targets of student anger. In the course of protests, language takes the form of extremist utterances that include words like death, kill, burn, and the borrowed "I can't breathe." One thing that became clear in the 2015–2016 moment was that the performance of politics off campus, such as in the routines of service delivery protests in municipalites, had blended seamlessly with the spectacle of student protests on campuses (Jansen 2016).

More than one South African scholar has tried to make sense of the politics of protest in South Africa in the context of the performing arts, as in Gerber's (2009) treatment of spectacle in musical works on Sara Baartman. For Helene Strauss (2014), an English studies scholar, "the spectacle of promise" by the first democratic government has been challenged and replaced by "the spectacle of disappointment," expressed in protest arts and action in South Africa. In the burning of things, Strauss sees "aesthetic activism" and makes it known that her work is to "depathologise" the expressive emotions of political protests (Strauss 2014, 474).

Adam Habib, a political scientist and Vice-Chancellor of Wits University, takes a completely different view on what he calls "the politics of spectacle," represented in the intense violence visited on his campus. For Habib (2016), the spectacle is a negative strategy of minority factions to gain control of a preferred narrative of protest but it also acts as "a means of silencing ordinary, pragmatic voices as it mobilizes others." More than that, citing the experienced of Wits as the national epicentre of the fees protests, "The mainstream press loved the spectacle, as did embedded journalists from the *Daily Vox* and documentary filmmakers, all of whom needed footage."

These scholarly treatments of the politics of spectacle underline that this particular demonstration of discontents was far removed from a strategy for challenging institutional authority, and even farther from making inroads against the institutional curriculum. The politics of spectacle in post-apartheid South Africa has its own internal logics, which may be to advance a factional cause (per Habib) or to express a political emotion (per Strauss). Spectacle in this context is disruptive and enflamed as it makes its political point for public attention. Whatever its merits, challenging and changing institutions is neither it's *primary* goal nor, certainly, its considered strategy. As Habib (2016) recalls, after he brought in a powerful team of mediators "to institutionalise the matter" – by agreeing to the gradual realization of "free, fully funded, quality, decolonized higher education" – the student leaders withdrew and the plan fell flat.

That is why the institutional curriculum, as reflected and sustained in the disciplinary curricula of the different universities, has changed little since the historic university protests of the second decade of the century. Institutions were not, however, neutral observers

How do institutions deal with and respond to the politics of performance? They recognize performance for what it is; hell, they might even pay for it. Venues are made available, speakers are compensated, and accommodation facilities are arranged. The Second 3rd Space Symposium at UCT carried the headline "Decolonising Art Institutions" with an unusual subtitle calling for "Papers, Disruptions, Performances, Interventions" (Institute for Creative Arts 2017).

Institutions know that performances come and go. Performance is non-threatening; it offers no incisive strategy for really changing things. The people who attend political theatre are the usual suspects, kindred spirits who share the passions and the projects of those leading the energetic presentations. Performances are fleeting. Participants blow off steam. Institutional leaders are lambasted. Whiteness gets unflattering treatment. Black lament and agency receive ample treatment in dance, poetry, and music.

Thereafter, academics and students settle back into the institutional routines of teaching and learning, of examination and assessment. Institutions, in other words, can wait out a potential disruption, and even participate in its external performance, for it hardly threatens the institutional curriculum – that core of knowledge which represents the epistemological bedrock of what gives the institution its identity and maintains its stability.

In his "Notes on Political Theatre: The Perils of Spectacle," the theatre critic Nelson Pressley (2016) observes that

In the public sphere "political theatre" is synonymous with "empty show." It's a gesture. Posturing. Grandstanding. Sound and fury … Policy specifics didn't matter. Anger did. And it was spectacular.

The drive for decolonization in South Africa never did articulate a theory of change in the face of institutions. Beyond the spectacle, its primary appeal was exhortatory, with statements, demands, and presentations burdened with the normative language of *what should be* in the curriculum: African content, achievements, languages, cultures, histories, and heroes. African-centredness instead of European-domination. The language of *what should be* was rhythmically presented alongside a corresponding language of *what should not be*.

There was little room for complexity in the student demands for decolonization. This was, after all, a language of protest, marked by very powerful moments of physicality (the toppling of Rhodes at UCT and of Charles Robberts Swart at the UFS). Things had to fall, literally. The lack of nuance in the directness of these physical demands explains why, among the things that "fell," were the burned photographs of the anti-apartheid activist Molly Blackburn and the covering up or removal under pressure of progressive artworks, such as the welded sculpture of *Sara Baartman* by the Black artist Willy Bester. That unnuanced demand, which came with the sound and fury of protests, did little to chip away at the epistemological foundations of the institutional curriculum.

This does not mean that the press for decolonization was reduced to mere public performance, though a good deal of the struggle was simply that. Most campuses were caught up in some of the most exciting curricular moments in the history of higher education, where auditorium-filling speakers and seminars brought students and academics into conversation around the urgencies of decolonization. However, these intense sessions of intellectual engagement were – from an institutional perspective – *extracurricular* engagements. While invaluable as a form of political education for those who attended, this kind of teaching and learning did not impact on institutional requirements for a degree. There were no discussions of regulatory standards or course assessments. In short, none of these intense interactions on the subject of decolonization made any systemic impacts on the institution, except, perhaps, to the extent that one or more academics might have found ideas worth taking into their normal lectures.

The fact that activist students could summon such excitement and interest in the extra-curricular sessions organized around decolonization certainly deserves a closer look. One of the long-established courses in UCT's Department of Archaeology is a third-year offering called "Roots of Black Identity" (formerly "The Iron Age of South Africa"). The curriculum promises to "problematize the notion of 'settler' and explore the rich and diverse heritage of the making of South Africa." (Department of Archaeology 2021)

Given the strident criticism of the resident curriculum as Colonial/Westernized/Eurocentric and the like, one would naturally expect that this institutional offering, among several others, would be in high demand, at least by activist students pressing for decolonization. It offers radical content on an exciting subject, it has been taught by a very eminent Black professor, it contains a richness of multimedia content, and it contributes a hefty thirty-six credits towards qualification.

But the course is taken mainly by American students interested in studying Africa. The professor who taught the course for a decade, Shadreck Chirikure, is perplexed. As he told us in an interview in 2020:

One would think that if I want to understand South Africa's problems of dispossession and inequality, then I would take this course on the roots of Black people, on the classical civilizations, that would foreground my education.

What explains this disaffection by students for a radical course on a campus that was the epicentre of the student protest movement on the fight for decolonization?

The first reason for the lack of interest in radical curricula on campus is that what drove the decolonization protests in the first place was the primacy of politics. The political critique of the curriculum turned out to be a powerful and effective way of mobilizing students behind a pressing cause and focusing institutional attention on a well-articulated set of grievances. Academics across institutions responded in a flurry of busyness. The dilemma was that sympathetic scholars published papers and articulated positions that ran way ahead of the protestors' more immediate political mission. Two examples of this kind of academic enthusiasm that was disconnected from the immediacy of student political grievances (like fees and shelter) were publications on the decolonization of assessment and the advancement of indigenous languages.

The second, related, reason for the uninterest in radical curricular options already available on campus was that these were institutionalized options for teaching and learning. To take AGE3006H was to enrol in a coded course, satisfy its entry requirements ("for third year students specializing in archaeology, otherwise with permission from the head of department"), complete its assignments, and meet its assessment standards:

- Essays and tests count 20%
- A long paper counts 40%
- One 3-hour examination in November counts 40%

For that purpose – participating in the institutional curriculum – students already had demanding class schedules and exacting commitments in, for example, engineering, medicine, or the accounting sciences. In other words, the institutional conditions of teaching and learning made such out-of-degree options much less attractive to all students but especially to those with the added difficulties of inadequate school preparation as they struggled to pass.

The third reason for the lack of interest in radical courses is that most South African students in the normal run of an academic year are much more concerned with completing the kind of degree that lands them a job that earns them adequate income. As the professor of the archaeology course observed of the decline of humanities enrolments compared to fields such as the commercial sciences, "At one point commerce was oversubscribed in their courses; they used to have about 1,000 students and they would offer 3 or 4 lectures a day to meet the demand." For him, decolonization was largely a rhetorical moment and confirmed "a misalignment" between what students said they wanted in the curriculum and what they actually pursued. This presents formidable challenges, of course, for the problem of change.

3.4 So, How Does Radical Curriculum Change Happen?

If the course of a radical idea through an institution is so fraught with difficulty, how do decolonization activists think change happens? One of the difficulties with the work of activist scholars concerned with decolonization is that so much of their published material can be described as *a politics of lament*. This lament was heard during both the anticolonial resistance of the 1960s and in contemporary struggles for decolonization. Many of the current laments are marked by repetitive references to the contemporary writings of Latin American intellectuals using the urgent language of decoloniality.

Consider, for purposes of this discussion, a presentation by one very important scholar in this expansive literature who submitted a crucial paper on the subject of the decolonization of knowledge for a symposium at the University of Johannesburg at the height of the student protests; her submission was titled, "Decolonising Knowledge, Democratising Curriculum" (Connell 2016).

The laments is as follows. The global north is the centre of intellectual authority as part of a hegemonic economy. Universities in the global south are followers and imitators, so that "it is not surprising that their teaching curricula have been largely built on models from Northern Universities" (Connell 2016, 1). As in economic transactions, Africa offers the global north the "raw materials," in the form of data that are accumulated and reworked in the metropolitan universities for their benefit, after which the "processed knowledge" is recycled back to the global south for consumption as applied sciences by dependent universities. Theory happens in the metropole, application in the former colonies.

As we have demonstrated elsewhere, this staid representation of international knowledge transactions is not only overstated but also repetitive, outdated, and misrepresentative of the weight of African scholarship, which in many places sets the terms of cross-border engagements in the twenty-first century (Jansen 2019). The major weakness of this scholarship is that in concentrating so much of its intellectual energies on the politics of lament, it has failed to give adequate attention to the politics of change when it comes to the question of institutions and the radical curriculum project.

So how *does* one do radical curriculum change under the weight of institutions? Or as Andre Keet (2014) puts it, "to write from within disciplinary knowledge and against the social structure of the academy"? For Connell (2016, 8), the starting point is "the democratization of the university as an institution." Few countries have had a flatter structure for curriculum participation by students and staff than democratic South Africa before and during the protest movement; participation, however, is not enough – because institutions, as we have shown, work to undermine processes of shared decision making.

Connell (2016, 8) rightly observes that "deep problems about knowledge formation" are not resolved by resorting to "showy, under-funded, feel-good programs," which, in the language of our arguments, is about mimicry on the margins of the institutional curriculum. Unfortunately, Connell then commends what South African students and staff did with tremendous political winds behind their backs but with so little to show for it when the protests died down:

Sustained discussion and experimentation among broad groups of staff and students, who themselves have power to make things happen on the ground, who can build courses and programs.

She concludes with a list of issues from her own experiences in sociology to "decolonize the discipline" that includes re-making textbooks and undergraduate course plans to include Southern perspectives; developing new research agendas based on postcolonial perspectives; and "reforming the institutional framework of the discipline" – by, for example, forging South–South partnerships, transforming journals, and reducing "Northern hegemony" in conferences and associations.

From the extended analysis in this chapter of *how institutions function*, using the powerful example of the institutional curriculum, it should not be surprising that these otherwise important initiatives stand little chance of success when it comes to a radical knowledge project like decolonization. This does *not* mean that enclaved curricula do not find expression on the margins of an institution or that new curricula initiatives do not carry the signage of radical intent.

What our argument suggests, rather, is that often the powerful discourses of lament cannot explain how a radical idea, such as decolonization, can even begin to unsettle the epistemological common sense that holds together the institutional curriculum. What radical change means, and how it can be achieved within universities as institutions, follows in the conclusion to this book.

4 | *The Contending Meanings of Decolonization and the Implications for Radical Curriculum Change*

> Just tell me what decolonization is, and I will do it.
>
> University lecturer

4.1 Introduction

It was not at all surprising that when decolonization made its appearance on South African university campuses in 2015–2016, few people understood what the construct might mean, and even fewer knew what the implications could be for curriculum change. At no point in South Africa's long struggle history did "decolonization" banner any of the protest movements. Those campaigns were better known for slogans such as anti-apartheid education, alternative education, People's Education, education for liberation, or in I. B. Tabata's (1960) memorable dismissal, education for barbarism. The language of decolonization was more commonly found in the political discourses of countries in East and North Africa, either as part of the drive against colonial occupation or in reference to the lasting effects of colonialism that prompted calls for the decolonization of the mind or the decolonization of curriculum. That language of decolonization had long faded in postcolonial Africa, but it enjoyed an unexpected reawakening on the South Africa political landscape during the historic protests of 2015. The question is, why?

4.2 The Political Roots of Decolonization

The early stirrings of discontent with the whiteness of UCT long preceded the 2015 agitation around the demands for decolonization. There were at least two earlier "sightings" of decolonization.

When postgraduate students protested the decision to merge African Studies at UCT with the departments of gender studies, anthropology, and linguistics, they not only complained about their alienation from the institution but "were saying we need decolonization; they used the word decolonization," recalled Ari Sitas, a senior humanities scholar in a 2018 interview. Another, Mark Fleischman, recalled that it was in the performing arts, "in themselves potentially radical," that that discourse of decolonization was used.

Still, while the concept was not used widely across the campus, its substantive concerns were raised on a regular basis through a string of connected controversies from the Mafeje Affair in 1968 to the Mamdani Affair in 1998, and eventually the Rhodes Affair in 2015. Archie Mafeje, a black anthropologist, was appointed by academics but turned down by the Council of UCT because of pressure from the apartheid government. Mahmood Mamdani challenged the "Bantu Education" premises of the African Studies curriculum and was forced to leave the university. And the statue of Cecil John Rhodes, British imperialist and one-time prime minister of the Cape Colony, was unceremoniously taken down, signalling the symbolic start of the decolonization campaign at UCT.

When decolonization eventually burst through the surface calm of UCT campus life in 2015, it was buoyed by a powerful moral cause and rhetorical language that drew attention to long simmering discontents. As an acute observer and supporter of this movement, Vasu Reddy of the University of Pretoria, put it:

When emotions are mobilized in such a way, anger becomes a driver and a tool to express anger, pain, frustration and resistance; logic doesn't enter the frame [and] dominant voices projected a particular type of moral perspective that any critique showing otherwise would be immoral.

When universities did attempt to open debates on the subject during the course of the student protest movement, they were often shut down, as Adam Habib, the Vice-Chancellor of WITS recalls:

It was probably the worst time to start a process because actually you couldn't have a rational conversation on decolonization because effectively there was so much emotion in the room.

Other observers also made the points that "decolonization was just a strategy to bring about change and to be heard in the academy," and that "the problem is that this thing [decolonization] was so ideological that it's not looking at the curriculum as curriculum."

The power of this moralizing discourse as a blunt political instrument explains not only the relative silence of academics who dared not raise concerns (see the following chapters)[1] but also the frustration of academics desiring a neat and tidy operational definition for a concept mobilized to serve other purposes. "Just tell me what decolonization is, and I will do it," said one frustrated academic.

Still, none of this explains why decolonization became the rallying point for student discontents in the mid-2010s in the first place. Put differently, in a country that does not lack words to signal radical intent, to what was decolonization responding? For this question, we turn to the perceptive voice of a major student leader in the protest movement at NMU:

Transformation became a decomposed concept that lost its radical rhythm. Management became comfortable with using "transformation" in everyday conversations, so transformation lost its intent.

So we realized that transformation is not enough. Something else must now be pumped in, which is why ... decolonization became the new theme.

The NMU activist was not alone, of course. A UCT student blamed the clash of political terms on the university leadership:

The university does not want to use "decolonization." They insist on using "transformation." Because they understand that this is an ideological battle that we are winning. (Ndelu 2017)

This view was shared among leading academics in other parts of the country. One senior administrator at a Johannesburg university, Kirti Menon, saw decolonization as "the term being used for the transformation that had not happened at our universities." Adam Habib, of Wits, underlined the difference between the two terms:

Decolonization is a rhetorical tool that has emerged from political activists to distinguish this project, which was basically a social movement, from what they saw as its precursor, that is, transformation.

That fact that decolonization as a term was a political standard for a growing student movement did not mean that it was one of "mere

---

[1] One of the authors received very hostile receptions on six different campuses for daring to question the utility of the concept of decolonization as an explanation for the complex layers of social and curricular injustices in universities. The arguments did not matter; it was the audacity of merely questioning the political merits of decolonization that raised hackles.

words" among associated terms, such as decoloniality. In fact, rich dialogues and deliberations on decolonization emerged on campuses, in both large auditoriums and small reading groups. There appeared for a moment to be a genuine attempt on the part of active students to grapple with seminal texts (e.g., Fanon, Memmi, and Ngũgĩ) and prominent thinkers (e.g., Mignolo, Ndlovu-Gatsheni, and Maldonado-Torres) on decolonization.

However, it must be stressed here that what inspired activist students was primarily the political ideas of the decolonial authors, not the curricular consequences of their thought. If the decolonization moment was about the desire for a less Eurocentric and more Africa-centred curriculum, there were already such radical courses on the books at the major universities, such as African Arts at Wits and Black Roots at UCT. And yet, as indicated earlier, such courses were the least popular on these campuses, with their main enrolments coming, ironically enough, from white foreign students. Decolonization was, in essence, a political moment for driving change; it was much less engaged with its rhetorical target, the curriculum.

It is important to remember, in this context, that on all the campuses, the decolonization activists were relatively small groups who, in one or two intense weeks, mobilized huge numbers of students to attend mass meetings. Over time, it would be the same core group of students who carried the momentum forward, in seminars, workshops, conferences, dialogues, and discussions. As one senior academic recalled, "When you go to these kinds of gatherings, it's almost like speaking to the converted, with the same faces, the same people attending." Another university leader at a university in Cape Town concurred that these public deliberations were "an experience of the converted." Eventually, even these gatherings of true believers gradually dissipated.

Even so, what the decolonization moment did achieve was to raise both awareness and alarm among academics, who, in the absence of clear and defined meanings for decolonization, made up their own definitions in the context of their particular disciplines and experiences.

This absence of a framework for the meanings for decolonization did not mean that there was no effort to take on the task of finding some conceptual anchors for the term, given the urgency of the political demands for change – as this next example illustrates.

The Dean of a reputable Humanities Faculty relayed to her academic departments the injunction from senior management that they "decolonize" the disciplines. "But what does that mean?" asked the Psychology Department. "I don't know," said the Dean in an email, "right now we're winging it." The sense among many academics at South African universities was decidedly that they needed to respond to student demands for changing the curriculum, or at the very least, to be seen to be responding.

In the process, the possible meanings association with decolonization, as a practical matter, were as varied as there were academic departments, as this selection of interviewee responses across our sampled universities reveal:

I try to teach my people to be the best math and science teachers possible, working with culturally relevant pedagogies, which maybe now I reconsider [to be] decolonialized pedagogies.

As a finance person, I never understand what decolonization fully means, right? For me it includes the apartheid issues, anything where there was this hierarchy, differentiation between the races – apartheid or colonization or whatever.

Decolonization has come to mean many things, often rhetorical, but it should be about new forms of knowledge that empower students to understand who they are, where they're coming from, and what they are doing with their lives.

I think of decolonization as the equality of voices, so you can decolonize the curriculum because everyone's an equal participant in that space.

Decolonization is about giving value to local knowledge, local ideas, and local research.

One of the key aims of decolonized teaching would be to develop a student that has critical thinking.

Decolonization is all about being inclusive of perspectives that had not been included before, which means ones other than Eurocentric and Westernized perspectives.

This chapter is decidedly not concerned with finding the "correct" definition of decolonization or comparing academic meanings of the term to some standardized or idealized conception. That would be a futile pursuit. Rather, what we find intriguing are the kind of meanings that emerged in the conceptual vacuum left by the decolonization moment, how those different meanings found appeal and attachment within particular academic communities, and what those varied meanings made possible in the context of radical curriculum change.

With these objectives in mind, we found seven different threads of meaning for decolonization within and across the ten universities studied.

4.2.1 Decolonization as Additive Inclusive Content

The most common response to decolonization was to add a module that academics deemed to reflect decolonized content to the existing curriculum. Nothing else changed within the mainstream curriculum except for this added module within the course. In the minds of the academics concerned, this was – if only in part – a response to the press for decolonization.

Engineering electives at UCT, such as "Social Infrastructures," "Citizen Professional," or "Engineering Professionalism," were justified as part of the "soft skills" provided for in accredited programmes. The thinking of academics was that the addition of courses would move beyond the technical aspects of the training to imbue students with a sense of responsibility, even activism, for involvement in communities. This additive model of curriculum was at times not one of choice but a course requirement, as in the common core engineering curriculum at Wits, which *all* first-year students had to take, regardless of specialization (civil, mechanical, electrical engineering, etc.), and where the focus was on "fundamental life skills, including methods of learning" (see Chapter 7).

In UWC's law faculty, the description of the new Introduction to Law module read that "On completion of this module students should be able to … discuss the possibilities and limits of social transformation through Africanization, decolonization and constitutionalization." Here a number of complex concepts are strung together in a way that suggests that the addition of decolonization is meant to signal the inclusion of something demanded. There was no "content" yet for this added concept, conceded the UWC academics concerned, for the idea was "to have an ongoing academic and intellectual discussion … on what they mean and how they might impact on the law."

When the Black urban campuses of Vista University were incorporated into the former white University of Port Elizabeth, the merger dissolved any of the "less colonized curricula" of the smaller entity. Vista "had one or two psychology modules that definitely brought the other worldviews into discussion, took account of African perspectives." But the Vista staff were small in number and had a limited voice when they were absorbed into the conservative institution under a new name, the Nelson Mandela Metropolitan University (now Nelson Mandela University). This view of decolonization as containing African content is worth a closer look, which it will receive in Section 4.2.2, but the expansion of the curriculum in "one or two modules" fits the conception of change as added inclusive content.

At the University of Pretoria, this additive understanding of decolonization amounted to as little as a single study guide in one faculty – "a type of window dressing, or paying lip service to the decolonial agenda," said a senior education scholar. The small-scale change not only allowed the mainstream curriculum to remain undisturbed but also signalled to the outside a responsiveness to the radical demand for change, even if it was contained in the smallest unit of the curriculum – the ubiquitous study guide. Such signalling also concealed a generalized resistance to change in one faculty, where the response to decolonization was heard in reactions such as "Do they expect us to go back to the caveman days?" or "How can we change proven scientific knowledge now to fit in [with] decolonization?"

Sometimes, a push for the mainstreaming of an idea considered to represent decolonization confronted the age-old curriculum question of whether to mainstream or give stand-alone status to an added component. This was the case with customary law at Stellenbosch University. If it were integrated into all modules, the argument goes, the added content would lose its visibility behind mainstream legal knowledge. The counter-argument was that the added content must be taught across the curriculum – something local academics like to call "cross-cutting themes" – in order to be fully recognized and incorporated. In either scenario, the inclusive content is considered an addition to the overall curriculum, not the transformation of established knowledge of the law.

In an effort to demonstrate radical curriculum change, customary law was the content of choice among legal academics at other South African universities – even though, as will be shown later, there is nothing to suggest that adding an "African" example to an established curriculum is inherently radical. For the academics, though, customary law offered radical possibilities: "We tried to create processes to be radical," offered a senior scholar at NMU; decolonization "doesn't come through any stronger than in customary law being turned into a full-year module." That radical move, from the academic leader's perspective, was also evidenced in the decision to allow students to take a non-law module "in order to broaden their thinking" or a compulsory module, added on, of course, in African Regional Law.

4.2.2 Decolonization as Africanization

The understanding of decolonization as Africanization is ubiquitous in South African universities. The demand was confronted with an interesting paradox: In the social sciences and humanities, and even the natural and biomedical sciences, much of the curriculum content was already "Africanized."

The rhetorical politics of the student movement was often based on an exaggeration – that *nothing* has changed. Nowhere is this more evident than in the sweeping claim that the curriculum is centred on Europe and the rest of the Western world. No doubt, that remains true in several disciplines and fields of study. But the broad claim comes up against an institutional reality – so much of what South African universities teach is, in fact, about Africa. How then does the political criticism make sense of what we shall call normal or everyday Africanization?

A top scientist at the University of Pretoria wearily made the point that "I study the South African fungi. My research is deeply embedded in the continent. Biologists in South Africa study South African flora and fauna." In this case, it is not simply that "examples" are African; the very biological sciences curriculum is based on African subjects. A world-renowned scientist at UCT made the point that her subject, archaeology, is "the stuff about colonization and decolonization," since humans leave and come to Africa. "Even without the new language of decolonization," she reflected, "we've been holding conversations about having a very Africa-centric curriculum for as long as I've been here." This was much deeper than a case of "adding discussions on the African butterfly and then you've decolonized," as a senior administrator at UJ put it. In many cases in the sciences, the curriculum was essentially African.

What these academics point to is not simply global scientific knowledge being applied to the African context but African distinctiveness in the natural sciences. So, for example, the UP scientist talks about the single recessive gene in the male and female leopard that produces the

King Leopard. This is "a beautiful example of a single recessive allele that is beautifully African and yet doesn't exist in most of the genetics textbooks that are written in the West." Similarly, a Rhodes University anthropologist teaches about the ethnography and indigenous knowledge systems of Nguni communities in the Eastern Cape, revealing alternative origins of African clans than those described by European and Indian men along the coasts. It is fascinating, original African research and teaching, which, for the scholar concerned, "absolutely fits in with the decolonization agenda." These and many other Africa-centred studies existed long before the decolonization moment announced itself on campuses in 2015.

The political claim of the decolonization activists – that little or nothing had shifted in terms of the Africanization of education – left the radical pursuit of curriculum change stranded on two fronts. First, it failed to recognize and build on critical efforts towards decolonization in the different universities. Second, it confused the mere inclusion of African content in curriculum with the deep transformation of knowledge (more on this later). The press for decolonization as Africanization therefore proceeded, carried as it was by the political moment of the mid-2010s, as if institutions were working from a blank slate.

Among academics and students alike, Africanization itself was understood in two ways – either as the re-centring of the curriculum knowledge with Africa (rather than Europe) at the centre, or simply as the use of local content in the teaching plan.

The re-centring project of Africanization was often driven by a strong sense of Pan Africanism among the decolonization activists. On some campuses, this drive for Africanization often came from students associated with the Pan African Student Movement of Azania (PASMA), who were the most prominent articulators of the idea – as was the case at UWC. Where a particular academic leader among the senior academics professed a Pan African worldview – such as the chairs of the decolonization task teams at UJ and Stellenbosch – the framing documents that resulted from their work reflected this perspective on Africanization.

In this hard turn towards Africanization, "students were not talking about decoloniality; they were meaning let's bring in more African literature, African authors, and a more African-centred content," said a UJ Task Team leader. This meant that while progressive academics were talking about decolonization in its more refined Latin American form – as decoloniality, or embracing many knowledges – the students in this instance understood their struggle quite simply as the Africanization of curriculum content. As a senior academic put it, "they want a curriculum that brings their worlds into the curriculum."

One particular group among the Africanization activists expressed its goals in the personal terms, "I need to see myself in the curriculum." This personalization of curriculum criticism targets many things – the content is foreign (curriculum), the lecturers are white (staffing), and the educational experience is alienating (culture). "I do not see myself in the curriculum" is, moreover, a quest for recognition; it is not surprising, therefore, that this expression of Africanization came mainly from within the historically white, English universities such as Wits and UCT.

Such a sweeping ambition for decolonization through an Africanized curriculum drew heavy criticism across the ten universities, and in particular from within the natural science and engineering disciplines. The reactions were at once petty and dismissive, expressed in statements such as "An atom is an atom," "You can't decolonize mathematics," or "1+1=2 in any culture."

While decolonization as the re-centring of Africanization carried some appeal in certain universities, a much less ambitious variation on the theme was simply to add African examples to the mainstream curriculum. This particular version was very popular among academics, for it was the least disruptive to the institutional curriculum. The examples are endless.

Sometimes the use of local references was minimal, what a commerce professor called picking "low hanging fruit," in efforts to decolonize the curriculum. In his words, "We were looking at an exam the other day and the question was asked why use Euros and Dollars; why not Rands?" The academic recognized this as "the sort of shallower level of curriculum engagement," but one that nevertheless constituted "quick wins." This is nothing more than what a medical school academic referred to as giving "an African flavour to the curriculum."

More often, localization meant adding "African content" to the existing curriculum through local examples, local authors, or local context. Some academics called this "Africanization," and others a recovery of "indigenous knowledge." This branding of the curriculum as local was often emphasized by academics as not meaning the substitution of Western knowledge for African knowledge or of one "canon" or "archive" for another. Localization of content, in other words, meant an African example or illustration or case study within the established curriculum.

This threadbare interpretation of Africanization as local examples allowed for a striking coincidence of thought between African nativist and Afrikaner ethnicist commitments. This is sensitive terrain, and we proceed with caution.

We noticed that whenever Africanization was raised with, especially, white academics, the default reaction was to reference, if not in so many words, "the primitive" as examples of how to "Africanize." We use the term *primitive* to describe an ideological position that frames African indigeneity as simple, elementary, and unsophisticated, even as it is upheld as a worthy contrast to its opposite, Western knowledge. The following is a long list of disciplinary examples raised by many of our academic interviewees whenever Africanization was explained by reference to local examples:

Field or discipline	Example mooted
Medicine	African traditional remedies
Law	customary law
Statistics	card games
Engineering	wheelbarrows
Accountancy	stokvels
Economics	spaza shops
Biotechnology	homebrewing
Conservation ecology	goats
Construction	shacks
Nutrition sciences	chicken feet
Mathematics	beads, stones
Architecture	Zulu huts
Electricity (static)	superstitions

The fact that white academics so easily default to these kinds of examples to signal an Africanized curriculum is problematic, on many levels.

First, the default to the primitive casts "the African" in a unidimensional existence of class, caste, and cultures that, of course, defies the richness of human existence within the Black African community.

Second, in the name of relevance, the African is locked into a description as basic, rural and subsistence-based, rather than *also* as urban, educated, and accomplished in the worlds of industry, finance, technology, innovation, medicine, fashion, etc.

Third, it reduces the African to its racialized and ethnic meanings – the apartheid "African" – to the exclusion of other Black South Africans and how they live their lives. All of the examples relate to one particular group of citizens, those classified as "African" under apartheid.

Fourth, it matches perfectly the apartheid stereotype of the racial African, whose station in life is preordained and of whom Verwoerd warned that they should not be trained "above the level of certain forms of labor," but "in accordance with their opportunities in life" and "according to the sphere in which they live."

The defence of this racialized version of Africanization is often made by contrasting extremes, such as in this reflection by a senior academic:

If a student comes from the deep old Transkei and you suddenly end up in Rondebosch [UCT's location], trust me, it's a completely different world.

It is not at all surprising, therefore, that a white academic from a conservative Afrikaans background would see the curricular response to this racialized view of Africanization as "culturally relevant pedagogies which maybe now I reconsider decolonized pedagogies."

Nevertheless, what makes such radical opposites – Transkei and Rondebosch – a problem is that most of UCT's students are not, in fact, from "the deep old Transkei," but from urban areas with middle-class aspirations, and they are often drawn from the elite schools of the southern suburbs of Cape Town and similar areas of the other major cities of South Africa. This raises the question as to why white academics insist on this contrast of the extremes. It is because it fits their predetermined and often unconscious framing of the African as sociologically "primitive," in accordance with deeply held beliefs about Black status and aspirations (see Rosenberg and Le Grange 2020).

This particular framing of the African as primitive is even reflected in
the traditional African language departments of universities, as one
Black scholar explained:

And so the world that is presented to students as African in the name of
decolonization is actually the world that they do not inhabit anymore ...
scholars in African languages are still ... kind of stuck into huts, cow herding
and milking as if that is something that is going to bring back the world that
we have lost due to colonialism.

The criticism of the racial essentialism of such a narrow view of
Africanization does not mean that there is not a case to be made for
reclaiming indigenous knowledge within the curriculum. Local knowledges and indigenous ways of knowing have indeed been subjugated
over the centuries of colonialism, as seen also in the cases of tribal
minorities in New Zealand and Australia.

In South Africa, however, the pursuit of what is indigenous to
Africa is made more complex by the association of indigeneity with
the racial and ethnic project of apartheid. There is nothing inherently
radical in the recovery of African knowledge, culture, and customs
within the established curriculum. Apartheid was, in fact, about
racial and ethnic distinctiveness, justified on the basis of the inherent
social and cultural norms and beliefs possessed by four races and ten
ethnic groups. Therefore, to enter this curriculum terrain without
eyes wide open is to be sucked into the quicksand of racial and
ethnic politics.

How then, asked the sociologist Zimitri Erasmus in an interview,
does one balance "acknowledgement of the disavowed" with alertness
to the dangers of race essentialism? With difficulty, she responded: "I
find the tension productive, but I have not yet come to a place where
I can live with this tension, socially and politically."

The readiness to embrace Africanization as the preferred meaning of
decolonization carried different agendas for different constituencies.
For the student political movement – and not only the Pan Africanists –
it meant placing African traditions, identities, authorities, and
knowledge at the centre of curriculum change. For the academics, a
minimalist interpretation of curriculum inclusion meant the passing
use of African examples (huts, wheelbarrows, stokvels, etc.) as a
demonstration of doing decolonization. In the first conception,
Africanization is a threat, and it floundered in the face of institutional

resistance; in the second, it flourishes, precisely because it is non-threatening in institutional terms and, at the same time, ideologically attuned to the idea of the racial African.

4.3 Decolonization as Good Teaching

In the confusion about meanings, many academics understood decolonization as nothing more than good teaching. Pushed to elaborate, academic teachers would talk about accessible teaching, relevant content, and fair assessments – the kind of things that a good teacher would do in almost any context. Instead of exerting themselves to find more challenging meanings for decolonization, this was something good academics could, in fact, already do: teach well. It was a practical way of responding to a potentially difficult task, or, in the words of one academic as she pondered the many and complex meanings of decolonization, "let's just do something sensible."

At a very elemental level, the pressure for decolonization enabled conversations about good teaching among more academics than the usual few innovators in a faculty or department. It helped that there was "the instruction from above that you will now think about decolonization," said a UJ academic, and therefore a motivation that doing so meant that "you tick that box in your performance indicators." In other words, the interpretation of decolonization as good teaching was a safe off-ramp into doing what was manageable in the cloud of contested meanings hovering over a complex term.

For at least one institution – Rhodes University – the *institutional* position on decolonization was very much associated with the "good teaching" conception of change. This does not mean that there were not individuals engaging in more radical curriculum actions, but the main thrust of the decolonization drive was focused on improving teaching. There were two reasons for this disposition towards decolonization at Rhodes.

First, the drive for decolonization came from within the Centre for Higher Education Research, Teaching and Learning (CHERTL), the anchor group in the institution for dealing with decolonization through its primary work, staff development. Second, it was CHERTL's explicit position that it would adopt "a soft touch to staff development at Rhodes," which meant "not making anything compulsory," for "we don't go in with a strong decolonizing discourse."

In the absence of a hard line on the decolonization of curriculum, Rhodes instead focused on pedagogy, assessment, and "challenging questions around knowledge." But nothing was pressed or prescribed, with the result that a major institutional publication meant to address decolonization published papers on topics such as scaffolding student learning in pharmaceutical chemistry, teaching for reflexivity in information systems, developing meta-thinking in mathematics, and group work in environmental science (Vorster 2016).[2] In other words, good teaching.

Outside of Rhodes, what were some of the examples of decolonization as "good teaching" on which academics embarked? At one university, it was about innovations such as teamwork and semester projects in engineering. The curriculum change started with "semester projects long before the decolonization discourse happened," and contained non-science components recognized by ECSA (the accreditation council for engineers) as important "exit level outcomes," which, in this case, referred to "soft outcomes." For the engineering academics, these components of projects allowed for the introduction of topics such as communication, ethics, economics, and the environment. But academics recognized that dealing with these topics in isolation from their broader social significance would amount to nothing more than "a little tweak here and there to satisfy the masses with a few lollipops," in the words of an engineering lecturer.

In economics at UWC, good teaching was expressed in being attentive to the scheduling of student evaluations: "We didn't consider the timing of our assessments, which was part of our conversation around decolonization." The problem was that, with large classes in the economics and management sciences, assessments were done in the evenings and on Saturdays to fit everyone in. But what the decolonization conversations raised was the inconvenience of these arrangements for students who did not have money to travel or who lived at some distance from the campus. All of which prompted this exchange during one campus interview:

---

[2] The publication is a selection of case studies from a series of "curriculum conversations" and describes itself as an attempt to "facilitate deliberations" on "whether it is necessary to reconsider what is taught and how, and what it might mean to decolonize the curriculum."

Interviewer: I understand the human issue but what does this have to do with decolonization?

Respondent (the dean): We see assessment in a holistic way because it's the connection between what you're teaching and what the outcome is … we see it as part of the conversation around decolonization.

For other academics, decolonization expressed as good teaching was about the pedagogic relationship between the academic teacher and the student. Good teaching in this case meant taking students seriously, listening to their concerns, and making the necessary adjustments in the curriculum in response to student voices. Students felt alienated on the former white campuses, and therefore closing the gap between the teacher as the authority and the student as learner was a vital element of a decolonizing curriculum. This was certainly the view of a dean (now Deputy Vice-Chancellor: Academic) at Wits: "I really understand [decolonization] as a curriculum that is responsive to what we're teaching and what students need."

Decolonization as good teaching also means giving attention to pedagogy, or, as a dean and economist at a major university put it, "transformation of the curriculum focused more on delivery than content." In his case, this meant deploying technology to make science accessible, such as the IT upgrade that would give students access to bio-informatics on a laptop: "that, for me, would be the ultimate transformation … that science is actually everywhere." Throughout this study, academics underlined the point that it is not only what you teach (curriculum) but how you teach it (pedagogy) that counts as decolonization.

Good teaching as an expression of decolonization certainly evoked a broad range of educational practices, including the use of more project work applied to community-based problems (relevance); translating study guides into the mother tongue; the generation of glossaries of terms in African languages; and simply "the habit of engaging with and a habit of speaking to students wherever I saw them."

This particular interpretation of decolonization allowed academics to work within the comfortable range of their professional experience and political comfort zones – the improvement of teaching practice. It did not, for the most part, require an interrogation of the purposes or politics of knowledge but simply the improvement in the delivery of what they were already doing: more tutorials, more application, meaningful translations, adjusted schedules, and lots of listening. This could be done without questioning inherited knowledge or disrupting the settled curriculum. "Maybe," as one NMU academic pondered, decolonization is simply "normal teaching methodologies."

4.4 Decolonization as Remediation

Decolonization arrived on university campuses where a long and continuing struggle was being waged – that of the large numbers of under-prepared students who came into higher education from poor school systems. More than half of them dropped out in the first year and fewer than a third obtained their degrees on time, if at all. It is in this context that a very powerful meaning assigned to decolonization was one of remediation, that is, of "making up" for what was lost or missing in the education of, especially, Black youth as they entered the elite universities. As a UJ academic insisted, "You can't have these [decolonization] conversations in the absence of the challenges of low pass rates and poor preparation."

Another academic activist put it more bluntly: "Their curriculum doesn't need to be decolonized, it needs to be provided in the first place." In other words, the more urgent task was simply providing disadvantaged students with the knowledge to succeed in university as a practical matter. They need "a knowledge base that makes them understand what they are doing and engage in productive ways when they are doing it." Some academics evoke the language of "powerful knowledge," from the sociology of education, or the more familiar local language of "epistemological access." *That* is the curriculum that needs to change – one that empowers young Black youth, in particular, with knowledge that gives them access to the disciplines and enables them to experience success in their studies.

Often, the notion of decolonization as remediation is associated with what has been known in South African higher education since the 1980s as academic development, and which has continued to exist under various names, conceptions, and methods ever since. It is very difficult for historically disadvantaged universities, such as UWC, to have a conversation about decolonization without falling back on a pressing institutional priority called "operation student success." It was, however, difficult for our academic interviewees to make conceptual and political connections between remediation and decolonization.

One proposal offered was to convince students in an extended curriculum programme that the remediation works to their benefit. An academic dean offered this argument: "I always try to explain to the students that they are in a position of privilege because they are getting the foundational material – the ideas, the concepts, the language – that the other students in the mainstream are not getting." It nevertheless remained a hard sell to link the urgent development needs of students and the political demands for the radical overhaul of the curriculum.

The language of the old academic development model slipped easily into the interviews; for example, that foundational modules offer "a bridge to English" through glossaries of terms. In order to deal with student anger about white staff teaching these bridging programmes, universities hired "multilingual teaching assistants ... where multilingualism [was] a kind of turnkey for resolving the resentment." There is a harsh irony at play in this difficult balancing act between remediation and decolonization, and it is this: The purpose of academic development was to induct underprepared Black students *into* the settled curriculum, not to disrupt it.

For remediation to function as curriculum induction, an African language is recruited not for purposes of transformation but to aid facilitation, as this NMU academic in information technology explained:

From a decolonization aspect, it is how we use technology and the way we are doing our classes; we have a lot of extra lessons with students who can explain in their own language to them and with videos in either English or Xhosa to help them navigate through the university structures. For example, where do I find my progress report and where do I go and find how much I owe the institution.

Decolonization as remediation leaves undisturbed the power hierarchy between academic teacher and disadvantaged student – a particular criticism made by decolonization advocates, especially in its expression as decoloniality. This established hierarchy is particularly visible in academic development, where the role of the teacher is to "bridge" the student into the mainstream curriculum.

When there was resistance to these arrangements at a leading university, the institutional response was to change the face of the facilitators (more black tutors and trainers) and the language of induction (isiXhosa, with or without English) without upending the settled curriculum or the hierarchies in the pedagogical relationship. With those adjustments made, many staff working in academic development programmes found decolonization as remediation to be manageable, something that could be delivered within their capabilities as academic teachers.

4.5 Decolonization as Critical Pedagogy

Within every university, there is an individual or group of academics actively engaged in doing some form of critical pedagogy. Often these are academics who were doing radical work long before the decolonization moment of 2015–2016. "We might not have called it decolonization," several would say, "but we've been doing it all along."

Critical pedagogy is used here as an umbrella term for academic work – including teaching, learning, and assessment – that starts with a critique of the settled curriculum. The critique is broad and includes perspectives on curriculum such as feminism, anti-racism, postcolonial and anti-imperialist theory, sexuality studies, and critical race theory. Critical pedagogy is concerned with how knowledge and power are reflected in the curriculum, and how agency and resistance can change the social, and indeed curricular, arrangements that privilege the few at the expense of the majority.

Critical pedagogy therefore means much more than improving teaching and learning (decolonization as good teaching); on the contrary, it challenges the very foundations of the settled curriculum on which mainstream education practices are founded. The different ways in which critical pedagogy is expressed on the ten university campuses vary not so much in their radical purposes but in the particular perspectives that each takes on the established curriculum.

In several cases, the approach to critical pedagogy references the ideas of the great Brazilian educator Paulo Freire (1970), expressed in his landmark book, *Pedagogy of the Oppressed*. For an activist group in the Health Sciences at UWC, Freire's critical pedagogy is "not just using local examples" but about "consciousness, helping the student become conscious of how the context affects them." Another senior academic, at UP, did her dissertation on Freire's work, and she tried to introduce this thinking in the education core module, but with limited influence across the faculty curriculum.

The notion of critical consciousness is fundamental to a Freirean approach, and it is conceptually linked to what, in the bygone struggles in the Cape, used to be called "awareness." The attraction of Freire is distinctive, though not widespread in programmes on some campuses, existing rather as "little pockets of awareness bubbling up here and there," as a UWC lecturer observed.

At Rhodes University, a psychology academic revels in the "disruptive" methods that she uses in her teaching on subjects such as race, ethnicity, poverty, and health. Her classes are packed (including with non-registered auditors), and she takes on critical subjects directly – such as the question of gender-neutral toilets. Would she call this kind of work decolonization? "I don't actually use that label. I use transformation." The academic feels that she is alone in teaching such a critical psychology, that white students doubt her, and that white lecturers are unsupportive. "I'm the only woman of color with a PhD in my department and so I have to literally have a slide where I list all my qualifications."

Every university seems to have its own "internal grammars," as a senior academic described the variety of critical pedagogies on campuses. NMU's "humanizing pedagogies" enjoyed much prominence in its Faculty of Education, but few were convinced that this construct enjoyed meaningful uptake in the rest of the university. The education faculty at Wits, on the other hand, spoke of "socially just pedagogies" as one approach to curriculum work with teachers. An academic at UCT reported on "post-humanism in education," which threads through her work in early childhood development. And in the history of art department at Wits, an academic draws on "post-colonial theory" to teach subjects such as slavery, memory, and identity.

These diverse initiatives are all *critical* in the broad sense of the term, but they do not easily fit under a single conceptual umbrella of radical pedagogies. Other critical initiatives encountered in this study included studies of the Marikana massacre in engineering courses at UCT, radical perspectives on occupational therapy at UWC, and the integration of transformative constitutionalism in law courses at NMU.

Exponents of each of these critical pedagogy initiatives, however framed, struggled when pressed to conceptually link their work to "decolonization." The political connection to decolonization was assumed, rather than established through connections with allied concepts such as decoloniality, Africanization, and even transformation.

One unusual intervention in the context of critical pedagogy came from outside the country, when the Mellon Foundation in New York invested millions of Rands (R6,172,387 million for the period 2018–2020) in decolonization projects in humanities fields at selected universities. This injection of money and ideas grafted onto the curriculum initiatives of academics already working from a critical perspective in their disciplines. The funded projects reflected Mellon's grand ambitions for radical work associated with what its Program Director, the former Vice-Chancellor of Rhodes University Saleem Badat, enthusiastically called "the decolonial turn." Here are some of the funded themes:

- The humanities and the decolonial change
- Africanizing philosophy
- Socially relevant curricula
- Interdisciplinarity and the decolonial (exhibition)
- Decolonial aesthesis as critical teaching methodology
- Talking about indigenous music
- Decolonizing spaces
- Visual redress
- Recovering subterranean archives
- Toppling visual regimes
- (De)colonizing power of portraiture
- Decolonizing anthropology at the margins
- Socially just epistemologies
- Creating African narratives

All of these bold themes carried direct or indirect connections to decolonization as critical pedagogy. The Mellon funding supported critical scholars working for the most part within their particular institutional enclaves. What cannot be claimed is that these very creative ideas had any broader institutional impacts once this well-funded initiative came to an abrupt end in 2019.

The notion of decolonization as critical pedagogy nevertheless allowed for the flourishing of small-scale, often radical curriculum initiatives, mostly on the margins of institutional life. Students and academics with critical commitments were drawn to some of these "decolonial hotspots" on campus for readings and seminars, or simply to gather together during the heat of the decolonization moment.

Critical initiatives that existed before that moment found themselves politically validated, though not beyond criticism, as in the dance curricula on one of the UCT campuses (see Chapter 3). These critical efforts also provided university leaders with a means for claiming that "something was being done" in response to the criticisms of student leaders that "nothing had changed."

4.6 Non-change: The Most Common Response to Decolonization

For most academic departments, decolonization carried little relevance for their work, because most scholars and scientists believed that this radical idea simply did not apply to the peculiarities of their disciplines. While many academics grappled to come to conceptual terms with decolonization and gave it various meanings in their own work, such as good teaching, the majority either went quiet and did nothing (the safe political option) or resisted outright.

One of the main reasons for "non-change" with respect to curriculum had to do with disciplinary beliefs. This means that academics were committed to foundational beliefs about the nature of knowledge in their disciplines that could not be shaken, let alone uprooted, by an alien concept such as decolonization. A UWC economist captured this position well in his response to decolonization:

There are certain core theories that are uncontestable, such as supply and demand. When Zimbabwe wanted to defy those basic economic laws, they had shortages. Those laws have been tested over time, centuries before us. You can't just throw them away. You do that at your own peril. Every discipline has certain core pillars and theoretical foundations.

The strength of these foundational disciplinary beliefs meant that decolonization was seen as irrelevant to some, and as a threat to others, as for another UWC economist:

So even in economics, there are areas in which I see no reason to respond, as far as decolonization is concerned. Some areas might even have a cruder response, such as econometrics, where they might say "these are our tools and that's what they are, and I do not see how you want to decolonize that."

The science faculties were the most difficult to convince of the need to decolonize, and academics often expressed their concerns sharply and dismissively. A colleague at NMU summarized some of those concerns: "What must we decolonize? Math is math. IT is IT. The atom is the atom." A more detailed and sophisticated criticism of the demand for decolonization came from a UCT mathematician who argued that the questions of science lie outside of social or political considerations, for they addressed questions like:

Will the bridge fall down when heavy lorries and buses cross it? Will this cell phone be able to receive a signal from that transmitting tower? Will this photodiode emit light? Does this computer program have a bug in it? (Ellis 2018)

Like the UWC economists, the scientists taking this position insisted that there is no such thing as Western science, and that expertise should drive curriculum considerations, rather than student views on science subjects; students simply cannot offer meaningful comment on things they know little about:

Do we need a quantum mechanics course before introducing astrophysics of radiation processes? Should Maxwell's equations precede the Dirac equation or not? Do we need to introduce Lie Group theory before studying partial differential equations? Is it necessary to study peptides before proteins? Or should amino acids precede both? In what order should one teach crystallization, drying, and evaporation in a chemical engineering syllabus? (Ellis 2018)

What was being defended, given the levelling demands of decolonization, was therefore both the universal knowledge of the disciplines, such as science and economics, and the authority of expertise. These were important arguments, to which the decolonization activists seldom provided a focused and coherent set of counter-arguments. More often, the defence of normal science took the form of sarcasm and dismissiveness, as two academics quoted the criticisms of their colleagues:

Let's just take-out Roman Dutch Law and put in indigenous law (UJ).

Is there African literature about the hard sciences? How can we change proven scientific knowledge to fit in with decolonization? (UP)

Emotions ran high as academics defended their curriculum turf during some of the decolonization debates. "Two academics from the same department almost came to blows – same department, different views. We had to separate them," recalled a senior leader at UJ. No doubt, the curriculum wars provoked by decolonization were often intense, pitting believers against resisters.

The resistance to decolonization was particularly acute in the professions, where the external standards of regulatory authorities loomed large over curriculum decisions. A medical dean made it clear that "you don't want to decolonize, in the true sense, a curriculum that is intended for a professional or for professional qualifications." These external demands of national regulators, as we will show in Chapter 5, also come with international benchmarks for the professions. The threat posed by decolonization was, however, not simply a challenge to what academics saw as the standards of the profession but also "the dilution of professional identity," charged a Wits academic.

So, five years later, what is the status of decolonization in the curriculum of South African universities?

In a nutshell, the pre-2015 curriculum has not changed in any significant ways. In most academic departments, it is "business as usual," according to activist academics supportive of the decolonization moment. Others would concede small changes in specific departments, such as the ways in which students are engaged in the classroom. Those who were doing critical pedagogy continue to do so, momentarily inspired by the decolonization moment, but continuing to do change work without necessarily referencing "decolonization" as the motivation for their academic labours. In the end, the curriculum status quo in South African universities was sustained not for lack of political pressure but as the result of a lack of political strategy with respect to formidable institutions.

4.7 Conclusion

The main observation from this chapter is that, given the indeterminate meanings of decolonization on campuses, academic teachers, under pressure to respond, created their own understandings of this *potentially* radical concept. The meanings that academics assigned to decolonization was, however, much less important than what such attributions of meaning allowed.

Our thesis is that these self-assigned meanings carried with them particular utilities for the academics concerned. That is, the *particular appropriations of decolonization fit within the ideological comfort zones and implementational capabilities of the academics concerned.* It is clear from this research that decolonization as a political force on campuses was often experienced as threatening and disorienting for many academics. There was therefore an acute need to respond, not only because of the student demands but also as a result of institutional pressures to comply with an executive requirement to "decolonize the curriculum."

Therefore, to define decolonization as good teaching, for example, simply continued and extended the work that academics did anyway. Interpreting decolonization as Africanization, and by that meaning the use of local examples here and there, did little to challenge the settled curriculum. A minority of academics embraced the political meanings of decolonization through, for example, one or other version of critical pedagogy. However, these were often academic teachers who were already doing this kind of critical work, using different conceptual labels, before the student protest movement of 2015–2016.

Needless, to say, this voluntary take-up and appropriation of decolonization in diverse academic communities had direct consequences for the possibilities of radical curriculum change at the level of the academic department or the university as a whole.

However, what kept the institutional curriculum in place was not only the preferred interpretations of decolonization among academic teachers on the inside but powerful regulatory frameworks from outside the university.

5 | Regulating Radical Ideas
The Role of Regulatory Agencies

5.1 Introduction

South Africa has a byzantine structure of regulatory agencies that directly and indirectly affect the university curriculum. At first glance, it would appear that these authoritative bodies are simply responsible for the registration or accreditation of qualifications by setting standards against which all university curricula are measured and with which they must comply. On closer inspection, though, it can be seen how the regulatory authorities exercise a powerful influence over curricula through a range of administrative procedures that contain and constrain any deviations from the institutional curriculum. In this chapter, we will demonstrate how exactly regulatory agencies "enclave" (Cuban 1999) or "defang" (Ahmed 2012) radical curriculum ideas such as decolonization.

5.2 The Path of a New Curriculum to Recognition and Accreditation

It is illuminating to trace the complex path followed through the education bureaucracy before a new curriculum idea becomes a reality for teaching and learning in the university classroom. We use a simple example and deploy the term *curriculum* in its broadest sense.

A professor decides to develop a new curriculum – let's say, for the sake of argument, a new masters' qualification on decolonization. The new curriculum first needs to find support and approval within the academic department, for example, the sociology department of University X. It then serves at a Faculty Board, which may or may not approve, depending on factors such as resources to teach the additional courses; available infrastructure, such as lecture room space; and the extent to which it articulates with (or links to) what the sociology department is already doing.

Assuming that approval is granted, the new curriculum proposal then goes to the Senate, which is the highest arbiter on all matters academic at a university. There is normally another hurdle to scale, and that is the institutional planning office, usually under a Deputy Vice-Chancellor: Academic, which has to ensure that new curricula satisfy all the technical conditions required for submission to the national government's Department of Higher Education and Training (DHET).

The government department then receives the new curriculum proposal from University X and considers approval, using an instrument called the Program Qualifications Mix (PQM) (Department of Higher Education and Training 2016). The PQM is the list of all approved qualifications and specializations already offered at an institution. Government approval for the new curriculum hinges on considerations such as institutional capacity (e.g., staffing resources) and institutional performance (e.g., throughput rates). Most importantly, the new curriculum has to "fit" within what the institution already does. The government department pre-approves the new curriculum, and the proposal can now be considered for accreditation by the Council on Higher Education (Figure 5.1).

The Council on Higher Education (CHE) is a statutory body responsible for quality assurance in higher education. The CHE accredits new curricula and also reviews existing curricula. It uses a long list of

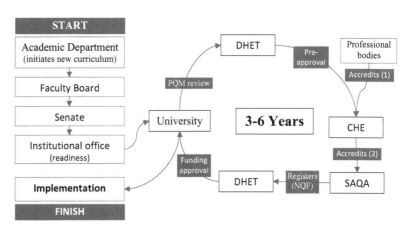

Figure 5.1 The generic path to curriculum approval in South African universities

nineteen criteria by which to assure the quality of a new curriculum, including technical considerations, such as credit values and learning outcomes; administrative concerns, such as infrastructure and support systems; and academic imperatives, such as staffing qualifications required to deliver the proposed curriculum. Once the CHE has accredited the new curriculum, the new degree qualification is sent for registration with the South African Qualifications Authority (SAQA).

SAQA is also a statutory body, and its task is to register the new qualification, with its curriculum essentials, on a structure called the National Qualifications Framework (NQF). SAQA looks for evidence that the new qualification promotes optimal access, through, for example, the recognition of prior learning; whether it "articulates" with other qualifications for learners to advance along more than one learning pathway; and whether, on completion of the qualification, the learner is competent to do a certain job. One of the key issues for the Authority is whether the new qualification enjoys international comparability. If successful, the qualification is registered on the NQF and is then visible and transparent to the public. Without registration, the curriculum cannot be offered at a university. Once the qualification is registered, it returns to the DHET.

The DHET puts the final stamp of approval on the curriculum. The registered qualification then becomes part of the PQM of University X, funding is approved by means of the state subsidy, and the curriculum can be offered to students. In the case of several professional qualifications, however, there is one more hurdle to scale.

There is a knot of professional bodies that set the standards for their respective professions, three of which were studied for this research. The Health Professions Council of South Africa (HPSCA) is a statutory body that, through its eleven boards, sets standards for doctors, dentists, medical scientists, and clinical associates.

The Engineering Council of South Africa (ECSA) is a statutory body that counts among its core functions the registration of engineering professionals and the accreditation of engineering programmes. Its central concern is that engineering students meet the prescribed graduate attributes on achieving engineering qualifications.

The South African Institute for Chartered Accountants (SAICA), by contrast, is a non-statutory membership body that sees its role as setting the education and training standards for future chartered accountants (CAs) and accrediting CA-specific programmes within universities.

What is the role of these professional bodies in the process of approving a new curriculum? In the view of the CHE, "they have to endorse a new program before it is properly accredited." In reality, the question of accreditation is a much more intricate political contest between rival accreditation authorities, as we shall see in a moment.

This complex process of approval – from initiation by an academic department in a university through review, registration, accreditation, and approval for funding by DHET – can take anywhere from 18 to 36 months. In the estimation of a senior administrator in the national accreditation authority, "All in all, it takes two years, and sometimes up to four or five years, before a 'new' program conceptualized by academics reaches the first student cohort" (Zawada 2020, 4).

This drawn-out process of administrative approvals obviously has a direct bearing on *comprehensive* and *institution-wide* curriculum reform in the face of the immediacy and intensity of student struggles for a more radical knowledge intervention, the decolonization of the curriculum. Such a radical reinvention of the institutional curriculum is therefore not only compromised by a convoluted process of bureaucratic clearances and professional approvals but sets the very terms for curriculum change, which, in the end, is inevitably modest, modular, and momentary.

5.3 The Politics of Accreditation and the Implications for Radical Curriculum Change

With the advent of democracy in 1994, there was only a semblance of planning in the higher education system in South Africa. The public universities at the time were not born of high-level technical planning befitting a modern state, but were in fact unwieldly creatures of apartheid planning marked by inefficiency, waste, and the duplication of resources. With the release of the National Plan for Higher Education in 2001, planning swung into high gear, and universities were introduced to concepts such as enrolment planning, higher education management information systems (HEMIS), and quality assurance.

In the fervour of post-apartheid planning, a new and formidable bureaucracy was installed to, on the one hand, root out past inefficiencies, and on the other to give direction to the emancipatory ideals of the democratic state. In this excited phase of higher education planning, any number of new "structures" were established, such as SAQA in 1995 and the CHE in 2004, which morphed into mega-organizations with complex infrastructures and impenetrable languages. Importantly, these new "democratic" structures were often created alongside well-established organizations with overlapping mandates and duplicate functions, such as the professional bodies. It is, to this day, a legislative and administrative mess that frustrates curriculum changes routinely proposed by universities. Those inside these complex regulatory authorities are very conscious of the problem.

"This is a huge conundrum," says the CEO of the principal accreditation authority at the time, for "it's where the regulatory function is breaking down." While legislative changes, such as the NQF Act of 2008, were supposed to sort out overlapping authorities, it did not work that way in practice:

It is one thing to create new legislation that empowers a new body like the CHE with accreditation matters, but you've got other statutory bodies and a whole lot of non-statutory bodies that also fulfil this function of accreditation and registration when it comes to theprofessions.

Nowhere is this political contestation over accreditation authority more acute than with the professions, such as medicine, engineering, and accounting. These high-status professions were established with legislative mandates before the advent of the democratic government in 1994, and they were well-regarded and entrenched among their practitioners. The attitude of some of these older professional bodies to the new ones was, in the words of a senior CHE official:

They say, "We will just fulfil our function [of accreditation] and to hell with you." So we've been left to slug it out with all the professional councils, statutory and non-statutory, and then to conclude memoranda of understanding with them. It is a huge frustration for the universities as well.

Why would the professional bodies disregard what the CHE sees as its overarching authority in accreditation? From the perspective of SAICA, a well-established professional body:

They [the CHE] don't have the capacity, they don't use the right people to do the accreditation [and] have very much a tick-box approach – have you got this? Have you got that? Whereas we say how effective is that in the delivery of the program?

This does not mean the relationship between the two accreditation authorities is hostile. Members of SAICA are invited to serve on accreditation committees of the CHE and are in fact valued by the Council. In the process, the two authorities find practical ways of working around overlapping functions; for example, SAICA limits its accreditation to the CA-specific programmes of universities and would not proceed unless the university and its general programming is accredited by the CHE.

The HPSCA, on the other hand, is in the process of trying to define its own accreditation relationship with the CHE. While its website makes clear that it is a statutory body with accreditation authority, one of its most experienced practitioners tried to spell out a new understanding of the relationship that revealed the messiness of a new deal:

> We feel that the power of accreditation lies with the CHE and that what we do is rather evaluations. What we do is to ensure the graduates meet the requirements to register with the CHE. So our role is more to ensure standards, while the CHE is geared to ensuring correct [sic] educational approaches.

In this maze of administrative complexity and overlapping authority, the CHE is left with negotiating "memoranda of understanding" with the professional bodies to enable some movement on vital accreditation decisions. Why is it so difficult to change these complex arrangements into something simple, accessible, and workable for universities?

One reason, it appears, is the status and standing of these professions among their members. It carries considerable weight to be recognized as a doctor or accountant or engineer by your professional peers. These bodies developed formidable reputations in their respective professions long before the CHE was established. Another reason is that there is a significant amount of money generated by these professional bodies through their standards-setting and accreditation functions. "It's a perverse incentive for them to maintain the status quo," maintains the CHE. And a third reason has to do with the turf wars that come with inter-ministerial politics, since different departments of government hold authority over the different professions. For example, the Health Professions Council works under the authority of the Ministry of Health, while the Ministry of Higher Education and Training has responsibility for university programmes as a whole; at the same time, SAICA is accredited by the International Regulatory Board of Auditors (IRBA), which falls under the Ministry of Finance!

Another example of curriculum contestation among government, accreditor, and the profession is the interesting case of nursing. University heads of nursing schools (departments) believe in a four-year science-based qualification that combines theory and practice with completion of all the hours to meet the professional registration requirements. The Ministry of Health, on the other hand, insists that three years of college-based training provides more practical and useful "bedside" training for patient health. Complicating matters is that the training of nurses is split between universities under one department (DHET) and public nursing colleges under a different department (the DOH). These complexities are not simply organizational but ideological for at the heart of the contestation is a curriculum question: What constitutes a well-trained nurse?

What this complexity of accreditation and the confusion of responsibilities mean is that the universities do not receive clear, comprehensive, or consistent guidelines with respect to curriculum change. Universities, at times, exploit this confusion for their own ends, as will be shown later.

In sum, a university's proposals for curriculum change have to contend with both a complex bureaucracy that weighs things down and a contested accreditation environment that further slows the process of curriculum change. A radical proposal for curriculum change therefore enters an arena in which the focus of a maze of regulatory structures is on exercising administrative control and compliance on the one hand, and on securing political turf and territory on the other. Neither of these dilemmas, bureaucratic or political, bodes well for academics seeking a fundamental shift in understandings of what the curriculum is for. One reason is that the regulatory authorities themselves have completely different ideological positions when it comes to the curriculum and the problem of change.

5.4 Regulation and Radical Curriculum Change: The Case of the Apex Authority

SAQA, as the apex authority in the regulatory system, requires a separate discussion. SAQA was established after apartheid with a strong activist rationale for its operations. "Freire is alive and well in this building," says the authority's head of research, referring to the famous Brazilian educator and author of the education activists' bible around the world, *Pedagogy of the Oppressed.*

The founding commitments of the authority spell out the ideals and aspirations of the democratic imagination. SAQA is about *access*, its officials stress, that is, opening up admission for those denied it in the past. The universities, as elite organizations, are charged with enabling access to their curricula for those who might not meet the formal requirements for admission but who have gained knowledge through experience and self-learning. The Authority calls this "the recognition of prior learning," and moving examples were cited during our engagements for this research of older people who were short-changed by apartheid, who dropped out of school but later in life became passionate about a particular area of training. One such example was a woman who learned about physical exercise from books, did short courses and workshops, and listened to experts on exercise physiology. Thanks to SAQA policies, she could show up at a university, seek recognition for her previous learning, and enter the first or second year of studies for a particular qualification.

This kind of example, for the Authority, is not simply about an older woman gaining access to the curriculum on the basis of an administrative accommodation; it is about social justice, in that a historical wrong is being corrected in the process. SAQA calls this *redress*, one of its founding values, which it sees as the fulfilment of a constitutional obligation.

In the democratic imagination of the Authority, a student should also be able to progress from one level of work to a much higher occupation. "From sweeper to engineer," is one of the most moving phrases used by SAQA officials in describing their mission; it comes from the early days of its establishment, and echoes the calls of the progressive unions of the time. It is not clear whether any sweepers actually became engineers, but this was the ideal around which the Authority mobilized its agenda as the apex authority in the regulatory field. No learner should be stuck in a dead-end of learning; *progression* therefore became a fundamental component of the new imagination.

Perhaps the most powerful of all the democratic ideals of the Authority has to do with *articulation*. In simple terms, articulation means a qualification in one field, such as vocational education in a technical college, should allow for transfer to academic education in a university. This is the whole idea of a National Qualifications Framework: it allows for seamless movement from one level of education to another so that a person's educational ambitions are progressive in the pursuit of life-long learning.

Finally, the national framework makes all of this transparent to prospective and current learners. *Transparency*, a core value of the authority, has democratic intent – it makes the rules of the game visible on the framework for what was often concealed from ordinary workers and students desirous of further and higher education.

In order to advance these ideals, SAQA relies on an extensive stakeholder model of participation. It uses its platform as a regulatory authority to bring together hundreds of stakeholders annually to deliberate on vital concerns in the education and training environment. It sees itself as the coordinating mechanism that assembles components of the education and training system; it is "the oil in the system" of moving parts, as one official put it. Workers, employers, academics, students, community activists, and others come together for purposes of deliberation. Position papers are generated, recommendations made, and actions taken.

These ideas for the transformation of education and training are indeed radical, but do they work in practice? In other words, *what can we learn about institutions and radical curriculum change* from the experience of this important regulatory authority?

The first thing to realise is that SAQA brings people together and charges them with certain duties on a voluntary basis. For example, while the recognition of prior learning has radical implications for curriculum, it cannot be forced on autonomous universities. For this kind of task, the Authority has no teeth. It is conscious of the fact that there are enthusiasts among institutions who run with RPL, such as in the celebrated case of the University of the Western Cape, and also places like the Central University of Technology. It really is up to the university representatives who attend SAQA conferences and workshops to take forward ideas like RPL, and here is the first problem: several of the elite universities simply do not attend.

As a result, the take-up of radical ideas is completely voluntary and lies along a continuum of institutional responses, as a senior SAQA official explained:

I could honestly name them [the defaulters]. I could name the ones that have embraced it [like RPL policies] and succeeded, the ones that have embraced it and are struggling and finding their way, and the ones who are really not interested.

There is the further dilemma that institutions which at one point were early adopters of radical curriculum ideas have invariably changed over time, as was the case with UWC, which for years was the poster child for lifelong learning and the recognition of prior learning:

Now those champions have moved on. The leadership is different. The student sub-committees that facilitated change have reformed and reshaped into something else. It's different now, though that was an era in which we achieved incredible things.

The critical observation to be made about the demise of such a radical curriculum idea at UWC is that powerful as it was, it remained enclaved on the margins of institutional life. It would become institutionalized through absorption into university structures and routines, thereby losing the sharpness of its appeal – an event powerfully reflected in this administrative record of a governance decision at UWC:

The disestablishment of the Senate Lifelong Learning Committee (SLLC): The functions of the Division for Lifelong Learning (DLL) will reside within the Teaching and Learning portfolio. The functions of the SLLC will reside within the Senate Academic Planning Committee (SAP) and the Senate Teaching and Learning Committee (STLC). (Walters 2018, 1)

In the same reflection, Walters observes of this radical project that "Mainstreaming or institutionalization, by its nature, brings about regulation rather than turbulence – this is not how substantive change works" (7).

This is by no means the only radical curriculum idea that lost traction within South African universities. In a superb review of radical curricula in institutions, Crain Soudien (2019) spends some time examining the course and fate of a Centre whose aim was to expand ("enlarge") an integrative approach to curriculum at the University of South Africa (UNISA). The university, however, withdrew funding despite "a commitment at some point to look at ways of institutionalizing it" (Soudien 2019, 148). In the UNISA case, the radical idea was not absorbed into the mainstream of institutional life but terminated on the spot when the resources dried up. As with all radical ideas, the absence of dedicated funding often means the end of an innovation.

None of this analysis suggests that SAQA as a regulating body had no authority to impose the radical ideals embedded within the policies of the Authority. As an official recalled:

We have a qualifications and standards committee that evaluates new proposals and in the beginning about half of them used to be sent back because they did not have RPL and articulation routes; they were dead ends.

The salient point is that once universities understood *how to become compliant* with these criteria, they would make the necessary adjustments for clearance without necessarily making changes in the day-to-day curriculum of the institution. In other words, compliance with progressive criteria such as access and articulation became little more than satisfying a checklist of requirements rather than any deep interrogation of institutional practice. The question had to be asked:

Researchers: Do you have a way of going into the 26 public universities to see whether they are doing what they promised to do?
Regulator (SAQA): No, that is the CHE's role.

This is a critical point that hangs over much of the work of any regulation authority: Can a regulatory framework that requires institutional *compliance* also be the stimulus for radical change, which by definition demands some degree of *deviation* from the institutional curriculum? The logic of compliance, moreover, implies deference to prescribed administrative minutiae, as we observed when a SAQA official recited the criteria looked for in determining whether a new qualification complies with what is required:

Criteria for registration . . . must have a title, must have a sub-framework, the level, the credits, the rationale, provide details of reasoning, indicate how the qualification meets the needs of the sector, typical learners, learning pathway, rules of combination, entry requirements, international compatibility.

It is in this context that prominent change activists and scholars make the crucial point that "the institutionalization of transformation has reduced it to the measurement of equity, monitored by institutional research units, which are not necessarily concerned with deeper issues of transformation" (Walters 2018, 6). This fault line in the regulatory function would be laid bare when the decolonization moment exploded on university campuses.

5.5 When Decolonization Came Knocking on the Regulator's Door

5.5.1 The Case of the South African Qualifications Authority

The student demands for decolonization of the culture, complexion, and curriculum of universities caught all the regulatory agencies off guard. Their responses were varied, with the more progressive authorities (SAQA, CHE) grappling feverishly with ways in which to respond, while the mainstream professional bodies remained largely unperturbed by what the spate of unexpected demands might mean for the curriculum.

SAQA, as has been discussed, was born in the throes of a new democracy with strong political rationales for its mandate resulting, in part, from the founding influence of the progressive trade unions that popularized the term "from sweeper to engineer" (Allais 2003). Alert to its social environment, the Authority became aware of the press for decolonization through the media and its network of partners, which spurred the organization to start collecting news clippings on decolonization for internal use. Then the Authority kicked into gear – "This is how SAQA works," said a senior manager – and rallied its stakeholders to attend a large public gathering of about 150–200 people that included government officials, regulators, professional bodies, universities, private higher education institutions, and more.

Like many universities at the time, SAQA invited an articulate advocate for decolonization as a main figure, even though Professor Sabelo Ndlovu-Gatsheni's (2018) political tilt seemed to lie more in the direction of Africanization. As the Authority saw it, "Decolonization is something that must be undone, Africanization is something that must be built." Out of the conference deliberations, a report was generated for action: "We don't just have events. We don't have talk shops. We always do something." The Authority was now in high activist mode. What should be produced? A declaration? An agreement? A working document? Or an action plan? Nobody would leave until some agreement had been forged on what to do about decolonization.

The Authority decided not to talk about decolonization but about Africanization. "We wanted to know what the African way of doing is." But was SAQA not concerned that it was tilting away from the preferred student slogan for the movement, decolonization? "Yes, but at the same time, I mean, we are also actors in our own lives. It's not like the institution we're in comes out of nowhere. It comes out of a particular history," argued a former SAQA director. With the confidence of its political standing, the Authority then proceeded to produce an organizational statement on the subject entitled *SAQA's* [2018] *Position On Decolonization*, which at its end declared boldly that "SAQA is committed to decolonization and transformation."

The Authority's emphasis in this one-page standpoint document is on re-centring education in Africa, recognising indigenous knowledge, and including broader experiences and ideas "rather than blindly following Western universalism." With respect to curriculum, the Authority makes clear that:

A decolonized curriculum must place Africa at the centre of teaching, learning and research and incorporate the epistemic perspectives, knowledge and thinking from the African continent and the Global South as well as the global world.

In true SAQA tradition, this document was the product of many hours of deliberation, not only in the stakeholder conference but in Management and Board meetings of the Authority that involved everyone, including the administrative and clerical staff as well as the workers in the building.

The test, of course, was how this profound statement on decolonization would be taken up within the curriculum of public universities. Put differently, did the Authority have the teeth to make this thoroughly consultative document a reality within university curricula? It was at this point that the Authority staff recognized that, despite the extensive and intensive work done on developing an agreed position on decolonization, it ended right there:

The universities out there pick what they want to pick. Some embrace it all, some embrace parts of it.

Sometimes it's up to someone's conscience.

We even ask them the question [at SAQA events]: "Who agrees to take it back to their organization?" People put their hands up. It's up to them and then they go away and forget about it. I hope it bothers them if they forget about it.

And so, despite all the hard work done to carve out a curriculum position on decolonization, SAQA simply did not have the authority to require, let alone enforce, the uptake of its progressive ideals within the curriculum practices of public universities in South Africa. What it did, at best, was to signal a position on the subject that might or might not have been taken into further consultations and implementation in the different universities. What this entanglement with decolonization reveals is that SAQA is left with a narrowed-down sense of authority as a regulator, which simply means registering institutional qualifications on the National Qualifications Framework. The "sending back" of qualifications happens only when the technical criteria for registration are not met, without any sense, even in such cases, of how those criteria are taken up in curriculum practice.

5.5.2 The Case of the Council on Higher Education

Like SAQA, the Council on Higher Education (CHE) was created in the post-apartheid period with a strong sense of its democratic mandate to be "a dynamic organization contributing to a transformed, equitable and quality higher education and training system" (National Government of South Africa 2021). Indeed, among its CEOs were prominent activists in the anti-apartheid struggle and others in leadership with a broadly progressive agenda for the transformation of higher education in South Africa. In fulfilling this broad social mandate, the CHE has three specific functions: to accredit new programmes (i.e., curricula, for the purposes of this study) submitted by each university; to conduct national reviews of particular programmes across universities (such as a review of the LLB law degree, in all seventeen universities); and to advise the Minister of Higher Education and Training on matters of national concern.

When the decolonization debates broke on campuses, the CHE was entangled in a related struggle at universities, and that was the uprising against fee increases. There was a critical standoff between the Minister of Higher Education and Training and the President of the country. The Minister wanted to impose a limited increase; the President had other ideas.

In this turmoil, the Minister approached the statutory body and asked for "advice from a regulatory framework" perspective. Doing this task with a limited budget – in fact, the Council would slide into a

R12.5 million budget deficit – the CHE found itself under considerable strain to provide an evidence-based recommendation to the Minister with the available resources and under the time pressures of an unprecedented political crisis on university campuses. The CHE advised on an increase for the immediate moment in line with the Consumer Price Index (6 per cent), while the Vice-Chancellors convinced the Minister to go higher, towards 8 per cent. To the surprise of the sector, the President promptly announced a 0 per cent fee increase for the immediate moment and instituted a Commission of Inquiry headed by Justice Jonathan Heher to investigate "the feasibility of making higher education and training free in South Africa." (Commission of Inquiry into Higher Education and Training 2017).

In other words, when decolonization came knocking, the CHE was engrossed in the fees debacle and rallied all its resources to advise the Minister on this other hot potato on burning campuses. "I suppose you could argue that the CHE, given its role, could have convened something on it [decolonization], convened some kind of Indaba on it, but our resources and capabilities were totally preoccupied," mused the head of the Council.

Of course, given its democratic mandate, the CHE was not going to remain on the sidelines of this intriguing challenge, and it generated an important document through a publication at its disposal called *Briefly Speaking* (Council on Higher Education 2017). The November 2017 issue of this periodical laid out the basic arguments for decolonization over twelve pages, citing liberally the most prominent advocates of the moment, from campus favourites like Ndlovu-Gatsheni to the early decolonization intellectuals, and from the post-colonial period scholars like Ngũgĩ wa Thiong'o to any number of South African academics at the English liberal universities. It was, without question, an advocacy position that did not cite a single critic of decolonization. *Briefly Speaking* laid out strident arguments calling for "systemic change to the parameters of the South African curriculum [as] a necessary precondition for achieving the goals of equity." Would this comprehensive statement on decolonization by the principal accreditation agency among regulatory authorities in fact influence the uptake of this radical curriculum idea within universities? It was a critical question to put to the organization, and we found that its pulling back from the heady and uncontested positions taken in *Briefly Speaking* was swift.

A radical engagement with curriculum was not the mandate of the chief accreditor, its leaders hastened to point out: "The role of the CHE is about processes and quality assurance of institutional processes. It would not be for the CHE to prescribe to institutions to follow a particular paradigm in curriculum." There was good reason for the accreditor not to move beyond the strong positions articulated in documents such as *Briefly Speaking* – resistance from universities that keeps the Council in its regulatory lane, so to speak:

The CHE is always under pressure from institutions regarding overreach, so we have to be careful to be true to what an assurance role is. When an accreditor moves in to decide on "content," then it is on thin ice, in the domain of academic freedom, and in danger of overreach.

It is not surprising, then, that none of the nineteen accreditation criteria speaks to issues of radical change in the curriculum, as envisioned in the press for decolonization, or even the claims represented in *Briefly Speaking*. Even with an upcoming review of those criteria, accreditor concerns about overreach, autonomy, and academic freedom loomed large. Being caught up in such contestations would "dilute the influence we have," says the CEO:

Can you imagine the consequences for the CHE if we had to get tied up in ideological battles and contestations? Questions would arise such as what intellectual resources are you drawing on? What qualifies you to make a value judgment on curriculum? So that's a barrier to the CHE being heavy-handed on these matters, being more assertive in this debate.

What is critically important in this (re)positioning of the accreditor with respect to decolonization is the understanding that the regulatory role of quality assurance is in fact at odds with any political stance on radical curriculum change. It returns us to a crucial question raised earlier in this book – that when it comes to curriculum, the logic of bureaucratic compliance as a regulatory requirement is inherently at odds with the logic of radical change as a political imperative. The accreditor's executive recognizes this dilemma with a particularly insightful reflection on the tension:

So in an assurance role, if something is controversial, you can't develop a method, an instrument, and apply it. It's a non-starter. As soon as it is controversial it is not a method or a process that can be consistently applied across the sector. You have to steer away from controversy and that is a limitation of the assurance role.

As in the case of the apex authority, SAQA, the principal accreditor understands that its limited role with respect to radical curriculum change is the airing of radical (or not so radical) ideas in the public domain, but not the steering of those ideas within the public universities. "We promote critical discourse and we have colloquia and conferences and so on where we deal with these controversial issues."

This is the critical point of our analysis: It is not simply that these regulatory agencies have no teeth with respect to curriculum implementation; it is that the very nature of their roles as government regulators proscribe interference with the curriculum of public universities.

Unless, of course, the radical impulse for curriculum change comes from powerful voices within the universities themselves. This was the case when it came to one particular curriculum moment in legal education known as *transformative constitutionalism*. This radical idea has its roots in an article written by the American legal scholar Karl Klare (1998) on "legal culture and transformative constitutionalism." A radical scholar and co-founder of a school of thought known as critical legal studies, Karl got the attention of progressive law academics in South Africa by punting an activist interpretation of the Constitution in the pursuit of egalitarian ends.

A one-time co-author with Klare on the subject of transformative constitutionalism, the well-known South African legal scholar Dennis Davis, defines the term as "pursuing significant social change through legal as opposed to other means" (Davis and Klare 2010). In this view, South Africa had a progressive Constitution, which, using the lens of transformative constitutionalism, could be leveraged to "renovate the entire legal system so that you have it pointed in the direction of reproducing more egalitarian results." What stood in the way of legally driven social change was "a very conservative legal culture in South Africa which was formalistic, unimaginative and possibly anti-intellectual."

This activist interpretation of the South African Constitution immediately came under fire from several quarters as imposing a singular interpretation among many other possibilities on the reading of the Constitution, of dissolving the important line between law and politics, and in consequence constituting a threat to academic freedom within universities (Roux 2009; Van Marle 2009; Van Staden 2019). But it did not matter; the progressive voices within the academic legal fraternity prevailed and had the audacity to demand commitment to the concept in the 2017 National Review of LLB programmes in South Africa (Council on Higher Education 2018). The opening lines of the review report state that:

The LLB Standard requires that "transformative constitutionalism" and its core philosophy are suitably understood by law faculties, appropriately embedded in curricula at all levels of the LLB programme, and internalized by law students.

This level of ideological prescription for the curriculum of any public university was unprecedented in South African history, and the demand that this thinking be "internalized by law students" would be hard to find in higher education even in the apartheid period. The CHE, based on the LLB review report, goes even further in that its recommendations task universities, in sometimes high-handed language, to

present to the CHE a detailed plan on how transformative constitutionalism is incorporated throughout the LLB curriculum and how staff members are brought to an internalization – respectively in their teaching and learning and socialization activities – of this foundational principle in modern South African jurisprudence. (52)

The critical observation here is that the accrediting authority allowed for such a particular perspective on constitutional law to be presented front and centre in its report entitled, *The State of the Provision of the Bachelor of Laws (LLB) Qualification in South Africa* (Council on Higher Education 2018). In other words, having made substantial representations to our research team about upholding academic freedom and steering clear of political controversy, the CHE nevertheless went along with a segment of the legal fraternity to advance, and indeed require, *transformative constitutionalism* as the required interpretation of the South African Constitution.

Which raises an important curriculum question: to what extent was this radical idea shared across institutions and taken up in the curricula of the seventeen law schools in the country? Would such an unusually forceful demand concerning legal content and the required "internalization" of a radical idea, *linked to accreditation*, be taken up in the curriculum of universities?

The LLB Report itself offers the first answer to the question when it names and lambasts four universities (the University of Limpopo, North West University, Walter Sisulu University and the University of Zululand) for not adequately addressing the concept, possibly due to ignorance, as expressed in this scathing comment, that they:

Do not adequately address the concept of "transformative constitutionalism." This may be the result of the inability to appreciate the difference between "transformative constitutionalism" and "constitutional imperatives." (18)

Beyond the case of the laggards, the report acknowledges that the curricula of the remaining institutions only address constitutionalism to a limited extent, some more extensively than others, and concedes that most universities probably "offer two or more modules," which "*may* cover aspects of transformative constitutionalism" (18). In the end, the requirement to teach transformation constitutionalism "expansively and systematically" was found only in three universities (the University of Pretoria, Stellenbosch University, and Wits University).

Experienced law professors, and advocates of transformative constitutionalism, are far more emphatic about the reasons for the lack of uptake of this radical idea in curriculum, as Dennis Davis explained:

Academics who share the vision of transformative constitutionalism are few and far between, and those who want to do it are in such a small minority. Some faculties have none, others have a few people and, if a student is lucky, they may get one or two courses that open their eyes in that direction. But they would be overwhelmed by the fact that the vast majority of teaching (constitutional law) remains as it was 30 years ago. I can guarantee you that.

The case of transformative constitutionalism was a "best case" scenario for institutional uptake in the curriculum. It was supported by leading scholars in the profession and it enjoyed "required" status in an official CHE report and yet the radical idea floundered when it came to institutional "take up" in the curricula of most public universities. This critical observation requires deeper analysis at the intersection of curriculum theory and institutional theory (see Chapter 8).

5.5.3 The Case of the Department of Higher Education and Training (DHET)

The Minister in charge of the DHET is also the strident and outspoken Secretary General of the South African Communist Party. The voice of

Dr Blade Nzimande is powerful within higher education and, after being dropped from this Cabinet portfolio following a standoff with the previous president (Zuma, May 2014–October 2017), he was returned to the same position by the next president (Ramaphosa, May 2019–) after a brief intervening spell as Minister of Transport.

The DHET, as established earlier, is the first gatekeeper in reviewing new qualifications and programmes against the PQM of the university concerned, and eventually the funding authority for any new initiative once it has been accredited by the CHE and registered by SAQA on the National Qualifications Framework. Given the prominence of its Minister in national political debates, how did the DHET in fact respond to the press for decolonization coming from students on campuses around the country?

It is safe to say that the Minister was preoccupied with the massive disruptions caused by the fees uprising. Student organizations were already raising hell about issues on their agenda, including fees increases, at a boisterous Second Higher Education Summit held in Durban in October 2015, from which Professor Adam Habib, Vice-Chancellor of Wits University and head of Universities South Africa (USAf), the Vice-Chancellors' Association, had to race back to his institution, where congregating students were demanding his immediate presence.

Meanwhile, the Summit drew to an end and the 2015 Durban Statement on Transformation in Higher Education included in its agreements the observations that:

- Curriculum change is the core of university transformation initiatives.
- University curricula and forms of knowledge production are not sufficiently situated within African and global South contexts, and are dominated by western worldviews.
- Research and dialogue on curriculum transformation must be supported and resources allocated to enable re-curriculation and curriculum development processes.
- Flexible curriculum pathways (and improved use of data analytics) are two important vehicles for student success.
- There should be an increasing focus on curriculum development initiatives which examine new and alternative contents and pedagogies which [are] relevant to the South African context.

What is striking is that none of the published "agreements" at this point make reference to "decolonization" as the standard-bearer of the student movement (the attack on the Rhodes statue, the symbolic moment for the decolonization protests, had already happened months before, in April 2015). In fact, the term decolonization does not appear in the Minister's Opening Speech at the Summit. Although it contains a broad statement on "Africanization" that refers to familiar "transformation" imperatives such as inequalities, the Afrikaans language, and the need for a differentiated university system, nothing in the speech references the idea of decolonization. The reason, explained a senior official from the department, is that "that speech was developed before the real call for decolonization came out with the demand for 'free, decolonized higher education.'"

What was not unexpected in this very long list of agreements emerging from the Summit was the primacy of student fees – the more pressing of the two concerns as universities headed towards the end of the 2015 academic calendar year.

It was impossible, however, for the Minister and his department not to respond to decolonization as a pressing political issue on university campuses. At least one of the regulators (SAQA) recalls a remit given by the Minister that the regulators "need to take into consideration the issues of decolonization" – as brief and bland as that. That instruction was a response to decolonization demands that came after the Durban Summit.

But did the government's Department of Higher Education and Training have such authority in the first place – to instruct the regulators on something like decolonization? Yes, indicated the recently retired CEO of SAQA, referring to the section of the NQF Act (Republic of South Africa 2008, 8[2][c]) that specifies that the Minister might provide "guidelines" and that SAQA was obliged to "publish guidelines which set out the government's strategy and priorities for the NQF, and which may be updated annually." The Department, on the other hand, saw such signalling as less of a directive from the Minister and more of a point for discussion among the regulators.

Responding to the Minister, the matter of decolonization was nevertheless placed on the Agenda of the Board of SAQA and was passed as a resolution, following which the Authority's research unit generated a paper on the subject and hosted a stakeholder conference that led to a position statement. In line with the remit of the Minister to the regulators, SAQA instantly put the relevant clauses into its NQF Implementation Framework 2015–2020 document :

Develop and report ... on processes to address decolonization and transformation of qualifications, inclusion of curricula in qualifications [and] how qualification standards can underpin the development and delivery of decolonized and transformed qualifications and curricula. (SAQA 2015, 4)

As already discussed, beyond such formal acknowledgement in policy as a response to a ministerial remit, nothing happened, for it was up to the universities to decide whether and how to take up decolonization, if at all. In other words, what SAQA had accomplished was the necessary policy signalling in response to the Minister's injunction, but its inclusion in institutional implementation plans found little purchase in the day-to-day curriculum practices of South Africa's twenty-six public universities.

More striking was the fact that the Department of Higher Education and Training (DHET), despite the high political profile of its radical minister, consciously took a soft and cautious stand on decolonization. Besides raising the matter as a point of discussion with regulators, the only other official action in relation to decolonization was to encourage universities to submit curriculum change proposals for funding under the Department's University Capacity Development Programme (UCDP). What explains this caution on the part of the department? "Autonomy," offered a senior official in DHET:

We did not put out a policy statement or try to regulate anything. That's not our job, it's the institutions' job to think about knowledge, knowledge production and curriculum.

Like a political hot potato, the department as the funding body had passed responsibility for dealing with decolonization back to the institutions, just as the Council on Higher Education stood back from the fray for fear of impinging on institutional autonomy. That leaves one more set of regulatory authorities. Could the professional bodies that regulate the standards and accredit the programmes for the various professions be expected to weigh in on the pressing matter of decolonization?

5.5.4 The Case of the Professional Bodies

All three professional bodies engaged for this study (ECSA, HPSCA, and SAICA) were established as accrediting authorities in the apartheid era and had built up for themselves formidable reputations for maintaining rigorous standards for their respective professions. While ECSA and the HPSCA remain direct accrediting authorities to this day, SAICA is accredited by the International Regulatory Board of Auditors (IRBA) to maintain this function. While the other regulators (SAQA, CHE, and DHET) were post-apartheid regulatory creatures, with a more activist disposition towards curriculum change and the knowledge project, the professional bodies were more conservative in the sense of protecting their authority over the established standards of their professions.

It was not surprising, therefore, that when decolonization came to the university campuses, the professional bodies largely ignored the fuss. There was not even much curiosity about what decolonization could mean for the curriculum of the professions. This became clear from the responses of each of the professional bodies when pressed during this study for their stance on the decolonization question:

Our international standards are what really drive us and what gives us our international recognition. So, you can't necessarily go and change the standards. (Chartered Accounting)

As long as we are confident that the graduates from that curriculum will be able to address the health needs of the country. So, I think in that sense the concept of decolonization has never figured very strongly in how we evaluate or accredit curricula. (Health Sciences)

When the protests arrivedECSA's response was "What are the different institutions doing to ensure that the graduates who feed out of the system meet the graduate attributes associated with the qualification?" We wrote to the Deans of Engineering to ask for their mitigating strategies with the time lost due to protests. (Engineering)

In other words, the primary response of the professional bodies to decolonization was reflected in a concern about the effects of the campus disruptions on the professional standards or graduate attributes that determine whether the graduating student measures up to the expectations of the profession. While there might have been some engagement with universities on the meanings of decolonization, the subject did not make it onto the board agendas of any of the three professional bodies. Perhaps, reflected one of the leaders interviewed, "we need to look into how decolonized our standards are leading to our graduate attributes." Nothing more than that.

What explains the positioning of the professional bodies when it comes to any push for the radicalization of curricula as expressed in the drive for decolonization? First, these are conservative bodies constituted by and for the established professions long before the democratic era. Second, the standards of these professions are in turn defined and determined by employers of graduates, whose primary concern is not the production of revolutionaries but students who can meet the high-level demands of the professional workplace.

In other words, can the graduate coming out of the institutions practice as a professional engineer or medical doctor or chartered accountant? Do they measure up to the standards? That's all. And third, the national standards themselves are benchmarked against international standards, to which each of the professions compares itself.

The professional bodies are keenly aware of their international obligations. They desire that a South African graduate be recognized internationally and be able to practise as a professional in any country in the world. There are accords and agreements to this effect. Ironically (or perhaps not), in the context of decolonization, the international standards that moderate the national behaviour of the professions are often set by regulators in the former colonial authorities themselves.

ECSA is clear that "our signature agreements with the Washington Accord, the Sydney Accord, and the Berlin Accord are cast in stone. We must meet those requirements." As a member of the International Engineering Alliance, the authority aligns the South African standards with their outcomes-based qualifications, which in turn reflect in the graduate attributes that a professional engineer must meet. In 2010, the London-based journal *Lancet* established a commission to examine health professions education. This commission was scathing in its criticisms of medical care; these findings heavily influenced the ways in which doctors are trained in South Africa. The self-assessment questionnaire sent to South African medical schools ahead of an accreditation visit reflects those standards as well. In the same way, the competency framework developed for chartered accountants was heavily influenced by Scottish and Australian authorities on the subject.

Even with this sense of their international obligations in defining a South African standard, all three professional bodies were eager to point out that they do not prescribe curricula for universities and that they take the autonomy of institutions seriously. But is this true? We decided to do a deep dive into the operations of the three regulatory authorities to test the claim that they merely set professional standards without prescribing curricula for the universities.

On closer examination, the professional councils play a powerful role in determining what goes into the curricula for the respective professions. When pressed, for example, ECSA conceded that it "prescribes knowledge content areas as they are presented in the standards." In other words, this authority, in fact, stipulates the minimum amount of basic sciences, engineering science, and design content that should appear in the university curriculum. Without meeting that requirement, there is no accreditation. Without satisfying the education demands for the qualification, a student cannot register, and therefore practise as a professional engineer. Withholding such approval, as a regulator can do, has serious consequences for any institution offering engineering and, of course, its graduates.

In no instance is the claim to autonomy and the non-prescription of curriculum more emphatically made than in the medical sciences. Once again, the senior authorities in the HPSCA started with the claim that "we are very careful not to be prescriptive, so we will not prescribe what a curriculum in the country should look like." But is this the case? Not really, as this interview exchange revealed:

Researcher: If a medical school decides it is going to abandon the basic medical sciences (a curriculum requisite), would you have something to say about that?

Regulator representative: Oh yes, absolutely. *Not completely autonomous* (emphasis added). The regulations give very clear guidance as to what should be the core in the medical curriculum.

In other words, the curriculum content is prescribed and "the autonomy lies in what they want to add to that curriculum and how they want to offer that curriculum etc." Then there was this conclusion:

Researcher: So an institution that says, '"We don't agree
                               with this core" – I take it they would not get
                               their doctors accredited by the Council?
Regulator's representative: No, they would not.

No university can afford not to have its medical school qualifications
enjoy accreditation or their graduates proceed to their hospital intern-
ships and eventually into practice. The stakes are high, and institutions
are in a bind. In cases of non-compliance, the regulators, in this case
the HPSCA, have a very powerful instrument at their disposal:
conditional accreditation. What this means is that institutions have a
limited period of time in which to comply or risk losing accreditation.
Worse, the conditional accreditation status is made public, sending the
media into a frenzy and paying parents into a panic about what this
means for their children and their investment. One institution tried to
be devious:

Regulator representative: The curriculum they got accredited for by the
                             HPSCA differed from the curriculum they sub-
                             mitted to the CHE for accreditation, and they
                             implemented a curriculum that was not at all
                             the same as the one we accredited.
Researcher: Now why would they do that?
Regulator representative: That's a very long story. *They are now on the
                             right track* (emphasis added).

What this analysis so far reveals is not only that regulatory agencies
play a direct role in curriculum determination but that they exercise
powerful levers – such as the instrument of conditional accreditation –
to ensure compliance with an external standard. And the authorities do
this in a way that leaves universities suspended between public embar-
rassment and official compliance, as an experienced professor of dentistry explained:

When we as a university indicated to them that we did not feel that
expanding the scope of the oral hygienist should proceed, they politely told
us to do as they ask or they would not recognize the degree, and therefore
our graduates would not be able to go into practice.

As far as this academic is concerned, "They determine the nature,
content, and depth of the curriculum. They want equivalence across
institutions." But how is this authority established and maintained

within a professional body, given the expertise and experience of senior professors who could make such curricular judgements on their own? Here a complex web of institutional power was uncovered.

The Deans oversee the training of health care professionals, and yet "the very same deans sit on the responsible boards of the HPSCA that give the accreditation." Within this closed network of deans, "an Old Boys club" is established, whose networks determine what happens in the curriculum. In countries like the United States, an independent state board examination gives you the license to practise as a professional. In South Africa, it is a closed circuit of authorities who serve as players and referees when it comes to the curriculum demands for accreditation. At first glance, investing trust in the professional accreditation of degrees in academic authorities sounds like a good thing. But what if the same group of people who define the curriculum also decide on its accreditation?

Given the pressure on universities to comply with external curriculum standards, institutions learn to fall in line with regulatory expectations. What this analysis further revealed was a subtle but consequential process of *self-moderation* on the part of universities. The mediating authority between the academic department and the external regulators is the institutional planning office that readies the Senate-approved curriculum for submission to the DHET. This is where judgements are rendered about the chances of success of a programme or qualification proposal, and where adjustments are made to increase the chances of accreditation success. This is how one dean recalled the process of self-moderation within his own institution:

We were told "this is important for the DHET" and on that basis they decide what goes forward to be accredited by the CHE; if they do not find that a curriculum is appropriate or commensurate with their thinking, it would not be approved.

The institutional planning office therefore acts not only to slow down a new curriculum proposal but to frustrate the efforts of academic deans in proposing changes to the curriculum. As one senior academic recounted,

Part of this inertia with respect to curriculum engagement has to do with people's positions [in administration] so that when we ask for a curriculum that meets market needs we get told that it is a PQM issue and will take 2–3 years to change and we must not waste time with that.

This powerful mediating role of the institutional planning office determines what goes forward so that "the practical, administrative requirements are raised as barriers to curriculum renewal and curriculum change." But what happens if a radical proposal does slip through the institutional moderation process and ends up inside the churn of mainstream regulatory review?

5.6 The Little Foxes and the Vines

The analysis so far has shown that while regulatory authorities begin by denying a prescriptive role in the curriculum of universities, they do in fact play a direct and influential role in shaping curriculum content. Digging deeper, this study also found that there are in fact small and invisible ways in which the curricula of higher education institutions are further affected by regulatory arrangements; we use here the biblical metaphor of "the small foxes that spoil the vines."

One of these small foxes operating in the curriculum vines is an invisible instrument of regulation called CESM, or the *Classification of Educational Subject Matter*. CESM functions to name and demarcate disciplines for classification and funding purposes. A new curriculum must fit into predetermined fields of study that set out the right teaching and research areas for funding purposes. In at least one study, it was argued that the CESM grid "rigidly controls the naming, and therefore indirectly the content, of (new) programme curricula at South African universities" (Zawada 2020, 8). By endorsing disciplinary structures that have existed over many years and by tying funding to curriculum "fit" with established categories, "the regulatory curriculum requirements are invisible statues of colonization," according to this study (Zawada 2020).

More convincing an argument for the operation of the little foxes in the curriculum vines is the powerful role of the instrument of peer review. All of the regulatory agencies depend on disciplinary peers to establish whether curriculum X at institution Y meets the standards of compliance for a particular qualification. These peer review panels might offer the illusion of *independence* in making accreditation decisions, but they also open up the possibility of *interference* in the curriculum decisions of an institution – something observed earlier in the discussion of the dentistry profession, where board accreditation members were also panel evaluation members.

In the case of law, it was observed how the panel members promoted a particularly radical view of constitutional law (transformative constitutionalism), even if the concept did not enjoy significant take-up across institutions. But that influence can go the other way as well, as a senior official in one of the accreditation authorities pointed out:

> It would not be for the CHE to prescribe to institutions to follow a particular paradigm. What is interesting though is the role of those peer evaluators. Because if you submit, say for example, a radical new program that is decolonial but it gets sent to a peer evaluator who has a traditional view about what knowledge is, they might give a negative evaluation to that radical or newly transformed programme. (Zawada 2020, 7)

While the accreditors seek to prepare their panel experts for adherence to a common set of accreditation standards, they are less likely to influence the ideological orientations of the various panellists or disciplines represented among the evaluators – as demonstrated in the case of the LLB review.

And a third "invisible" instrument by which regulators moderate radical curriculum change is through *enframing*, by which we mean the setting up of bordered conditions within which legitimate knowledge is included and through which non-conforming knowledge is excluded. For example, the CHE as accreditor defines nineteen criteria that frame the evaluation of every new curriculum. The professional bodies have ten or more "competency frameworks" or "graduate attributes" that prescribe what counts as acceptable knowledge. What this means is that institutions are forced to prepare and submit their curricula *within that frame* in order to stand any chance of approval. By setting the outer bounds for approval, the frame automatically excludes ways of framing knowledge that falls outside of them.

When pressed with the question "Do any of your criteria speak to the issues of decolonization?" all the regulatory agencies were hard pressed to find such accommodation within the standards or criteria that frame the accreditation exercises. Those framing elements (standards, criteria) are, on the one hand, broad enough to accommodate any curriculum ideas through references such as "responsiveness to societal needs" and yet narrow enough to define those needs as what a trained doctor, engineer, or chartered accountant needs to know (competency) and how to behave appropriately (code of conduct).

Enframing, in short, standardizes attainments and regulates behaviours in ways that are antithetical to the disruptive ideas that come with radical curriculum change. As Shirley Walters (2018, 4) argues in defense of "decolonizing education," radical curriculum ideas cannot be contained within compliancy frames, for their qualities are "informality, playfulness, turbulence, disruption, unpredictability, and relationality"; that is, qualities at odds with regulation.

5.7 Conclusion

This systematic account on how regulatory agencies contain and constrain radical curriculum ideas remains underexplored in the curriculum change literature. The study also brings to light new conceptual insights about the institutionalization of knowledge that is worth recapping in this concluding section.

What if one examined convolution and complexity not as an unfortunate characteristic of education bureaucracies but as something that exists by design? This means that the byzantine structures of regulation function to frustrate radical curriculum change despite the ready recognition of officials within these agencies that the problem must be *fixed*.

With a skilful use of metaphor, Sara Ahmed (2017) writes of obstruction as intentional, for "This is how power works: you don't have to stop people from doing something, just make it harder for them to do something. Deviation is hard. Deviation is made hard." The convoluted accreditation authorities, as we have shown, are not simply unnecessarily complex structures frustrating universities; they are circuits along which power is distributed among state regulatory agencies, across government departments, and in contested relationships with professional bodies.

And yet, surprisingly, in this jungle of regulatory bodies, all of these authorities work towards the single purpose of keeping a check on radical deviation from a professional standard or an accreditation norm. Deviation is, indeed, made hard.

This is not, however, about individual behaviour, for there is more than enough evidence that among the more progressive regulators (SAQA and the CHE) there are emancipatory impulses that drive the work of these agencies and their leaders, such as in the commitment to lifelong learning for the marginalized or the pursuit of transformative constitutionalism in legal education. It is, rather, about the "collective intentionality" of institutions, where "individuals are involved in collective settings qua roles and positions and not as persons" (Abdelnour, Hasselbladh, and Kallinikos 2017, 1784).

As we discovered, however, the logics of regulatory compliance conflict inherently with the logics of radical change. This means that there is something within the very act of regulation that is intolerant of disruption, deviation, and dissent. Regulation is about imposing order on messiness, not inspiring radical deviation from administrative standards. By institutionalizing regulatory norms and standards, the regulatory agencies seek to reproduce institutional behaviours by "stabilizing the requirements" for continued operation and, "once those requirements have been stabilized, they do not have to be made explicit" (Ahmed 2017, 10). Put differently, the regulatory norms and standards assume the status of common sense, and institutions, remarkably, fall in line.

This study further makes visible the instruments of regulatory compliance by which institutions are pulled into, and kept in, line. Those instruments include the power of (conditional) accreditation, disciplinary classification, peer review, (international) standards referencing, and enframing. As we have seen, some of these instruments of compliance are imposed on institutions as a matter of threat – you could lose your accreditation, or not get it in the first place, and your students might not graduate or practice – but also a matter of self-moderation. Over time, *institutions learn compliance*, or how to behave compliantly, in order to win the awards of recognition and accreditation of curricula. In this regard, the institutional plumbers, to borrow again from Ahmed (2017), are the university technicians in the administration that press gang a radical curriculum into compliance and conformity with regulatory standards.

The fact that institutions might formally comply with the regulatory standards for programme approval does not mean that *curriculum practice* will necessarily conform to what has been signed off by the accreditation authority. The demand for transformative constitutionalism in the LLB is the most obvious example. One of the reasons for this discrepancy between "what is required" of curriculum and "what actually happens" is the place of autonomy as a resident value in the post-apartheid university. As we have seen, autonomy is both acknowledged and trampled on in the formal accreditation process. There would, in some circumstances, be outright resistance, however, if the insistence on compliance was enforced in curriculum practice beyond what is formally required for accreditation purposes.

This raises the question, of course, of how autonomous institutions deal with radical change in instances where the proposed curriculum might have complied with the conditions for recognition or even accreditation.

6 The Uptake of Decolonization
The Case of the Humanities and Social Sciences

6.1 Introduction

While the uptake of decolonization in the institutional curriculum was observed to be uneven, superficial, and, across most disciplines, non-existent, it is the case that in all ten universities there were specific instances in which academics took seriously the charge of decolonization in *doing* curriculum change. Who were these academic teachers? How did they understand the decolonization imperative? What did they actually do to change the curricula of their specific fields or disciplines? What are the characteristics of these "institutional hotspots," as these curricular spaces will be called? How do these progressive academics manage the contradictions of assessments and examinations against the emancipatory claims of a decolonized curriculum? And what do such radical initiatives imply for curriculum change in universities? These are some of the questions pursued in this chapter.

We start with a sample of five enclave curricula from different institutions and five different disciplines – politics, psychology, philosophy, media studies, and the visual arts. All of the enclave curricula come from within historically white universities, since those institutions were the primary targets of the decolonization activists.

In each case, we place the curriculum change project of the five academics in the context of their personal biographies. That is, we ask what we can learn about their commitments to a decolonized curriculum from insights into their intellectual formation as academic teachers.

6.2 Decolonizing the Politics Curriculum at Rhodes University

Sally Matthews teaches politics at Rhodes University. When the demands for decolonization first came, she was already alert to its tensions and possibilities. She had an advantage over many other academics: As a scholar in African Studies and, in particular, African politics, contestations around the Western dominance of literatures in the teaching of African Studies had long engaged her field. She invokes the concept of "the colonial library" to refer to texts and representations of Africa that see the continent as not only different from the West in absolute terms but also uncivilized, undeveloped, simple, and backward. This was not only a negative political construction of Africa but a knowledge problem, or what she calls "the epistemological component of the damage done by colonialism" (Matthews 2018, 49).

Here's the problem, as Matthews acknowledges: As much as the critics of the colonial library might want to move away from these stultified constructions of Africa, they are entrapped within their very language. There is no neat split between colonial knowledge and decolonial knowledge. The African Renaissance idea once touted by President Thabo Mbeki draws on a word whose original meanings emerged from continental Europe. To speak about pre-African civilizations is to take for granted the European construction of what it means to be "civilized" in the first place. To cast the problem as colonialism and the colonial other is to commit binary thinking, "the categories and dichotomies presented to us by Eurocentric thinking" (51). The colonial library, in other words, reaches into the present and inevitably constrains the thinking of its most ardent critics.

How does the decolonial critic step out of this bind? Matthews does not hesitate to take on the racial essentialisms that underpinned the curriculum demands and proposed alternatives that emerged in the student protest movement: An African university with "our" own knowledge; rejection of European knowledge; the notion that there are basic differences between Westerners and Africans; and the idea that only Africans can study Africa. Is this not a case of epistemological ethnocentrism?

There is another possibility, argues Matthews, one that recognizes the dominance and dangers of European-centred knowledge while at the same time avoiding the pitfalls of ethnocentrism. All knowledge is political and therefore never neutral. Knowledge is socially constructed, so universal claims to the truth must be approached with the necessary vigilance. A different possibility is to use the very concepts and methods of the colonial library against itself; that is, critically engaging received knowledge and acting on it. There is a good reason for such action, and that is the interdependence of knowledge of the world, which requires recognition of Western knowledge in the course of exposing its violations.

What does all this conceptual and political discussion have to do with the exigencies of curriculum change under decolonization? This is where Matthews gets practical about "an actual course" (58–59). What, in other words, would a decolonized curriculum actually look like in the study of politics?

Matthews describes five steps she has taken in the course of decolonizing her politics curriculum:

1. Broadening the curriculum to include scholarship from other parts of the world, i.e., beyond the West. This, for her, means "being vigilant" against what comes easily to many academics – using principally established scholars and their texts from the western world – and being conscious about author origins and identities, including race, gender, geographies, "and other social characteristics" (59). Matthews is clear that simply choosing indigenous texts or those by Black authors, for example, does not mean that their work is by definition "decolonized."

2. Presenting knowledge as contested, rather than as a given or true, which, she argues, is what many students coming into universities often think. Knowledge is by definition political, and therefore it needs to be critically engaged rather than having its truth claims accepted at first sight. There is therefore nothing that dictates that Western texts or scholars should enjoy unquestioned pre-eminence within the curricula of South African universities. In her words,

   we need to unsettle students' certainties about the very possibility of identifying completely objective, wholly accurate, final accounts of the world (60).

3. Introducing different perspectives on a particular subject or topic. This includes studying traditional texts alongside critical texts in comparative politics. In this way, students come to appreciate a critical study of comparative texts and their subjects. Literature on Africa as a collection of failed states, for example, is thereby countered in student readings by literature that questions the failed-state narrative. In the process, students learn that the production of knowledge is by its very nature contested, rather than settled.

4. Including biographies and photos of the authors being read in course readers and class audio-visuals. That is unusual, Matthews concedes, but she argues that such information makes the point that knowledge and its production has an identity and that it is generated under particular conditions that are not the same for everyone. Such a curricular strategy, moreover, highlights the link between knowledge and experience.

The strength of Matthews' approach to the decolonized curriculum is its simplicity and elegance, on the one hand, and its humility and caution on the other. She is aware of the pitfalls of "an excluding essentialism," in which race or other forms of marginalization can claim exclusive insights into the knowledge of subjugated peoples. She recognizes that getting students to read and study within these curriculum frames can be intellectually challenging – such as reading texts for and against a position. And she makes the point that the curriculum is not enough – that how you teach (pedagogy) matters almost as much as what you teach in this critical mode. In the end, she argues,

Decolonising the political studies curriculum is not just about studying Africa differently within political studies, but rather about completely reorientating political studies as a whole (62).

6.3 Decolonizing Philosophy at the University of Pretoria

Leonhard Praeg teaches philosophy at the University of Pretoria. Praeg must be one of the first department heads in South Africa to directly try to secure a decolonized curriculum in all the undergraduate, as well as postgraduate, curricula of his department. Most heads of departments (or deans, for that matter), even those with an activist flair, would provide general directions on curriculum but never dare to become involved in, and offer direct comment on, the decolonial content or preferred direction of every course and module in their space. That hands-off attitude reflects, in large part, a respect for the individual autonomy of the academic teacher in a university (as opposed to a school), and more broadly the ethos of higher education – a professor decides what to teach based on their personal intellectual interests and in line with what their own training allows.

That is not the case in the philosophy department at the University of Pretoria (UP). Praeg explained that it was his mandate to decolonize the philosophy curriculum at the university. From the moment of his appointment, that was the charge from his dean, himself a prominent national advocate for the decolonization of the humanities and social sciences. Praeg took this mandate seriously, and the academic staff in philosophy understood that it was his brief. "That made it easier," Praeg explained, when pressed about the reactions of members of his department to this leadership-driven curriculum change project.

Praeg describes his commitment as "the project of a decoloniality engaged curriculum" (Praeg 2016), and in his prepared remarks for a June 2016 lekgotla of the department, called "Just Teaching," he provided a dense and detailed philosophical rationale for his colleagues to read ahead of time:

> I will not talk much by way of introducing this discussion. That was the whole point of writing it out in all its complexity. I want to request that you carefully study this proposal and come to the conversation with notes, corrections, alternative suggestions, and so on. (38)

It is important to note this brief, because Praeg is doing something unusual here –leading the radical curriculum change project from the front and more prescriptively than most academic heads, albeit with the invitation to bring to the deliberations "notes, corrections, [and] alternative suggestions." What exactly was this directed curriculum change all about, and what were its prospects for success?

Praeg wanted his colleagues to start with a review of the under-graduate courses in his department in 2016 before proceeding to postgraduate education in 2018. His focus question was sharp: *What do we teach?* He recognizes that this question is closely tied to *How do we teach?* but initially his attention is on the content of teaching. In a lengthy conceptual elaboration of his ideas, Praeg starts by questioning what a department is before delving into the curriculum. Are they individuals who happen to come to work in the same space or "a community, of sorts?" (2). This is important, because it goes to the heart of what he is trying to achieve – a communal approach to curriculum change where individuals find themselves working together as the basis for re-generating knowledge in the department (5).

Praeg then invokes a fairly conventional view of curriculum – "intended experiences" – to question whose experiences form the basis of the knowledge that a department teaches and produces. Here, he invokes – through the title of his lekgotla presentation – the dual meanings of "just teaching": that is, simply doing teaching (like everybody else), as opposed to teaching for justice, though always with the focus on knowledge – hence his constant reference to epistemic justice.

To illustrate his position, Praeg launches into a complex discussion of Ubuntu and decoloniality and their different meanings. Praeg calls on his colleagues to "rethink our undergraduate curriculum through the lens of the many variants of the cosmopolitan conceptual persona," by which he means a comparative, inclusive approach to the question of *what it means to think Africa and to be Africa(n)*. This does not mean that Africanizing knowledge can cut it off from its western origins; as Praeg puts it, "the desire to Africanize knowledge without leaving any political DNA at the crime scene was doomed from the start" (19).

Praeg makes an interesting and certainly challengeable case for a shift in South African society from Africanization to Transformation to Decoloniality. He dismisses the idea that decolonization was, to put it colloquially, a *gatvol* response to the neutering of transformation within post-apartheid politics. Decoloniality, he argues, seeks to link the local struggle for social justice to global struggles, thus "hook[ing] up with the same struggle all over the world" (23). After taking his colleagues on a long and complex detour into the philosophical underpinnings of his own thoughts on the knowledge we teach and the knowledge we produce, there remains "the practical concern of curriculum review" (23). Like Matthews in political science, Praeg has his own practical steps for how to decolonize the curriculum, using the lens of epistemic justice:

1. Identifying the processes of producing and disseminating knowledge that have allowed western knowledge to dominate and remain at the centre of the curriculum. This means making explicit the ways in which the history of a discipline contributed to colonialism. "This politicizing of western content," says Praeg, "has to find its way into teaching at both under- and postgraduate levels" (24).
2. Identifying the marginalized traditions that had to make way for dominant, western-centric content over time. In other words, western knowledge could not dominate without pushing aside non-western knowledge, and that *process* needs to be made explicit.
3. Establishing decolonized knowledge rather than simply critiquing it, as given in the two previous points. This means actively teaching previously marginal knowledges and traditions for their own value in the curriculum.

4. Demonstrating how formerly marginalized knowledges or traditions are better placed to yield understanding of the postcolonial condition. This entails showing that "non-western epistemic constructs are more suited to interpret non-western constructs" (24).

In sum, for Praeg,

The above four steps constitute the four major moments in the decolonisation of knowledge and there is absolutely no reason why the fundamental or core insights they represent cannot be incorporated into both under- and post-graduate curricula in any discipline.

It should be mentioned that a key commitment in Praeg's conception of curriculum practice is its insistence on non-essentialism, for "a curriculum that narrowly focuses on (pan)Africanity will be unjust" (24), and it is not sufficient to signal African content as different "without doing the hard work of connecting the dots between recognition and emancipation" (4).

Another vital part of Praeg's understanding of curriculum change is the insight that the decolonization of knowledge is pursued within an institutional context. This means that undoing the apartheid, colonial curriculum must take cognizance of "the institutional arrangements created for the production of knowledge" (Praeg 2017, 1). What Praeg does not do, unfortunately, is explain how exactly a radical curriculum approach will wrestle with, and come away from, an encounter with "institutional arrangements."

That he recognizes the problem is an important step forward – "Universities are troubled spaces because they are . . . the places where the past epistemic injustices are institutionalized" – but it is a completely different challenge squaring up to a centenarian, such as the University of Pretoria, which has successfully brushed off institutional threats to curriculum stability over the decades (Jansen 2009). The answer may lie in what Praeg actually does, and concedes, in dealing with the practicalities of change in the undergraduate curriculum.

Praeg tells his colleagues that he has examined all of their course outlines, and he suggests ways in which they could be brought "in line" with the conceptions of knowledge and curriculum that *Just Teaching* outlines. This was an exceptionally courageous move by an academic head, and one rarely taken in higher education anywhere. What is the intellectual basis for this steering of the department's curriculum in philosophy? For Praeg, such steering is not "to obliterate pluralism"

(Praeg 2016, 26) in the work of academics, but to promote curriculum coherence – "to bring this pluralism in line with the requirement of a coherent curriculum" (26). He continues:

Where I have suggested modifications to a course I have in some cases also included a reading that could be pivotal to enhancing the engagement with decoloniality (26).

The academic head goes on to make specific suggestions on each course in the philosophy curriculum, from the starting point of the results of a UP study titled "Curriculum Transformation in the Humanities: Student Voices Survey," whose findings, he claims, are largely in line with some of the arguments contained in *Just Teaching*. One of the survey prompts was: "Indicate which of your current modules you think should be transformed and describe how they should be transformed." The student responses included the teaching of African philosophy, more culturally diverse philosophies, Eastern philosophies, and the differences among all of them. The survey data having been shared, Praeg then outlines "basic principles of a coherent curriculum" (27), which essentially involves "making visible" the political foundations of western philosophy and those of the black experience of colonialism, racism, etc. This, for Praeg, is "the first principle I look for in a good philosophy curriculum" (27). The second principle is coherence, and this means a clear conceptual line should thread together ideas in the first year of studying philosophy and across all four years, extending into the honours qualification.

Praeg then critiques each of the courses, for example:

Phil 100: *What does it mean to know?*

- I would like to see the concluding cycle on epistemic justice.
- Why the apolitical question *what is philosophy?*
- I would like students to acquire a very basic introductory familiarity with the many philosophical traditions.
- I do not know how the question of epistemic justice is dealt with in the existing course.

Phil 120: *What does it mean to be?*

- I had extensive conversations with X (lecturer) about how to rethink this course in relation to . . . engaged decoloniality.
- The course will start with African ontology in the third term.

Phil 210 and 220

- There is a real sense in which these two courses deal with the crux of colonialism and decoloniality.
- My first suggestion is that we change the title of Phil 210 and 220 from "History of Philosophy I and II" to "Contesting Modernities I and II."

The point is made – that the leadership engagement with curriculum change is firm and directive and concerned with the political dimensions of philosophy that should thread through all courses. But what if – and here is the institutional question – the academic teachers do not share these particular interpretations or approaches to the teaching philosophy, or they simply do not have the capacity to deliver on these mandates? At this point, Praeg makes a number of administrative concessions that speak to these very practical dilemmas, for example:

The lecturer we appoint to replace X may not be ready to do so in 2018, but will be expected to prepare and present [the courses] in 2019.

I see the appointment we make to fill Y's position to teach the course. We may not get someone who can immediately do this.

In concluding his conceptual review of a "decoloniality engaged curriculum" applied to an analysis of the undergraduate philosophy curriculum, Praeg returns to his two major themes: first, that "just as a department is not a random collection of individuals, so a curriculum is not a random collection of modules" (35); and second, that what holds the curriculum together is a sense of coherence that does not undermine the pluralism of intellectual and methodological interests represented by the academics who teach philosophy.

The question is, does Praeg succeed in this leadership-driven dictation of the content of curriculum, justified by an appeal to coherence? Does pluralism not imply the accommodation of contrarian views of knowledge, politics, and philosophy that not only might include perspectives that are critical of decoloniality but also allow for paradigmatic positions that have nothing to do with it at all? Is coherence therefore not a fig leaf for imposing ideological compliance in the philosophy curriculum? In short, is the academic head not forcing his particular politics of knowledge on departmental colleagues? And, for the purposes of this study, is such authoritative steering of a "decoloniality engaged curriculum" actually reflected and sustained in curriculum practice? We will return to such questions in our conclusion.

6.4 Decolonizing Social Psychology at Rhodes University

Liezille Jacobs brings to her teaching a very strong sense of social justice that was forged through her experiences as a working-class child growing up under apartheid. Her father was a "Coloured" construction worker in and out of jobs who sought and eventually, in 1993, found work at the University of the Western Cape (UWC) to enable Liezille, the first in the family to go beyond school, to study with the financial relief offered to staff. As a high school student on an activist campus, she eagerly learned about apartheid and the struggle during those turbulent years.

When Liezille enrolled as a university student at UWC, her political education continued, for "our lecturers always brought it back to the struggle." She is clear that "I would not have the mindset" of a critical scholar were it not for those formative experiences. Liezille, in other words, teaches a decolonized curriculum from within the resources of her own biography.

Her approach to social psychology is marked by a critical, engaging, and – for some students – a rather provocative approach to social identity theory. "If I can get the students to understand who they are and how they behave in a social context, then I am happy," said Liezille. This process of identity formation is both political and practical for the social psychology lecturer, so she has students read Trevor Noah's (2019) *Born a Crime*. "He looks Coloured but does not identify as Coloured." This, for South Africans, is an interesting and puzzling take on identify formation, and Liezille pushes the envelope in confronting comfortable assumptions about race, ethnicity, and identity.

Liezille's classes are packed, often with students who are not registered for social psychology, and there are sometimes complaints from those who feel uncomfortable with these radical ideas. "People started coming to my class to audit it, because they found that my methods were disturbing students." It does not help that she looks like a young student herself, or that she is a Black woman – the only one with a PhD in the psychology department at Rhodes University.

I literally have a slide where I list all my qualifications, all the different places where I've been in order to get the people to relax. And only then will you see the smiles on their faces.

In the YouTube video *Trevor McDonald: Return to South Africa: White Poverty After Apartheid*, students learn that some white people say that things were better under apartheid. Some Black students in the class claim that their parents also say that things were better in the past, because food was cheaper. This is the kind of subject matter that would bring heat into any South African undergraduate classroom – and it is what gets students active in the class and on the Instagram account where Liezille continues the discussions.

After Liezille nurtured the social psychology undergraduate class, it was handed over to another lecturer. Liezille now teaches critical health psychology, which raises the question: how does she identify herself? "I am a social scientist and a research psychologist, but cannot use the latter designation because I have to be registered as such." Liezille's academic journey has taken her through research fellowships in the study of "substance abuse disorder"; monitoring and evaluation studies in the non-profit sector; and appointments in science councils, such as the Medical Research Council and the Human Sciences Research Council. She is broadly trained and approaches all her work with a critical social science lens.

Still, it is social psychology that is Liezille's first love, and her course outline for Psychology 102 gives a clear sense of the intellectual interests that underpin the radical curriculum she designed, including topics such as:

- Poverty and ethnicity
- Different types of love relationships
- Psychological experiences of poverty
- Social construction of gender
- Gender-based violence
- Feminism and masculinity
- Violence prevention
- Social psychological frameworks on peace processes

It is, however, in her pedagogy that Liezille brings the curriculum alive, thereby offering critical insights into how to do radical curriculum change – content means little in decolonized teaching unless the concepts are practically applied and critically engaged. This is reflected in Liezille's outline of module objectives in the social psychology course:

- To have in-depth lively class discussions on the understanding, integration, and creativity of major themes and methods in social psychology
- To be able to identify new examples of social psychological concepts and theories in real life situations
- To recognize the application of concepts and theories of social psychology to one's experiences and to social problems and issues
- To demonstrate an oral/written understanding of the major on-campus, South African, and international social psychological debates and concerns

What stands out in Liezille's curriculum work is the determination to locate theories, concepts, and methods in social psychological debates within the South African and African context. She recalls her own graduate training, which was dominated by international textbooks: "What upset me during that time was that we were using American textbooks" for teaching South African content. It is something, she claims, that her colleagues at Rhodes still use in much of their teaching today – the abstract teaching of mainstream social psychology using standard topics in other contexts, such as consumer behaviour.

That is why two of her guiding "texts" are those of Trevor Noah and the visit of the British journalist Trevor Macdonald to informal settlements in South Africa. Her prescribed readings are by South African authors, including two prominent Black psychologists, Normal Duncan and Cheryl de la Rey (Swartz et al. 2016). In the same way, Liezille's course outline for "Critical Health Psychology" emphasizes South African texts but also African scholarship more broadly, such as health psychology in Ghana. At the same time, her delivery platforms for teaching include, according to the course outline, blended teaching methods, on-campus debates, and social and other media platforms.

Why does Liezille not call this radical work *decolonization*? "I see it as part of decolonization," she insisted in one interview, but in another she conceded the formative influence of her own political socialization:

I don't actually use that label (decolonization). I use transformation. And it's really not difficult for me because I started in 1995. I was like that hopeful generation, the first free generation entering university. I was just following that example in the way I set up my curriculum.

Teaching to disrupt comes at a personal cost to a young Black woman, and the interviews provided an opportunity for sharing her burden: "I want to talk. It's such a painful thing for me." A few white students threatened to stone her on an Instagram post she was warned about by some Black students. The matter was reported, and the university did not act on the matter, she says. The implicated students have since graduated. For Liezille, there is a heavy toll for doing radical curriculum work, such as raising the controversial issue of gender-neutral toilets under "the psychology and gender" theme in her course outline.

This is the kind of topic that could land a lecturer on the Rhodes Confessions Page, a one-time trend among university students on several campuses to raise personal and sometimes hateful comments in a public forum. For students, Liezille said, the allure of decolonization as an interpretive tool for radical work was not necessarily something to which they were attracted. However, they handled its demands: "There's resilience from the students with decolonizing our curriculum"; although some are just as happy not to see such political language infuse their critical studies in social psychology,

I don't think they understand what decolonizing means, because they tell me that they're happy that I'm not focusing [on that], that I criticize Freud or whomever from a South African point of view, let's say, from a traditional healer's point of view.

And finally, Liezille's commitment to radical change is reflected not only in her *curriculum* and *pedagogy,* but also in her methods of *assessment,* as this essay assignment on the Trevor Noah book reveals:

Case Study
  Trevor Noah's unlikely path from Apartheid South Africa to the desk of The Daily Show began with a criminal act: his birth. Trevor was born to a white Swiss father and a black Xhosa mother at a time when such a union was punishable by five years in prison. Living proof of his parents' indiscretion, Trevor was kept mostly indoors for the earliest years of his life, bound by the extreme and often absurd measures his mother took to hide him from a government that could, at any moment, steal him away. Finally, liberated by the end of South Africa's tyrannical white rule, Trevor and his

mother set forth on a grand adventure, living openly and freely and embracing the opportunities won by a centuries-long struggle.

The assessment questions are themselves lodged in a critical reading of the sampled text and the personal challenge to change, such as the following:

• What personal experiences do you have relating to the book?
• Give examples from the text that describe the causes of prejudice, discrimination and inequalities.
• How does the author challenge the reader to change?

In sum, unlike the head of the Philosophy Department at UP, Leonhard Praeg, Liezille Jacobs is a junior academic with much less authority to drive curriculum change beyond her own courses, or even to retain her own preferred course (social psychology for first years), which was "taken away" and given to another lecturer to teach. Her junior status also makes her much more vulnerable to student criticism, particularly, in this case, from a small group of white students who questioned her authority to lead the class and complained about her disruptive teaching methods:

After every class I had to sit with the course co-ordinator and the class reps, and the class reps would tell me that, really Dr Jacobs, there was nothing wrong with what you taught us. It's only that most of the white students find some of the things you say offensive – offensive meaning "stop talking about what happened in apartheid."

This sense of vulnerability in doing radical curriculum change does not go away, and Liezille has had to weigh the costs of teaching the way she does in the institutional context of Rhodes University. Yet Liezille persists with transformative teaching, drawing on the core ideas from her earlier assignment, social psychology, conscious of the fact that this kind of curriculum labour is part of the broader decolonization moment; yet, she is not beholden to its language or prescripts in any doctrinal way.

6.5 Decolonizing Media Studies at the University of Johannesburg

Born in Malawi but raised in Zimbabwe, Sarah Chiumbe remembers always having a questioning mind, which she put to work during her days working for a non-governmental organization called *Freedom of Expression* in Harare. While her undergraduate studies were in English and French literature, it was when she went to Oslo in 2004 to do a PhD in media studies that she developed a vocabulary to express her intellectual discontents in a thesis on the information society, the precursor to today's Fourth Industrial Revolution (4IR). Her research questioned the power relations that underpinned the new information politics in the West, and its influence over developing countries.

In 2008 she took up a media studies position at Wits University, but it was a 2013 summer school in Barcelona that would give Sarah a coherent language (decolonization) for making sense of troubled knowledge. "It [the summer school] sounded interesting, so I applied and Wits gave me the funding." For three weeks, she studied the teachings of names that would soon become familiar in South Africa's decolonization moment – Maldanado-Torres, Grosfuguel, Mignolo. Also at this conference were other academics from South Africa who themselves would become featured speakers on campuses when the student protests broke out in 2015 – such as UNISA's Sabelo Ndlovu-Gatsheni. On their return, this group of Barcelona conferees formed a reading group on decolonization under the banner of the African Decolonisation Research Network. "I realized I now had a language; at that time South African universities were not even talking about decolonisation and, at Wits (where I was working), there was very little interest."

But by the time the student protests erupted on South African university campuses, Sarah had moved to the Human Sciences Research Council (HSRC), where she was preoccupied not with decolonization and the politics of knowledge but the mundane routines of contract funding and government research. "When *RhodesMustFall* came," she recalled, "I was outside of academia."

In 2019 Sara came back into the academy, taking up a senior position in the School of Communication at the University of Johannesburg. She found that UJ had adopted decolonization early on in the protest movement. This was certainly different from the way Wits was in 2014: "UJ felt like a place that was trying."

At the level of faculties and departments, Sarah found fear and discomfort among academics – "especially those from the former RAU"[1] – but they had to do it. She observed that the commitment of

---

[1] The Rand Afrikaans University (RAU) was the conservative white institution that was merged with other entities to become the University of Johannesburg in 2005.

academics to decolonization became a kind of "tick box" exercise: "You had to report twice a year on how you were decolonizing your curriculum." Then these academic responses were put online "and we laughed and made fun of the superficial ways in which people were reporting on their attempts to decolonize the curriculum."

All of a sudden, a new Vice-Chancellor was appointed, and "4IR became the new mantra. The decolonisation agenda was taken over by 4IR, and decolonization died a natural death." The tick-box form changed, and Sarah realized that it was now up to individuals with their own interests and efforts to decolonize their curricula – which is precisely what she did.

Sarah became Head of the School of Communication in 2019 with a clear focus: "I would push (the decolonization) agenda across the three departments (Communication Studies; Journalism Film and Television; and Strategic Communication)." With a curriculum review underway, this was the ideal time to examine once again the extent to which the departmental curricula injected a sense of criticality into the content of their teaching. It was, however, in Sarah's own radical curriculum work in media studies that the example was set.

The first thing that strikes a reader of Sarah's radical curriculum is that it is lodged within a much broader frame of critical theory. The 2020 study guide for the Communication, Media and Society (CMS8X12) course, under the heading "Introduction to Critical Media Studies," directs students to readings on critical theory in general, and the Frankfurt School in particular. Other readings locate this critical work in the context of her own field, such as Ott and Mack's *Critical Media Studies: An Introduction.*

It is only in week 5 of the course that students are introduced to the "D" word, in a teaching session titled "Digital Technologies and the Decolonisation Debate." The seminar topics are themselves revealing of Sarah's critical approach:

• What is decolonization?
• What is coloniality?
• The politics of technology from the Global South
• Envisioning decolonized technologies at the local, transnational and global level

The required readings for this session combine conceptual and practical work and draw on authors (mainly) from developing countries;

the recommended readings include African and non-African authorities as well. So, for example, students read Maldanado-Torres' well-
known "Theses on Coloniality and Decoloniality" alongside Achille
Mbembe's *The Internet is Afropolitan* and Syed Mutsafa Ali's intriguing writings on decolonial computing.

Another important observation about Sarah's approach to radical
curriculum change is that it is not doctrinate. The curriculum not only
introduces students to a broader theoretical canvas for exploring decoloniality (that is, critical theory), but it also teaches students the practical dimensions of media studies, albeit through a critical lens. "My
colleagues," she said, "feared that decolonization is about 'throwing
away Western knowledge'," which it is not; it is about incorporating
other knowledges in ways that "start from where you are" – in Africa,
in South Africa. The nuts-and-bolts topics in her curriculum include
subjects such as big data; the digital transformation of everyday life;
and, of course, social media.

The content on which Sarah's curriculum is based is therefore
immersed in the African context. Here it is important to note that she
does not simply *apply* theories and concepts from the West onto African
contexts; the continental context *is* the content of the curriculum itself. In
her Honours course for 2020 on *Global Journalism Ethics* assigned
readings included published works on journalism ethics in Zambia,
media ethics in Ethiopia, and African Ubuntu as a framework for normative media theory. For example, students read Kasoma's (1996) article on
"The Foundations of African Ethics (Afriethics) and the Professional
Practice of Journalism" from the journal *Africa Media Review*.

Sarah is further distinguished among the many academics coming to
grips with the decolonization of curriculum by her strength as a senior
scholar in her field and an expert on the topic. She co-edited the book
Media Studies: Critical African and Decolonial Approaches (Chiumbu
and Iqani 2019), which outlines systemically the key ideas framing her
curriculum theory and practice:

- Media, development, and decolonization
- African-language media in orality, print, and broadcast
- Decolonizing visual culture
- Decolonizing democracy, media freedom, and freedom of expression

Her authoritative leadership in the field enables Sarah to speak from a
body of knowledge in which she is a co-creator of critical approaches

to media studies that include but are not limited to decolonization. And because of her intellectual confidence in the subject, she is not dependent on the male gurus from Latin America who have come to define decoloniality for some South African academics.

It is, moreover, the same confidence that enables Sarah to bring in knowledge from other contexts without being self-conscious about the borrowing or the lending of ideas across national borders. Most importantly, her confidence as an authority in critical media studies means that when new curriculum doctrines come in the wake of a new university leader, Sarah can continue her critical work, because it is not dependent on compliance pressures from above but on a steady conviction about the politics of knowledge in her field of expertise.

But what about assessment? Sarah requires class attendance, gives semester marks, and convenes a final examination. We asked her directly, "How do you live with the contradictions of a curriculum that is emancipatory and an assessment system that is top down and authority-driven?" She replied:

I live with the contradictions and I have not solved the contradictions; you can say that again. Its more about the dynamics in the lecture room, between lecturer and student ... it is still is not resolved. I have not found a solution; if I said so, I would be lying. What does it mean to assess a student's work from a decolonial perspective? Students have to follow a certain formula, and when they disrupt that, when a student goes outside that, they don't pass. It goes to the issue of ethics, for which UJ has a rigid system. We have not even talked about decolonizing those. I live with these contradictions on a daily basis.

6.6 Decolonizing the Visual Arts at Stellenbosch University

Elmarie Costandius is a product of Die Hoërskool Louis Trichaardt (in the eponymous town named for the Voortrekker leader), and an unlikely candidate to lead one of the most effective campaigns for the decolonization of the visual arts at the historically conservative Stellenbosch University. Her social consciousness was forged by an open-minded mother, who kept pressing the question, "What is a good human being?" and by studies overseas, where she was particularly impressed by the ways in which the Czechs thought about the arts: not merely for display and personal acclaim but for community impact and social change. Elmarie's intellectual biography, with its foundations in those important life influences, is reflected in her radical curriculum work.

At its heart is the concept of "critical citizenship," which she defines as a social justice commitment. Critical citizenship asks, "What is a just way of being, doing, and thinking?" In the context of the visual arts, critical thinking presses the questions "How much are you affected by things around you?" and "How do your actions affect the things in your world?" Her Critical Citizenship Group (CCG) was formed some time before decolonization came marching onto campus, but when it did, the protest movement did for it what it did for so many other critical initiatives on the margins of the institutional curriculum – played them onside in the institutional politics of the day.

Before the protests made decolonization an issue, Elmarie's CCG group had received its share of cynicism and snide remarks from some members of her academic department. The more traditional approach to the field valued the *gallery arts* as opposed to the *community arts*, which underpins this radical curriculum. So why did Elmarie hitch her critical citizenship wagon to the decolonization movement? "I did not use that language [of decolonization]," she argued, but, indeed, there were points of agreement; "It was not strange."

What is distinctive about Elmarie's work in decolonizing the arts is that she took the curriculum out of the classroom to make vital connections to the campus and to the broader community. In her words, it was about "taking the students out of the studio." Her concept of community is, however, a critical and transformative one, not at all lodged in the usual "*opheffing*" (upliftment) logics of what the old Afrikaans universities understand to be community engagement.

Her "History of the Arts in Stellenbosch" project took students into the areas surrounding Stellenbosch to document the material culture of disadvantaged communities. The textual (works of art), spatial (architecture), performative (theatre), and sensory (food) are objects and events that exist within communities but that have "hardly ever been shown as examples at educational institutions" (Costandius 2019b). Students, however, do not enter to "tell" communities, but to ask and engage, in order to figure out how they would survive under their living conditions. It is a subtle but powerful course instruction, for the students become dependent on community members for guidance and help, rather than entering with the salvation logics of typical university outreach programmes. They are not giving "things" but being taught about them; the tables are turned.

In one curriculum project, Visual Arts students were informed that the old Arts building was on the very site of a home from which Coloured families were evicted, in a general area called *Die Vlakte* (The Flatlands). This powerful fact had not been well known to the students – the very place where they studied was a political crime scene. Costandius describes the event in graphic terms in a presentation:

- For decades, the removals from Die Vlakte and The Battle of Andringa Street[2] were not part of the official history of Stellenbosch.
- In addition to the 3,700 Coloured inhabitants, 6 schools, 4 churches, a mosque, a cinema and 10 businesses were affected by the forced removals.
- Many buildings on the current campus are geographically linked with Die Vlakte. (Costandius 2015a)

Thus, *Die Vlakte* becomes an art project as much as it is, inevitably, a political project, one in which the material culture of a displaced people finds its way into the art works on display within the Faculty itself. A permanent exhibition now memorializes the forced removals from *Die Vlakte* under apartheid.

Taking students "out of the studio" also meant engaging the campus itself, through the Visual Redress project, which had as one of its goals to "contribute towards the integration of social and academic (curricula) transformation on campus." Now the focus was on image, signage, and installations as the target for "changes in the visual language of the campus." This meant a dialogue with campus citizens, the exploration of "sensitive issues" with fellow students, and addressing the fear and anxieties of students and staff. And yet, strikingly, at the heart of this "public art as curricula" (Schmahmann 2019) is a radical account of symbolic restitution that seeks "redress" even as it acknowledges the hindrances that might be posed by "settler anxiety" (Costandius 2019a).

---

[2] The Battle of Andringa Street was a 1940 incident in which Stellenbosch University students clashed with Coloured residents of the town, with men from the *Dagbreek* residence entering and damaging nearby homes "to teach the Coloured people a lesson." (Grundlingh, n.d.)

The radical curriculum is all about process, doing things with people like the student leadership (SRC) and the activist student group called Open Stellenbosch (2016–2017). So, the visual arts curriculum invited campus students to re-imagine the campus in the course of many interviews, surveys, and suggestions, which included:

- Plant trees and create water-wise indigenous gardens
- Signage by the Arts & Social Sciences building should acknowledge Die Vlakte
- Sculpture of past and present leaders sitting on the ground in a circle in deliberation
- Campus benches welcoming students in sixteen different languages

The formal curriculum, in the form of the course outline, gives a sense of the content of what students read and are taught; this is important not only because of the criticism of European-centred texts it features but also for the insights it gives into the critical orientation of the Visual Arts curriculum. We take, for this discussion, the MA in Visual Arts (Art Education) offered in 2020. What does the course content reveal beyond what we already know from the curriculum-in-practice? In this respect, Costandius clearly teaches students from a range of critical texts, as reflected in these titles:

- *Remodeling Learning on an African Cultural Heritage of Ubuntu*
- *The Routledge International Handbook of Critical Education*
- *The Postcolonial Studies Reader*
- *Institutional Racism in Higher Education*
- *Towards a Framework for Critical Citizenship Education*
- *Critical Theories, Radical Pedagogies, and Global Conflicts*
- *The Critical Pedagogy Reader*
- *Educational Research for Social Justice*
- *On the Conditions of Anti-Capitalist Art*

While this content is critical and the pedagogy transformative, what about assessment? This Costandius regards as a problem that is difficult to resolve. Assessment makes judgements and places the academic teacher in an authoritative position over students and their futures – they pass or fail, depending on a decision of the lecturer. Her position is that there is no need for assessment, for the purpose of visual arts education is simply to prepare students for life and work as critical artists in communities. In the Czech context, she insisted, they have done away with assessment in visual arts altogether. It remains, however, a powerful institutional control over the lives and learning of students, about which Elmarie feels very frustrated.

Finally, on the broader campus, Costandius is a curriculum activist in public forums concerned with the transformation of Stellenbosch University. At a campus seminar, for example, she addressed the topic "Socially Just Pedagogies and Community Interaction," in which the framing question was:

How can academics make a difference in society in a socially just way? And how can lecturers facilitate discussions around critical assessments of community interaction as a learning experience? (Costandius 2015b)

In sum, Costandius's outstanding example of decolonial curriculum practice is distinctive from the rest we have examined in that it extends the radical critique of knowledge beyond the classroom or, in the case of the visual arts, the studio. It is not simply an application of disciplinary knowledge to an African context but the transformation of resident knowledge in its application to campus and society. Is this capacity for criticality in a humanities subject such as the visual arts inherent in the nature of the discipline itself? Yes and no, argued Elmarie. No, because mainstream visual arts education still promotes the individualistic, profit-generating idea of gallery art, where exhibitions attract attention and advance careers. Yes, because "art helps you to lose yourself a bit; working with materials allows you to let loose."

The soft-spoken Costandius knew that she needed support from senior management for her radical ideas, and she found some backing for addressing critical issues on the campus conscience (e.g., the forced removals and the public artwork) at the very time that student activism was escalating, through groups like Open Stellenbosch, in the years leading up to the decolonization protests. In the broader sense of curriculum as art, the project had significant social impacts, such as in *Die Vlakte* exhibition. In the narrower sense of challenging the institutional curriculum, the visual arts remain an example of an enclave curriculum.

6.7 Conclusion

The most important finding that emerges from this chapter is that the academics who were engaged in decolonized curriculum work in the humanities and social sciences were indeed doing so *before* decolonization as a political movement came onto campuses in 2015. None of them necessarily used the language of decolonization in the pre-2015 years, even though some had exposure to the concept outside of the country (a summer school in Barcelona, in the case of Sara Chiumbe) or in the very nature of their discipline (African Studies, in the case of Sally Matthews). Some, like Liezille Jacobs, sat uneasily with the concept of decolonization, given their own political upbringing in the struggle for transformation. All of them, however, found political resonance with decolonization, even though none offered a conceptually coherent or consistent account of the term in relation to their own work.

Another critical finding is that the five scholars doing radical curriculum work had each had an intellectual journey that transformed their own thinking about the politics of knowledge. They were not simply doing curriculum change as an academic activity; they were themselves challenged and changed as academic practitioners. This observation is crucial, because it raises the question as to whether academics can be instructed to "decolonize their curricula" (as was done explicitly at UJ, for example) when they neither understand nor commit to what is, in essence, a political project that requires much more than technical proficiency alone.

The Road to Damascus moment, for Praeg, came during a teaching appointment at the University of Fort Hare. He was handed a curriculum to teach that included Western thinkers such as Michel Foucault. He taught his heart out, but the students struggled. Either I am a poor teacher, he thought, or the students are really weak, or maybe both. Then he realized that the reason the students were struggling was because he was teaching philosophical questions that did not resonate with their own life experiences; it was, in effect, a foreign curriculum. From that moment on, he changed the *what* and *how* of philosophy that he taught to South African students.

For Liezille Jacobs, it was her social struggles in a working-class home and her political struggles on an activist campus that shaped her intellectual commitment to radical curriculum change. By virtue of being an African Studies scholar, Sally Matthews became aware early in her career of questions related to the politics of knowledge and of the debates on Africanization. Elmarie Costandius found her world turned upside down during travels to Europe and, in particular, by the ways in which Czechs understood the vocation of the artist as a public figure and a community activist. Similarly, Sarah Chiumbe, with an already questioning mind, found an intellectual and political language through her travels as a postgraduate student in Oslo and as a young academic in Barcelona that she could wield to make sense of her own academic interests and with which she could design a critical, decolonized curriculum. The link between curriculum and biography is vividly demonstrated in the academic work of these five scholars.

All five of these exemplars of radical change have created enclave curricula best described as *institutional hot spots*. Common definitions of *hot spot* drawn from online sources are suggestive, such as "a small area with a relatively high temperature" or "a place of significant activity," among others. In times of crisis, activist students are drawn to these curricular hot spots, places where connections can be made (as another definition has it) by gathered groups. University leaders, we found in the course of this study, are quick to point out these areas of "significant activity" that exemplify the transformative change for which institutions wish to be known. Those hot spots, by an extended definition, can be places of danger, even violence, as Liezille Jacobs discovered when she was alerted to threats against her from some students.

But do these hot spots radiate their radical heat over the institutional curriculum? There is little evidence of a broader curricular influence in the institution, the faculty, or even the department in the normal course of an academic year. The case of Leonhardt Praeg is an exception, in that he acts on a mandate to change the philosophy curriculum with a strong, directive hand; but can such authority-driven intervention in a university curriculum work, and can it be sustained? It is too early to know whether this kind of mandated change will work.

On the other hand, Elmarie Costandius is a refreshing example of how curriculum influence can stretch beyond the classroom (or arts studio, to be precise), both by stretching her work into the surrounding community and by extending her reach to the senior management of her university. She approached two senior executives with a document about visual redress and gained their attention; in the course of time, new art works appeared on campus in an effort to make the place welcoming for new students. And yet, it is precisely because these initiatives, important as they are, represent the extra-curriculum – that is, "additional to the normal course of study" – that they are absorbed into institutional life. They do not displace existing symbols of the past; they simply add to the collection and, in this case, outside of the disciplinary curriculum. In the meantime, the settled curriculum remains undisturbed.

The question remains: Is there something in the humanities and social science disciplines themselves that lends them more readily towards critical perspectives on knowledge, in general, and the politics of knowledge in particular? Put differently, how does a decolonized curriculum show up in the natural sciences?

7 | The Uptake of Decolonization
The Case of the Sciences and Engineering

7.1 Introduction

There is a general perception among the academics in this study (and outside of it) that the social sciences and humanities are the best candidates for the decolonization of the curriculum. These are, after all, areas of inquiry in which concepts such as agency, values, conflict, interests, power, and culture resonate immediately with the intellectual and political claims of decolonization. The natural sciences, health sciences, and engineering, on the other hand, are the "hard sciences," in which the scientific method claims to yield objective data through experimental studies that eliminate bias and subjectivity. The universal laws of science apply across time and space. As we often heard in the course of this inquiry, "an atom is an atom" and "a bone is a bone."

What this study found, however, were some powerful examples of attempts at the decolonization of curricula in the so-called hard sciences. This chapter offers analyses of the decolonization of knowledge in five diverse fields – engineering, computer science, occupational therapy, organic chemistry, and archaeology – from five different universities, Wits University, Nelson Mandela University, the University of the Free State, Stellenbosch University, and the University of Pretoria. Archaeology is taken up in this chapter as a science field though it is often classified either as a social science discipline or a natural science discipline (or both) depending on the leanings of a particular university.[1]

The questions pursued are the same ones as in the previous chapter on the social sciences and humanities. Who exactly were these courageous curriculum innovators in the different universities? How did they come to be known as critical scholars? That is, what is it in their intellectual biographies that gave each of them a critical disposition

---

[1] At the University of Cape Town, for example, archaeology can be taken as part of a BSc or BA degree.

towards the politics of knowledge in general and the decolonization of curriculum in particular? After all, some of these academics came from conservative homes, schools, and universities in the apartheid era. What were the outside influences on their lives as citizens and scholars that led them to advance radical curriculum change within their universities? How were these radical scholars similar to or different from other academics within their departments? How did their proposals for decolonization differ among their peers represented in this chapter? To what extent did their radical work infiltrate other academic units or the university itself? And how did they see the value proposition held by the majority of their peers – that scientific laws cancel out social peculiarities or political interests in making judgements about observed phenomena? We begin with archaeology.

7.2 Decolonizing Archaeology at the University of Pretoria

Like most African students of his generation, Innocent Phikirayi was taught the history of the continent through Western eyes, whether through the school curriculum or the university curriculum. In fact, during his undergraduate years at the University of Zimbabwe (UZ), Innocent recalls that "I was doing World and mostly European history." This emphasis shifted somewhat when he did his master's degree at UZ, when he learned more about Africa with a mix of pre-colonial and postcolonial African history.

What fascinated Innocent then, as now, was what he calls "deep time," that is, the periods of history long before the starting point of most texts on Africa, which was colonial settlement and postcolonial history. In his postgraduate studies, Innocent's introduction to pre-colonial history was mainly about Egypt and the classical world of the Mediterranean, "because we were taught that is where the home of the entirety of archaeology is." His inquisitive mind told him that there must be more, and that he should pursue digging up the "deep time" history of the African continent.

It was this pursuit that led Innocent towards a lifelong study of the great African kingdoms, from Great Zimbabwe in the pre-colonial period to Mapungubwe in South Africa. During his doctoral studies at the University of Uppsala, in Sweden, he combined history and archaeology to study a kingdom that was a successor to Great Zimbabwe, the Mutapa Empire, which he regards as a continuation of the culture established at Great Zimbabwe that Europeans encounter and write about.

Innocent has little interest, however, in studying ancient African kingdoms merely for their historical value. What motivates his study of archaeology is the links he sees between the past and the present:

> When I look at the past, I also look at the present, how that past intersects with the present. Without that, I don't see any relevance in doing archaeology at all.

Like all disciplines, archaeology was at the heart of intense political disputes during the apartheid era. On the one hand, it was a colonial discipline whose authoritative knowledge was constructed by colonial scholars using colonial methods and drawing on colonial theories that together constituted what counted as archaeology. On the other hand, it was a discipline whose professional community felt increasingly uncomfortable in the 1980s with the presence and prominence of white South African archaeologists within the international community of scholars. It was in this context that the World Archaeological Congress was launched in 1986 – a movement for the decolonization of the intertwined disciplines of history and archaeology; this was followed by another meeting, this time of the American Anthropological Association (the triple A, as it's called), where an activist scholar named Faye Venetia Harrison pressed the question of whether an authentic anthropology could emerge from the critical intellectual traditions and counter-hegemonic struggles of Third World peoples, and also whether a genuine study of humankind can arise from dialogues, debates, and reconciliation among various non-Western and Western intellectuals. It was the kind of initiative that would lead to popular publications such as *Decolonizing Anthropology: Moving Further towards an Anthropology of Liberation* (Harrison 1992).

As a result, by the time decolonization was demanded on the main campus of the University of Pretoria, Innocent had long since engaged with its critical ideas through his earlier participation in these international associations, in which the subject had already come up. To his colleagues at UP he responded to the directive to decolonize with, "This is what we have already been doing but no one was taking notice!"

A close-up analysis of the archaeology curriculum that Innocent has constructed shows that it places decolonization at the centre of the teaching programme. In Issues in African and Global Archaeology (AGL 753), decolonization is defined as

a process of learning and unlearning, knowing and unknowing, especially where knowledge production and consumption has been shaped by colonization, dominant ideologies, and socio-political systems.

What does a decolonized archaeology look like? For Innocent, the challenge for students is to engage the decolonization of archaeological knowledge, what he calls "an epistemic question" as it relates to the colonial history of the discipline. In other words, decolonization is not simply about replacing Western knowledge with African knowledge, or applying existing knowledge to African conditions; rather, students are charged to "revisit or rethink established canons."

There are three texts for this unit of the course, *Decolonizing Anthropology*, *Handbook of Postcolonial Archaeology*, and *Decolonizing Methodologies*; its discussion topic is: *How can we decolonize archaeological research and the teaching of archaeology at university?* But this unit exists among other units in the course, which goes beyond the third week's focus on decolonization to include topics such as ancient societies, monumentality, heritage in Africa, and climate change. While the entire curriculum carries an unmistakable thread of criticality, it is not dogmatic in its application of decolonization across the course but devotes a concentrated "week" of study to the concept.

In a similar vein, the course called Advanced Archaeological Theory (AGL 751) hardly mentions decolonization except in a discussion of theoretical approaches to the study of Africa in archaeological theory:

It should be recognized that "antiquarian" and "traditional" approaches to archaeology impacted on Africa significantly, underling the European and largely colonial origins of the discipline.

And so, while the curriculum is not doctrinaire on the subject of decolonization, its themes run consistently through the course and its selected readings. Students learn how archaeological theory is used in Africa and indeed "how some African models use Western theoretical approaches." In other words, the simplistic choice of African versus Western theory is replaced with a more nuanced account of the entanglements of South/North theory in archaeological studies.

Concepts from broader critical theory, such as "theorizing agency," nevertheless run through the curriculum, and students learn important distinctions of method, such as processual archaeology (i.e., using the scientific method to make objectives findings of human *processes* that produce material artefacts) versus post-processual archaeology (i.e., using interpretive methods to render subjective accounts of the social practices and cultural traditions that explain the material world). A critical disposition, in other words, does not require a dogmatic attachment to a new term on the block:

I'm one of those persons who doesn't subscribe to a definition as such, but broadly to an explanation or an understanding that asks, "what does it involve?" You know, let's say, there's the bigger picture in terms of what decolonization is.

For Innocent, the distinction is a simple one – decolonization as a historical process in which former European colonies became independent, and decolonization as a legacy concern where "you see the perpetuation of colonial elements as well as attempts to remove colonial influences not just in politics but in scholarship, in learning, and in research." This means rethinking the subjects of research.

In addition to "deep time" as a curriculum emphasis in Innocent's decolonizing work, there is another, his commitment to community archaeology, which he spells out in a range of related scholarly and professional publications. In *Listening to Great Zimbabwe's Local Histories and Its Toponyms*, Innocent decries "the silence of unheard voices and untold stories" (Pikirayi 2017) when it comes to accounting for the rich pre-colonial histories of ancient kingdoms. By listening to indigenous people in the areas surrounding these ancient kingdoms a much richer account of the meanings of those sacred landscapes emerges.

Excavating such knowledge requires a very different set of methods, one that prizes *archaeological listening* over "the extraction of data" and values the language of local communities rather than relying only on written texts or stone structures. Respecting the memory and remembering of disparaged communities is exactly what the decolonizing of research methods implies; otherwise, "we're also acting as colonial agents by not letting the community tell us about things as they were," rather than the researcher's agenda, which is to tell "how things should be." Once again, Innocent's approach is about reconciling the knowledge of the researcher and that of the researched in ways that lead to "more authentic ways of knowing and thinking." As he puts it,

All in all, this is how I want to look at decolonizing knowledge. Decolonization without even inserting the world "decolonize" in a text. You don't have to write that particular term to be seen to decolonize; it's just the way you do your theory, your methodology, your pedagogy, and your approach to communities.

But it is precisely the institutional need "to be seen to be doing decolonization" that led the University of Pretoria to put on mega-seminars on decolonization under the bold heading of The Decolonial Turn that raised concerns.

It was a reaction to the [political] circumstances to say "how best should we be seen to respond" rather than to say "how should we respond robustly to this challenge since we have been caught napping?"

Among students, this critical approach to knowledge inevitably caused problems when Innocent first introduced decolonized thinking through the archaeology curriculum. "I was reported twice, I had to walk out of a class," he reports. The student complaints ranged from the complexity of the subject matter to the discomfort caused by the topics covered. "Before 2010 things were very problematic for me when I tried to challenge conventions through these study guides (course outlines)." Since that time, things have improved, as undergraduate students are now more attuned to these topics in archaeology, and the postgraduate students, having chosen to pursue research in these areas of inquiry, were never really a problem.

Innocent's colleagues were caught on the backfoot when decolonization came knocking on the department's doors. Some simply accepted the instruction to decolonize with "an attitude of resignation" and asked, "What can we do?" Others behaved like typical academics and engaged the new demand with the question "What exactly is being asked of us?" And there were those who claimed that "We are already doing this," as a way of "covering their footprints." At UP, as elsewhere, the lack of definition, or at least of coherent intellectual direction for decolonization, meant that anyone could claim to be "doing it."

There are few places where this lack of curriculum transformation is more evident than in the university's traditional evaluation system.

Assessment is conventional, and measures of progression require compliance with often standardized protocols set for each module. There is no deep thinking at UP (or most other places) about the decolonization of evaluation and assessment. Following these mostly quantitative measures ("box-ticking, templating") is tied to personal advancement:

If you want to be promoted to becoming a senior member of the academy, you have to produce a portfolio indicating that you have met or exceeded the minimum requirements for being a good teacher and you include all these [conventional] instruments.

There is a critical set of insights to be gained from Innocent Pikirayi's approach to decolonization. Like other academics advancing decolonization in his discipline, there are powerful influences in his intellectual biography that preceded the 2015–2016 protest movement. Like others, such as Sarah Chiumbe in Media Studies at UJ, an earlier induction into the language of decolonization happened during his formative student years outside South Africa, in Zimbabwe and, later, Sweden. As a result, he was genuinely "doing" decolonization before the language of curriculum change came to South Africa via students' voices.

Innocent's approach to archaeology also reflects a very mature attitude towards the curriculum change project, one that resides in a broadly critical approach to the problem of knowledge. In this approach, decolonization, if the term needs to be deployed at all, is simply one approach for rethinking teaching, learning, and the conduct of research in the presence of a largely conservative community of scholars.

His deployment of the conceptual language of decolonization is, moreover, conciliatory rather than confrontational towards the Western canon, its theory, and its methods. Importantly, Innocent's critique of the colonial project is devoid of the bombast of more strident critics and, throughout, is very simple and practical in the search for a just and respectful practice of archaeology within communities.

Finally, the case of archaeology at UP suggests that what the mid-decade student protests might have done was to prepare more fertile ground for the reception of radical ideas such as decolonization, especially in undergraduate communities – provided, of course, that there were academic teachers who were bold enough to take on the decolonization of knowledge within their curricula.

7.3 Decolonizing Occupational Therapy at the University of the Free State

Tania Rausch van der Merwe comes from a politically conservative family, though it had some openness around the edges. She could bring home library books on forbidden subjects such as reincarnation, for example, and though her mother raised her eyebrows, "she did not reprimand me." Tania remembers how her paternal grandfather, an apartheid-era police detective, took her to meet his friends who were, nevertheless, racially diverse. Small things like this registered with the young student from traditional Afrikaans schools including Laërskool Thabazimbi in the Lowveld and Welkom-Gimnasium in the Free State.

It was, however, on a visit to the USA as a young white woman that

my head just opened up and my worldview was turned on its head; the world became so much bigger and I could see South Africa and South African patterns. It was like a real mind-break, an incredible liberation of the parameters of my thinking. It had a huge impact on my worldview and the way I thought and saw things.

As a result of this transformation in her thinking, Tania brought to her later studies in occupational therapy a set of critical social and intellectual instincts that caused trouble among her academic peers. When, for example, she embarked on master's studies, Tanya proposed doing an ideological critique of occupational therapy. The Chair of the Ethics Committee called her in and demanded to know "What type of research is this?" Such a critical disposition towards the discipline places Tania at interesting crossroads in her intellectual development, or what she calls "intersections" of ideas and people that offer new foundations for thinking about occupational therapy.

Professor Theresa Lourens at UCT saw the potential in her master's research and found funding for Tania to participate in human rights education focused on "training the trainer" with scholars such as Lesley London. Shortly thereafter, the profession of occupational therapy decided that human rights should form part of the OT curriculum. "I introduced that into the department with mixed outcomes," she says.

Two other points of intersection in her intellectual development came in the form of formidable PhD supervisors – Andre Keet (a former Commissioner for the South African Human Rights Commission), then at the University of the Free State, and Elelwani

Ramugondo, an eminent OT academic and one of the drivers of the decolonization of curriculum at UCT. Another intersecting influence in her thinking was William Mpofu at Wits University, a political theorist of decolonization.

Gradually, Tania came to understand that the political innocence of her discipline was anchored in a single, heroic story of the origins of occupational therapy. Between the two World Wars, occupational therapy came into its own in the treatment of wounded soldiers. It was a pioneering field that stood up to the more elevated medical profession. In the context of industrialization, OT became known for addressing problems of social justice, such as by responding to the exploitation of immigrant labour.

That is the heroic narrative of the discipline, says Tania, but there is another story – that of a profession whose history is marked by "the ideological imperatives of docility as a virtue" (Rauch van der Merwe 2019, iii). That unreflective, even uncritical, disposition of the profession emerges in the context of a paternalism that runs across time and space and expresses itself in gender power relations. Tania discovered in the profession what she calls "The bedrock of a Victorian family trinity [with] the 'medical doctor as father,' the 'occupational therapist as mother,' and 'the patient as child.'"

This stable and unyielding hierarchy of power relations in occupational therapy clearly riles Tanya. Overriding such power arrangements in the profession was its harsh exclusionary patterns, such as that on her own campus, where 95 per cent of students were white and female, a profile reflected as well in the staffing of the department, despite all kinds of external regulations and institutional directives to transform these legacies of a racially exclusive past. Tania therefore found herself fighting on two fronts – "the profession, grappling with its Eurocentric origins and embedded norms," on the one hand, and "patterns of (un)just exclusion/inclusion against a backdrop of calls for the decolonization of curricula" (Rauch van der Merwe 2019, ii).

As a result, when decolonization came marching onto campus, "it was sort of a relief that we could call it [hierarchies of power and patterns of exclusion] by a name." The availability of a critical conceptual language for making sense of the profession was, for Tania, a valuable resource but also a source of concern. What worried her was the dogma that came with the decolonization discourse and that it appeared very often to be little more than the flip side of what it was critiquing – colonization. Here she points to the exclusionary impulses of decolonization and, in particular, the disinviting of white voices into critical conversations on campuses. "It just sounds like something that's a little more of the same … the reification of the colonial logic for me."

Tania is cautious about, but also very conscious of, her positionality in these debates as a white academic of middle-class privilege. She does not push her concerns very hard and acknowledges that "I'm not sorted about decolonization actually." For Tania, what should rather occupy significant space in the OT curriculum is what she calls epistemic justice. If a critical history of the profession needs to enjoy prominence in the OT curriculum, then epistemic justice is its twin concern.

This does not mean that Tania does not recognize the colonial roots of occupational therapy and its troubled expression in the apartheid context. In fact, she is clear that

Occupational therapy is colonized in its construction of professional knowledge. Its knowledge project is tied up with epistemologies of women, and of white, middle-class women in particular. There were atrocities that happened in health care, committed by doctors, committed by healthcare workers.

But in her OT curriculum, she seeks something deeper and more transformative than simply a flipping of the colonial coin. Epistemic justice begins to address these concerns. For Tania, it means practising human dignity in occupational therapy. It requires recognition of the fact that the student in the classroom is not a blank slate but a human agent who brings a reservoir of knowledge into the pedagogical situation. The legitimate knowledge of the student constitutes the basis for a flat (not hierarchical or paternalistic) dialogue in which "we bring everybody's knowledges together" for purposes of reason and exchange.

In her course outline titled the Foundations in Occupational Therapy (OCT1514), Tania gives full expression to her critical approach to the study of the profession. Students are required to narrate the origins and history of the OT profession in Europe and North America, and its origins in South Africa. In addition, students are encouraged to grapple with the troubled philosophical underpinnings of occupational therapy. It is in this Foundations course that students also learn about ethics, human dignity, and the Bill of Rights as critical underpinnings of a new professional practice.

The curriculum moves towards difficult subjects that would not have been taught in her former Department of Occupational Therapy at the University of the Free State – race, culture, gender, and "the inherent power relationship between the therapist and patient." The class of overwhelmingly white, Afrikaans-speaking women students now learns about "engaging patients from diverse political, socio-economic and cultural backgrounds." In addition, they are taught how to formulate arguments that explain "why epistemic justice is part of practicing human dignity."

In her PhD thesis, *The Political Construction of Occupational Therapy in South Africa: Critical Analysis of a Curriculum as Discourse*, Tania launches a stinging conceptual and historical critique of the occupational therapy curriculum and underlines the many other ways in which students learn *how to be* in the context of the profession. In this regard, it is not only the formal course content on anatomy or physiology that matters but also the dispositions acquired from the powerful hidden curriculum that governs professional training. She teaches by example, to make this point:

One of the first things that I say to my students in the beginning of the year, especially when I meet my first years, is that my transactional posture towards them is from one adult to another. I am not their mother and I am not going to mother them ... I am interacting with them as one adult to another.

It would be difficult for an outsider to appreciate the radical departure that this statement conveys to students at the UFS, a once-conservative, white, residential university in the Afrikaans heartland, and especially difficult to appreciate its impact on what was a white woman's profession, as reflected in the historical enrolments at her former university. Tania has since moved to a senior position in OT at Wits University.

It is in this context that the focus of Tania's Foundations curriculum is not merely on teaching the normative practices of occupational therapy but also on introducing students to *occupational justice*, as in her course on Occupational Therapy and Mental Health (OCTM 3708). The curriculum objectives represent a radical departure from the settled curriculum for the discipline:

Revisiting the foundations of ethical practice (i.e. ethical theories, ethical values, human rights and legal aspects) and start to develop deeper understanding of these foundations in relation to occupational justice and the OT's role of advocacy in order to apply in global Southern context.

This and more are to be achieved through an evaluative framework for the OT curriculum that includes "critical thinking and argumentative writing" – a shift that sends shockwaves through the departmental curriculum. Important as this radical curriculum in OT is, it will be difficult, because of its enclave status, to disrupt the broader training of young professionals, precisely because of the "reproductive machineries of the department," as Tania acknowledges:

There's definitely a cycle that goes not only from student to lecturer but also from these graduates of the UFS who become the supervisors working in the hospitals around the city (Bloemfontein) and returning to teach students with the same epistemologies, the same model, the same worldview. (Rauch van der Merwe 2019)

In devising her curriculum, Tania sees her task as exposing the defensive discourses that sustain occupational therapy as a profession through the taken-for-granted status of professional knowledge itself. By unveiling a critical history of occupational therapy that is attentive to matters of demographic exclusion and epistemic injustice, Tania sees a way forward for "liberating the profession and its knowledge from its colonial and apartheid past" (Rauch van der Merwe 2019, iv).

In Tania's story, there is once again evidence that curriculum and biography are closely linked in explaining the intellectual openness and critical dispositions of the scholar when it comes to the decolonization project. Yet Tania's critical orientation towards knowledge also makes her cautious about an uncritical embrace of decolonization. While it offers a helpful language for describing observed dilemmas of knowledge and power within occupational therapy, decolonization as advanced in South Africa often comes across as a mirror image of its object of criticism, that is, the colonial project and its exclusionary tendencies.

What makes Tania's approach to radical curriculum change different from many other academic teachers is that she draws from a much deeper well of theorists, beyond the decolonial figures per se, to make sense of the shaping of occupational therapy over time. For example, much of her PhD thesis applies concepts and methods from the work of the radical French philosopher Michel Foucault to the analysis of her profession; such application is reflected in the titles of chapters such as "The Archaeology of Occupational Therapy in South Africa" and "The Genealogy of an Occupational Therapy Curriculum."

7.4 Decolonizing Engineering at the University of the Witwatersrand

It was immediately clear that Anne Fitchett and Rodney Genga, the two academics who drive the decolonization of engineering at Wits University, work as a spirited team of curriculum innovators in a field not widely known for a strong social science orientation. Yet Dean Ian Jandrell, an enthusiastic backer of his academic team, was clear in more than one interview that "engineering is actually a social science ... it is about using a skill to serve humanity; we lost that."

What is it in their biographies that endows Anne and Rodney with these critical dispositions towards engineering knowledge? Anne explains that her background in architecture en route to qualifications in construction economics and management (master's) and civil engineering (PhD) enabled her to bring a broader social science perspective to curriculum deliberations in the faculty. In her view, "The engineer is a social creature who has to solve society's problems."

Rodney, on the other hand, explains that even though he showed early aptitude in the basic sciences, it was his courses in literature and critical thinking that expanded his understanding of the human condition and what this might mean for engineering education.

This broader education gave me a competitive advantage among my peers, a robust understanding of multiple disciplines. I could break with the colonial mindset of engineering that separates civil, mechanical, chemical engineering. Africa's problems are complex and require a multidisciplinary and holistic approach. For students to have a really good foundation in engineering education, they too needed a holistic understanding of physical problems.

These engineering academics did something that would be very difficult in any university, and that was to introduce a core curriculum for engineering students that combines traditional first-year subjects (chemistry, physics, and mathematics) with a set of electives that include African languages (isiZulu and Sesotho), history (global encounters), philosophy (ethics), and international relations. Every incoming student has to choose one of these electives as a foundation for later learning in engineering. Importantly, the first-year students do not enter by way of their specializations (civil, electrical, mechanical engineering, etc.) but are identified by their electives, as the history cohort or the international relations cohort, etc. For Rodney, "this is the first level of the decolonization of the curriculum" – the dissolution of disciplinary boundaries and the reorientation of engineering students to approach problems using a broader social lens.

The history elective teaches students about their place in the world and includes topics such as "the nature of colonialism, decolonization and its legacies." In the international relations elective, students are taught about the decolonization era and the role of the Non-Aligned Movement and African states in global politics. And in the ethics elective, engineering students learn about topics such as African ethics, the philosophy of race, equality, justice, and virtue. Even in the other introductory courses, such as mathematical modelling in applied physics, it is not simply about developing "mathematical descriptions of simple real world situations" but, fundamentally, about "developing problem solving skills which enhance the intellectual self-reliance of each students."

In the core curriculum, students are introduced to a completely new way of thinking about engineering knowledge. Scientific knowledge is not simply something that must be applied in practice; the very nature of engineering knowledge itself is the subject of inquiry. The starting point for these academic engineers is the foundational question: What does it mean to be a good engineer?

The core curriculum attends to this question not only through the electives but also in the reconstitution of subjects like applied physics. For these curriculum workers, being a good engineer is much more than competence in a set of traditional skills – it is having the capacity to think, and think critically, beyond the confines of the discipline.

At the heart of their conception of a decolonized curriculum is a new pedagogy of engineering education. A required project in the first year brings together students from different disciplines (digital arts, engineering, etc.) to attend to problems that need to be addressed in a particular community of Johannesburg. A subtle but important shift takes place right away: The client is the community being served, not simply the large company to which the graduate is contracted. Here students learn how to pose powerful questions, such as: What is the nature of the problem? What does the community identify as the problem that needs to be fixed? What is the appropriate engineering solution, for example, a water purification system? In this process of engagement, students have agency.

The locus of power therefore shifts towards the engineering students. They are placed in charge of their identified projects and, in this way, "the hierarchy is broken down, as students take charge of their own learning." The role of the academic teacher is that of a resource person, a facilitator in the process of community engagement and student learning. "A lot of decolonization comes out of the students writing the scripts of their own knowledge," says one of the core curriculum leaders.

In addressing the practical problems of a designated community, context matters. "For us," says one of the academic leaders on the core, "one of the biggest elements of decolonization is context." But it is more than simply the context of application; it is the social, economic, and environmental context for the generation and application of knowledge in a Gauteng community. "Everything is context-based, right here at home." For the designers of the core curriculum, it is especially the challenges of the environment that constitute the principal threat to sustainable communities into the future. Professionals from the field are brought in to talk to first-year students about things such as environmental impact long before they learn the advanced competencies for doing engineering in their respective specializations, such as mining engineering.

An engineering graduate must be able to grapple with such problems, rather than with ones that are fixed within imported textbooks from the West. The students, in this model of education, "are rewriting the textbook."

How do academics engineers justify a set of humanities electives to fee-paying parents and to incoming students for whom the public perception of engineering is one of learning concrete skills to solve real-life problems? For these curriculum innovators, there is a ready defence for every elective, starting with another basic question: What is a well-rounded engineer? The profession demands that engineering students undertake "complementary studies," which are, specifically, not studies in the pure sciences.

Students who take the international relations elective are told that contemporary engineers graduate and take up jobs around the world, and this particular course prepares them for careers worldwide. Students who take philosophy as an elective are taught that a key to critical thinking is understanding how other people, such as future clients, think. Students who take an African language come to understand that communication skills within the diverse contexts of local South African communities are critical to being a successful engineer.

Surely, such a radical revisioning of the engineering curriculum must have caught the attention of the regulator, which, for engineers, is the Engineering Council of South Africa (ECSA)? In the calculation of the curriculum innovators, ECSA is only concerned about exit-level outcomes, including the kinds of graduate attributes that the students leave with at the end of their studies. How an engineering curriculum "gets there" is less important.

Of course, content matters for all the accreditation agencies, so no professional qualification would enjoy a blank slate with respect to *what is taught*. The Dean clarifies: "We make sure that we meet all the requirements in a formal way," and with that commitment the Wits engineering programme sees ECSA as a partner in rethinking the curriculum for the training of engineers. The role of the regulator thus becomes simply one of confirming through the accreditation process that "we are doing what we said we would be doing."

But surely this radical conception of the engineering curriculum must have drawn fire from some academic colleagues? It took eight years to bring the core curriculum to fruition. The daring initiative held major implications for the faculty of engineering and the broader university. Existing courses would have to be dropped in favour of new ones and that kind of change spells trouble on two grounds – the financial implications of a department losing revenue when a course is dropped, and the felt impact on the professional identity of academics when an established teaching unit is replaced.

The first-year core curriculum also had implications for other faculties, and this required senior leadership intervention, since some of the basic sciences would be lost (with implications for the science faculty) and new courses would add to the workload (though also to the revenue streams) of the humanities faculty. The Dean of Engineering would have to run interference for his two curriculum innovators inside and outside the faculty.

Inside the faculty, a curriculum war was brewing. "There was a level of extreme resistance" from some of the senior engineers and "we almost had a rebellion from one of our schools" that could have buried the core curriculum idea. "There was this massive resistance where angry words were spoken and written." Fortunately, when the bold

new curriculum plan was taken to the broader faculty, there was
sufficient support, provided the innovators could prove that they could
implement the change effectively. In the end, "being engineers, we ran
models and simulations to test whether the new curriculum plan
would work."

Implementing a radical curriculum would not have been possible,
the innovators emphasize, without an enthusiastic and involved Dean
who shared their beliefs about the broader purposes of engineering,
and who made possible what was long postponed under previous
deanships. It was especially important to have his leadership backing
across schools in Engineering and across faculties in the university,
because "the common first year [curriculum] had a massive knock-on
effect on all degrees; some courses had to leave the program."

What won the day among detractors was the argument that the
core curriculum would produce better engineers, especially when it
came to knowledge of the social, economic, and environmental considerations that should form part of an engineering qualification. As
students from other fields, such as the biomedical sciences, joined the
programme, the multidisciplinary model demonstrated the value of
such broader deliberations; for example, a student in the digital arts
would learn both mathematics and game design, a trend into the
future. With these new skill sets for the engineer of the future, "all of
a sudden the old colonial pillars [the conventional disciplines] look
much less secure."

How does an innovative curriculum that breaks down the legacy of
disciplinary structures and empowers students to generate their own
knowledge deal with the vexed issue of traditional evaluations in institutions? Anne believes that the portfolio review of work done – something she also borrowed from her earlier work in architecture – offers
students the opportunity for continuous assessment over the course of
the academic year. The project-based work referenced earlier is one
example of an alternative to traditional examination-based assessments, in addition to short tests on a topic as required. Students with
borderline-failed assessments also have the opportunity to take an oral
examination. Most important for the two innovators is giving students
regular feedback on their academic work outside of the examination
context, and this relieves the pressure of summative assessments alone.
Since the new curriculum is centralized, an added advantage is that
assessments can be synchronized among the different academic courses

and course coordinators, so that the process of evaluating student work is not overwhelming.

There can be little doubt that this core curriculum for engineering students is a highly innovative and, indeed, courageous effort within one university setting. The idea of disciplinary boundaries as colonial constructions would find support from scholars such as Lewis Gordon (2014, 87), who holds that "the teleological suspension of disciplines are also epistemic decolonial acts." The positioning of students as creators of knowledge and the conscious attempts to soften the evaluative blows of traditional assessments represent among the best practices of any critical pedagogy.

And yet, the core curriculum, foundational as it is to later learning in the engineering sciences, and even with evidence of some spillover effects to other fields – e.g., mining engineering is recurriculating with the important question in focus: What does it mean to be a mining engineer? – exists within the confines of traditional university structures (for regulation, evaluation, disciplines, and governance) that students encounter over the four years of the degree.

What the undergraduate core curriculum nevertheless offers a traditional research university is a demonstration of what is possible through leadership and innovation, even if constrained within a first-year engineering programme.

7.5 Decolonizing Organic Chemistry at Stellenbosch University

Mags Blackie did her PhD in chemistry at UCT and then joined a mixed religious community of nuns and Jesuit priests "teaching people how to pray." A two-year postdoctoral commitment in medicinal chemistry was followed by postdoctoral studies with Jenni Case, then a UCT scholar in engineering education. Mag's goal with the "postdoc" was to write the perfect first-year textbook in organic chemistry, but then a fundamental shift took place in her thinking – the answer was not the perfect textbook but a recognition of the fact that any teaching or text would come up short if it did not take into account the students' experiences, that is, what they brought with them to the teaching–learning encounter. "There was something in the being of the students" that was not being taken seriously.

Mag's sense of education and social justice was also shaped by her experiences as a white Zimbabwean whose father was a judge in that country during the Mugabe years. Judge Fergus Blackie had sentenced a senior politician (Justice Minister Patrick Chinamasa) to jail and was promptly arrested two months after his retirement. Mags found herself wondering whether she would have acted any differently from her father's persecutors if she had had the same experiences as Black Zimbabweans over the years of white colonial rule only to be subjected to the authority of a white judge in the independence era. As with her students, Mags grappled with what learning means when you place yourself in other people's shoes.

When decolonization came to the Stellenbosch campus, this senior lecturer in organic chemistry felt an immediate resonance with the moment. "The element that got my attention was, 'How do we value the experience of the student?'" she says. By this time, Mags had been introduced to the work of Australian-based scholar Karl Maton (2014) who had developed the idea of Legitimation Code Theory (LCT) for making sense of scientific knowledge. Maton built his theory of knowledge on the work of the French social theorist Pierre Bourdieu and the English sociologist of education Basil Bernstein, both of whom had made signal contributions to the sociology of knowledge.

LCT holds that all knowledge (or knowledge practices) is based on a set of organizing principles that is not obvious to those who research new knowledge or teach from a new base of knowledge. What LCT does is to make visible or explicit those principles that underpin scientific knowledge. Two of those dimensions (there are at least four in Maton's taxonomy) of scientific knowledge are specialization and autonomy.

Specialization is concerned with the question of *what counts as a legitimate knowledge claim*. There are those who take the scientific claims on knowledge very seriously and this dimension is called *epistemic relations*; this is the typical claim of a traditional scientist who believes in the objectivity and neutrality of science, which is governed by immutable laws and where the only real knowledge is produced by what is called the scientific method.

At the other end of the spectrum are those who take the social claims to knowledge more seriously, and this dimension is called *social relations*. For this group of people, science is more than what scientists claim to be legitimate knowledge; it is also the knowledge of those who are not traditional scientists but whose lives and work are also governed by science. Science is not only laboratory knowledge but the lived experiences of people often on the margins of society.

To make these complex concepts real, Mags draws on one unforgettable moment during the decolonization debates in South Africa when a non-science UCT student condemned the totalizing authority of Western science, questioned the uncritical acceptance of Newton's laws of gravity, and raised for legitimate consideration the use of magic to invoke lightning to strike an enemy. The four-minute videoclip of the event received the short-hand notation on social media as #ScienceMustFall (UCT Scientist 2016).

The traditional scientists were furious with this propagation of non-science, and a white student was reprimanded at the campus event for exclaiming that the magic claim was not "true."

Mags concedes that the student's understanding of science was naïve ("*I have to say that*") but argues that it was the social understandings of science that demanded another look at her contentions. For the traditional scientist, the specialist view of science that elevates expertise and expert knowledge typically downplays social claims to knowledge; such practices result in a *knowledge code*. On the other hand, for the student activist who regards social experiences as sensible and legitimate in their own right, such a view constitutes a *knower code*.

In *the knowledge code*, where hierarchical knowledge structures govern scientific work, "it is the explanatory power of the axioms and theorems that is valued." In *the knower code*, the legitimacy of knowledge derives from horizontal knower structures where who speaks and whose knowledge counts are grounds for the recognition of other ways of knowing.

The problem arises when these two positions – that of the traditional scientist and the social activist – are so entrenched that they become absolute positions; what results is *a code clash*. For the scientist, the scientific method is what matters. For the activist, science must be re-examined from an African perspective. Under such conditions, "It is impossible to find common ground because the nature of the ground itself is contested, even if not explicitly so." Who can bridge this gap is a scientist with an appreciation for the social or, as Mags puts it, "a scientist who has the appropriate social gaze," meaning the stance that a participant assumes in relation to knowledge.

Maton's conceptual schema is in parts dense and difficult to grasp, but Mags makes the core concepts of LCT accessible in a book chapter titled, "Decolonizing the Science Curriculum" (Adendorff and Blackie 2020). Her goal is "to find a way of explaining decolonization to scientists" without the difficult language of LCT. Indeed, Mags and her collaborator, Hanelie Adendorff (an education advisor in the SU science faculty), conducted workshops on LCT and the decolonization of science to university-wide seminars on their own campus in September 2018 ("Decolonising the Science Curriculum: Can Legitimation Code Theory Show a Way Forward?") and to various Deans of Science the following November ("Science Must Fall: A Clash of Codes") on the campus of the University of the Western Cape. Both presentations make simple and accessible the more theoretical language of LCT.

Returning to their academic exploration of LCT among its theorists, Mags (and Adendorff) spend some time elaborating on Maton's concepts of specialization and autonomy.

If *specialization* was concerned with the question of the nature and content of legitimate knowledge (the epistemic versus the social), *autonomy* has to do with the relative strength of the boundaries around particular knowledge practices. The following are examples of how science curricula might engage decolonization depending on boundary strengths:

- A science curriculum that teaches students how to think and act like scientists (strong boundaries, insulated from outside ideas)
- A science curriculum that is open to using indigenous knowledge systems (IKS) to teach scientific concepts (strong boundaries, open to other ideas)
- A science curriculum that uses ideas from other disciplines (such as the social science disciplines) to teach science (weak boundaries, open to other ideas)
- A science curriculum that uses the concepts and methods of science to overcome "false beliefs" such as religious ideas in science (weak boundaries, closed to other ideas)

But what does this mean in practice? Mags argues that if you looked at the curriculum documents she uses to teach organic chemistry, it would appear be no different from what a typical course outline looks like for the subject. The difference lies in the pedagogy used to teach students important scientific concepts. Her starting point in teaching is "to valorize students and their experiences" in relation to the curriculum – to bring in their views and to start with their understandings of a concept. "Is this decolonization?" asks Mags of her own work; "I'm not sure, but it points in that direction."

At the heart of the decolonization of the science curriculum is the notion of learning in community, and therefore group work features prominently in her approach to teaching organic chemistry. Here, she also draws on the work of the Canadian Bernard Lonergan, a Jesuit theologian and philosopher of knowledge. Lonergan identifies crucial principles about coming to knowledge that involve experience, insights, judgement and decision-making – all of which are mainly about learning in community, rather than simply individualized learning. It is, no doubt, with Lonergan in mind that Mags made this appeal to the Science Deans Forum that science education has to move beyond discovery:

If our graduates are going to contribute meaningfully to society, we cannot stop there. We need to help students to evaluate their knowledge, and learn to make good decisions based on that knowledge. We need them to ask themselves: "Do I need more information? Or can I render good judgment?" (Kruger 2018)

It follows that how learning is organized is at the heart of a decolonized curriculum. For Mags this means that

curricula might venture into using science for purposes other than advancing or learning science, through projects or service learning components aimed at fostering a variety of graduate attributes.

But this seldom happens, because of the way in which science is conceptualized as neutral, objective, and universal, an insular and bounded product of the scientific method that has little to learn from other views of science. The consequences are dire:

It is this very positioning which affords the strongly polarized positions over whether science is inherently neutral or blindly colonizing ... Decolonization scholars have described science as both colonized and colonizing.

Mags remains cautious in her approach to radicalizing the science curriculum. In fact, she argues that "tinkering with the curriculum can be the start of a decolonizing process." Yet the cases she cites are powerful examples of what a decolonized curriculum might look like; two from her own practice are worth describing.

First, students develop science projects in which they apply scientific knowledge to their own lived experiences to benefit the community. In this case, "materials, actors, and practices from inside science are used for outside purposes such as social justice." Students decide on the topics, and while the lecturer gives up some of her authority, she is also sharing authority in the pedagogical context, thereby creating a more equal distribution of power in the classroom. More than that, students are now co-creators of knowledge in this practical application of the curriculum.

Second, students generate a timeline of the history of conservation science in South Africa. In the hands of a knowledgeable academic teacher, that history necessarily begins before the arrival of Europeans in 1652. This simple act corrects an important perspective on the history of (conservation) science in Africa. New knowledge is added to what students know about the science in question and its early origins. In this cautious approach to the decolonization of the curriculum, "not too much of the integrity of science [is sacrificed] and therefore it is more likely to be accepted by academics teaching science classes."

While the *curriculum* itself is not dismantled in this steady approach to the decolonization of curriculum, the *pedagogy* certainly contains radical forms of engagement with knowledge, authority, and community. But what does such a progressive pedagogy mean inside a traditional system of assessment? Mags is acutely aware of the problem and feels that group-based project work to some extent mitigates the worst features of individualized, competitive, and standardized assessments. The tension between pedagogy and assessment remains real, however, and it is not completely resolved in the way the university accounts for learning in terminal examinations. Traditional scientists would expect nothing less than a rigorous evaluation system for science teaching and research.

In that light, how do Mags' colleagues regard her approach to the decolonization of science? She works, after all, in a Department of Chemistry and Polymer Science with a somewhat conventional division of academic labour in five divisions: organic chemistry, inorganic chemistry, analytical chemistry, physical chemistry, and polymer chemistry – the latter being unusual as a separate division in South African universities. While her perspective is novel, Mags enjoys credibility as a chemist for the high standard of her work, and since her entry point into the academic debates is through education, she holds the attention of her colleagues.

What insights can be gained from Mags Blackie's approach to the decolonization of science? There are three things that are striking about Mags' rather unusual approach to a decolonized science curriculum within a traditional science faculty and department. First, Mags' ability to speak with authority on a subject most natural scientists struggle with comes from her exposure to science education in her postdoctoral experience (where she encountered theorists such as Maton) and her experiences in the Jesuit community (where she engages the work of Lonergan, the philosopher-priest). In other words, there are prior formative experiences that shape her understanding of science and society that enable Mags to bring a critical lens to the decolonization of knowledge in the classroom.

Second, Mags is able to play the role of bridge builder between the natural scientists and what has been, for the most part, a social science concept of decolonization. Her patient, methodical, and measured approach to curriculum change in the sciences is what keeps the scientists at the table. She gives regard to both the settled world of the traditional scientist and the urgent arguments of the student activist. She holds in tension the knowledge claims of the natural sciences and the knower claims of the human sciences. And she brings those worlds together not through the arcane language of the high humanities but through simple examples that carry the concepts in questions.

Third, what enables movement towards a decolonized curriculum in science is real change that does not upset the epistemological applecart of Western science: "there are real risks in rushing into decolonizing science," warned Hanelie Adendorff on the occasion of the Science Deans' Forum. The idea is to include and extend the curriculum from its more familiar referential authorities – the science of Europe, to put it bluntly – to seek both the application of familiar knowledge and the generation of new knowledge through a more open, inclusive, and participatory process of scientific inquiry.

7.6 Decolonizing Computer Science at Nelson Mandela University

Darelle van Greunen obtained her PhD in computer science and spends much of her time advancing the use of information communication technologies (ICT) in poorer communities. A graduate of *Die Hoërskool Despatch* in the Eastern Cape, Darelle did her first degree in German and learned to become critical in the course of language learning:

I had this East German lecturer who always used to say to us, "You have to challenge every statement that I make, do not just accept it because I said it." That stuck with me throughout the years.

Armed with a Higher Diploma in Education (HED) from the former University of Port Elizabeth (now Nelson Mandela University), Darelle became a teacher in schools of the Department of Education and Training – the racial designation of an apartheid government department set aside for urban African children. Following graduation, Darrelle found herself teaching English and introducing technologies in New Brighton township, where she started the first computer literacy classes at Ithembelihle Comprehensive School.

Even at this early moment in her career, Darrelle saw a disconnect between "the foreignness of the terminology" for technology concepts and the language children used in their African environment:

I always relate the story of being an English teacher and asking, "How do you teach Shakespeare to children in a township who have not even crossed the railway line?" So, I tsotsified Shakespeare in many ways and carried that experience through to the university environment in later years.

For Darelle, the problem of language lies at the heart of the decolonization project, and whether as a schoolteacher then or as a university academic now, she holds that "the colonized terminology [of technology] doesn't actually make sense to anybody other than those who created it." Her task, therefore, is to take a traditional scientific concept and transform it "to make sense to the person in the street so that they can identify with a very simple concept which they can relate to."

The use of language in learning new technologies is, for Darelle, more important than technical skills or mathematical abilities. "We need to go back to the vernaculars of people and what they are familiar with," she says. This enables people in communities to more easily grasp the syntax and structure of what is effectively another language – that of the computer scientist or the information technologist. Accordingly, "we cannot remove language from decolonization, for it has nothing to do with the English language because you can still colonize even if you are explaining [technological concepts] in isiXhosa or Sesotho."

What does this mean? That the decolonizing power of language only makes sense to the extent that a new technology connects with and becomes meaningful to ordinary people far removed from the modernities of urban life. In Darelle's framework, the *deep rural Eastern Cape* is a constant reference point in explanations of what decolonization might look like in practice:

So how do I explain to teachers who are working in the rural Eastern Cape words like Internet Browser or things like that which do not exist in the Xhosa vocabulary and therefore cannot be translated into Xhosa. So, I need to be more descriptive, using local terminology that is familiar to people and so create a link between language and visuality.

Darrelle's approach seems to advance the idea that one should create a *mental model* of a concept in the minds of the users of technology with language appropriate to, and meaningful within, the local context:

And that translates for me to decolonization, because the expression creates a certain image in your mind so that the language of description will determine the kind of image ... a decolonized image if the wording that you use is correct.

This heightened sense of the role of language in concept formation is very much part of Darrelle's biography and her critical posture with respect to the decolonization of ICTs:

I speak seven languages, one of which is isiXhosa and another of which is Sesotho, so I have a big passion for languages. Language becomes important because, as South Africans and Africans, we are people of orality. We like to use analogies and stories to convey messages and to get ideas across.

Her growing ideas about the disconnect between ICT concepts and user experiences were bolstered during work for an international technology research unit in Germany, where she again observed "the disjunct between ICT tools and how humans respond to them, as well as who has access to them and who does not" (Centre for Community Technologies 2019, 7).

In addition to language, the concept of *the user context* is key to understanding Darrelle's approach to decolonization. This user-centred approach focuses on technologies already in use in contexts such as the homes, clinics, and classrooms where people live, work, and learn. Context is therefore everything, and for Darrelle and her university's Centre for Community Technologies (CCT), it is about technologies by and for Africans in African contexts. User-centredness is thus about users' experiences of technology in everyday life, and she feels that perhaps the word decolonization is a distraction that gets in the way of this powerful idea:

Maybe we should remove the word decolonization, because the moment you say you are decolonizing your curriculum everybody's hackles rise and they think that you are saying "throw science out the window." That's not what I am saying. All I am saying is, "think about how you are presenting your content. Are you making it real for your recipients?"

Now the leader of the CCT at Nelson Mandela University, Darelle understands her academic identity as straddling the worlds of the natural and social sciences, although the CCT itself falls under the Faculty of Engineering, the Built Environment and Technology (EBET). She regards herself as a product of both the sciences and the humanities, or as a social scientist with an interest in technological innovation. Technology, she argues, is merely a social tool for solving human problems.

There is a fourth element, in addition to language, mental models, and user-experiences, in the decolonization rationale of Darelle's work with community-based technologies: that it solves local problems for Africans, in Africa and by Africans. However, solutions to those problems are not understood as simple, technical ones among local peoples but as connected to much broader purposes of equity, sustainability, and social justice. In more forceful accounts of her work with colleagues and students, those broader purposes are made clear:

Dominant Western and Eurocentric literature sees Africa as danger, chaos and instability, and Africans as people who have no capacity, initiative or hope for survival without the handouts and the know-how from the global North. (Fatyela and Van Greunen 2017)

In response to this perception of Africa, "Colonial rule has delegitimized and erased native knowledge systems that formed the basis of who Africans were and are" (Fatyela and Van Greunen 2017, x). What now needs to happen is for Africans to start "decolonizing their minds, their systemic and structural spaces as well as the knowledge systems that are still heavily influenced by the Eurocentric 'leftovers'" (Fatyela and Van Greunen 2017, x). It is this powerful connection between technology education in rural communities "on the ground" and its broader social, economic, and political purposes that drives the decolonizing work of the CCT.

What does this incisive criticism of colonial knowledge mean for interpreting the very practical work of Darelle and her team as they advance technologies in deeply rural communities? That the current curriculum

detaches African students from their reality, their communities, their world, and its needs. Students are expected to learn to "speak well," gain skills and Eurocentric knowledge that allow them to enter the marketplace but not allow them to make fundamental changes to the status quo in the society (Fatyela and Van Greunen 2017, x)

One way to redress an unjust curriculum is "to build an Afrocentric knowledge base around ICT [because] we are not contributing enough to contextualizing ICT within our context of Africa." This means empowering students through research and development to establish a very different knowledge base that tells us how to do ICT in African communities.

Such commitment to decolonizing ICT runs through the work of Darelle's students, such as the Dutchman Gertjan van Stam, who takes its applications into the region through his dissertation research on "A Strategy to Make ICT Accessible in Rural Zambia: A Case Study of Macha." All of the staff working in the CCT are involved in projects that make similar incursions into disadvantaged areas, including the following projects:

- Designing and creating training materials and wordless picture books using visual design methods
- Producing digital music as well as video production and recording for community use
- Introducing programming to primary school township and rural learners
- Developing digital solutions for community problems
- Conducting user testing for digital apps
- Building community skills development programmes in community-hubs
- Creating positive user experiences with digital solutions

- Generating digital solutions to support community-based health care
- Designing school health assessment tools

In taking the curriculum to the community and bringing the community back to the campus, Darrelle is able to give legitimacy to the lived realities of, especially, rural communities through their encounters with technologies in a language that is accessible to them and that resonates with their experiences as end users while solving real problems in the local environment. For Darelle, this is what is meant by the decolonization of the university curriculum – not one that is imposed on communities but one whose very content derives from a recognition of the experiences of those far removed from elevated language and Eurocentric knowledge that still frames computer science as well as information and communication technologies.

The pioneering work of Darelle van Greunen is distinct from other decolonization initiatives in that the immediate audience is not students on campus but communities far removed from the institutional curriculum. This means that Darelle's approach allows for much more flexibility in pursuit of the ideals of a decolonized curriculum that falls outside the regulatory apparatus that keeps settled knowledge sheltered in place, and away from the academic contestations that might restrain a more radical practice when it comes to formal qualifications on campus.

That, of course, is the point of our thesis – that retained within the confines of institutional life, a radical curriculum would find its course through institutions to be much more difficult and contested than when it is perceived as a service offering to rural communities at a distance. At the same time, the degree of freedom granted to the Centre allows it to make a powerful impact on community development. What this detached project experience also means is that there is little institutional friction or threat perception to the mainstream curriculum on campus.

7.7 Conclusion

The single most important finding from these five cases of curriculum decolonization is that each of the innovators involved has a strong sense of the social dimensions of the natural sciences. While they all respect the basic value proposition of the sciences as generating scientific knowledge based on rigorous methods of inquiry, these scientists also recognize that science is a social construct that holds rich meaning and significance for improving the human condition.

Each of these scientists comes to their field or discipline with an intellectual biography shaped by many forces, including an inquiring mind from their early years; an openness to reading and thinking within the home; exposure to social environments abroad; intellectual ferments within their disciplines; and previous training in social science fields that broadened their personal knowledge landscapes as science practitioners. None of these activist academics (in the sense of doing radical curriculum work, whether or not they embrace the term) started from scratch; their earlier socialization very much explains their later practices in advancing curriculum change within the five institutions. This simple observation at once raises the question as to whether the managerial directive from the top leadership of a university to "decolonize the curriculum" is meaningful, achievable, or durable in the absence of such earlier transformations in the lives of ordinary academics.

This review of the science curriculum in institutions also offers the first insight into a faculty-wide push for decolonization, in the case of the core module for first-year engineering at Wits University. This is an impressive initiative, because it breaks the mould of a course-based (e.g., archaeology) or departmental locus (e.g., philosophy) for doing radical curriculum change. Inevitably, this radical initiative generated intense resistance from more established academics and took a long time to come to fruition. It is, however, enclaved in a special way – the core is self-contained within the general engineering curriculum and does not easily infiltrate the faculty-wide curriculum. Its scope for change is also limited in that it combines normal science with content that is more open to critical thinking and radical perspectives. But those additional course inputs to the common core are offered from the humanities faculty at Wits University and lie *outside* of engineering. In this sense, new knowledge is added on from an external source, rather than upending the traditional engineering curriculum on home turf.

What is striking in these cases is the sensitivity with which the science academics approach their colleagues. The engagement is patient and understanding – which explains the slow pace of change, as in engineering. The change strategy, moreover, is one of intellectual persuasion rather than political confrontation, as is the drive for decolonization on other campuses in this study. This change-by-persuasion approach is most evident in the push for the decolonization of organic chemistry, where Legitimation Code Theory offers a conceptual framework that allows scientists to see the change problem lying on a continuum from the epistemic to the social dimensions of knowledge. That model encourages understanding of rival viewpoints in which the role of academic activists is to bridge understanding among colleagues.

These cases also present an intellectually fascinating range of thinking and action with respect to the politics of knowledge. In the case of engineering, the knowledge challenges are about the employment of multi-disciplines or fields to solve complex problems. For archaeology, they are about extending knowledge beyond its familiar anchors to take account of suppressed knowledges, those of local communities around historic sites. In computer science, the issue is knowledge expressed in the cultural media of rural communities through languages that have meaning in dispersed areas. Organic chemistry finds powerful knowledge in an appreciation of the social understandings of science. And in occupational therapy, knowledge itself is the subject of interrogation, through its historical power in creating and reproducing hierarchies and assigning destinies.

Strikingly, none of the science disciplines examined here are ideologically doctrinaire in their advancement of the decolonization. In fact, some of these academic activists are downright suspicious of decolonization as a new orthodoxy of exclusion, while others draw on the new terminology as one among many ways of grappling with knowledge and power in the curriculum. As in the social sciences and humanities, decolonization has often been welcomed as a critical language for making sense of epistemological or knowledge dilemmas with which some of these critical scholars were already engaged.

What do these riveting case studies of decolonization mean for institution-wide change? That is the subject of the next and final chapter.

8 | How Does a Radical Curriculum Idea Travel through Institutional Life?

New Insights into the Politics of Knowledge

8.1 Introduction

When decolonization advanced onto South African university campuses in 2015, it appeared that all the conditions were in place for a rapid uptake of its core demands. Propelled by two powerful ideas (both a free and decolonized education), the decolonization moment enjoyed considerable support among academics on the different campuses. The executives of universities responded with unusual alacrity, setting up tasks teams to advise on the implementation of decolonization. Financial resources were released to support seminars, symposia, and conferences on the subject. Academic senates were charged with oversight of the decolonization project.

Several universities made "decolonization" a part of their curriculum monitoring reviews and even a component of individual performance assessments. Major funding came from outside the universities to enable decolonization, such as a generous multi-university, multi-year grant from the Mellon Foundation. Students at the different universities organized themselves in reading groups and brought in prominent authorities on decoloniality to address them.

Five years later, what can be said to have happened? In this book we have traced the complex path of a potentially radical curriculum idea, decolonization, through the university *as an institution*. What did institutions do and how did they behave when decolonization came knocking on the door?

In this final chapter we synthesize the key findings from the study, interpret those findings through the lens of institutional theory, and draw out some of the implications of this research for radical curriculum change in higher education institutions beyond the South African case.

8.2 Making Sense of the Institutional Response to Radical Curriculum Ideas

We start by re-presenting seven different but interconnected ways in which institutions responded to decolonization as a radical idea for curriculum change.

8.2.1 Posturing as a Response to Radical Ideas

Decolonization arrived on campuses not with the patient logic of persuasion but as a set of pressing political demands calling for immediate institutional attention. Those demands were experienced by university leaders and academics as strident, assertive, and sometimes threatening to ordinary campus citizens. The decolonization moment was further buoyed by a strong moral discourse that called on institutions to respond as a matter of urgency. Confronted by student revolt, the reactive responses of the sampled universities took the form of *institutional posturing* – that is, a set of stopgap decisions made in response to immense institutional pressures that nevertheless remains "non-committal in the long term" (Anderson 2018).

Of all the protest actions, nothing concentrated the minds of university executives more than the very public toppling of the heavy bronze statue of the imperialist Cecil John Rhodes from a prominent place on the upper campus of the University of Cape Town. As statues were being defaced, artworks destroyed, and buildings set alight on several campuses, the demands for "a free, decolonized education" compelled university leaders into action.

It was important for university heads to be seen to be doing something in response to these incessant pressures from protestors once the demands for a decolonized education (since April 2015) and free higher education (since October 2015) were rolled into one. The hastily instituted *task team* became the primary vehicle for carrying the institutional response under the authority of the highest academic body of a university, the Senate.

On every campus, decolonization debates, seminars, workshops, symposia, and conferences ignited an intense and exciting intellectual ferment around the idea of decolonization – why it is necessary, what it should replace, and, on occasion, how it should be done. On many campuses, there were occasional tense standoffs between concerned academics and student protestors on issues such as the universality of scientific knowledge or the place of white scholars in the South African academy. At the height of the protests, the radical idea of decolonization came to enjoy unprecedented attention on the learning commons of each university (Chapter 2).

The task teams took themselves seriously. They engaged students and academics. They attended faculty board meetings and open seminars on decolonization. They read or reread the major theorists on the subject. They prepared their final reports and handed them over to senior management, senates, and councils; sometimes those reports, in whole or in part, were placed on institutional websites "for comment." In all cases, university leadership released the reports to faculties for implementation. The radical idea for the decolonization of curriculum was then in the hands of the academics.

Institutions, in short, responded with considerable energy and commitment under pressure for change. Initial, if somewhat superficial, assessments confirm the more substantive findings of this multi-year study: that there was little concrete take-up of decolonization in the form of radical curriculum change (Hendricks 2018; see also Vandeyar 2020). What we call institutional posturing, other studies refer to as "decolonial-washing" (Le Grange et al. 2020). Institutions did much more than posture publicly in the face of pressure for decolonization, however: They tried to take the very sting out of this radical idea.

8.2.2 Diluting the Meaning of Radical Ideas

It became clear from the very start that the idea of decolonization would falter in the hands of the academic teachers. While diverse and nuanced understandings of social science concepts are not at all unusual in the academic world, this moment was different because of the political urgency that pushed the idea of decolonization.

But what does decolonization mean? Without having some fix on the meaning of this political idea, how could academics know how to "implement" it in quantum mechanics, immunology, or econometrics? There was more than a little anxiety among academic teachers who understood the importance of the decolonization moment and did not want to appear to be unresponsive to the political charge. Yet they struggled with the reality of Gary Howard's (2016) concession that "We can't teach what we don't know."

But no manual of meanings was available, nor any operational guidance given to those who taught across the range of fields and disciplines that constitute the curriculum of the modern university. Some academic teachers, in their enthusiasm to become part of the political moment, did not pause to reflect at all, revealing in some institutions "the oddity ... of intellectuals stressing the importance of 'decolonising' higher education before discussions on what it really means" (Long 2021, 91).

As a result, in the space that opened up, academics made up their own meanings for decolonization (Chapter 4). Some took the idea of decolonization simply to mean good teaching practices, and others the use of local, African examples in the curriculum; not a few assumed that a pedagogy of remediation satisfied the demands of a decolonial curriculum. It was in making such calculations that the political meanings of decolonization as a radical intervention in the institutional curriculum were diluted (Chapter 3).

These watered-down meanings of decolonization meant not only the affirmation of mainstream curriculum ideas, such as remediation, but even the entrenchment of the positions of conventional academic teachers. Here, indeed, "The radical imagination [was] stunted and diluted in those who enjoy the greatest privileges" (Khasnabish and Haiven 2014).

To be sure, some of the radical seed fell on fertile ground, and there were academics on all the campuses that interpreted decolonization to mean one or other form of critical pedagogy, in which questions of power, privilege, inequality, and justice could be taken up in the curricula of the different disciplines (Chapters 6 and 7). This is where the political meanings of the idea of decolonization found their most productive expression.

The problem was that these allied curricula shared two essential features. First, such radical initiatives existed on the margins of institutional life as enclave curricula – that is, they did not penetrate the mainstream curriculum of the university. Second, most radical curricula existed prior to the coming of the decolonization moment, even as their academic teachers welcomed the new political movement. These more critical academic teachers believed they were already "doing decolonization," even if they did not necessarily use the term.

While the decolonization of knowledge as a radical idea found ready attachment to allied curricula in the various universities, how did it fare within the university as a whole? This study found that from the moment the senior leadership of universities handed over task team reports or managerial directives to the faculties, the fate of decolonization as a radical curriculum idea was sealed – "devolved to those who [had] no vested stake in seeing it to its logical conclusion," as a Curriculum Task Team leader at a Johannesburg university emphasized (Hendricks 2018, 34).

In every institutional account of the fate of this radical idea, the political energy that came with the decolonization moment gradually lost steam as the incentive for fundamental changes to curricula passed. Put differently, as the political pressure for immediate change subsided, institutions returned to the steady-state curriculum, now subjected only to those routines of incremental, cyclical curriculum reforms found in any university.

This does not mean that the demand for radical curriculum change did not leave some trace in institutional practice. Across the ten universities, academics shared singular examples of changes made here or there to their curricula, from using rands instead of dollars in commerce lessons, to implementing flexible timetables with adjusted content for commuter students, to including an African text in a course.

But these dilutionary examples stand out precisely because, in universities as a whole, there was little evidence of fundamental changes to the institutional curriculum. Universities didn't just passively accommodate radical curriculum initiatives on the margins of institutional life, though; first they tried to institutionalize them.

8.2.3 *Bureaucratizing Radical Curriculum Ideas*

Even as the political press for decolonization commanded the attention of university management, the first steps towards institutional containment were being put in place. University managers, through human resources (HR) departments on several campuses, revised their performance management policies to take account of compliance with the new decolonization imperatives of the institutions.

By making a political demand for curriculum change part of the institutional routines of performance appraisal, the "box ticking" that followed meant the normalization of the radical project. "Decolonisation is not about ticking a box: It must disrupt," bemoaned the activist Foluke Adebisi (2020) in an Issue of *University*

World News. Indeed, one academic after another regarded this administrative move depressurizing the political moment of the moment while appearing to incorporate the student demands for radical change. Sometimes the managerial directives bordered on the comical, as in this puzzling instruction from the top at North West University: "A decolonized curriculum should be implemented in quotas of 5%, increasing annually" (Le Grange et al. 2020, 34).

Invariably, the indication of compliance was read as a sign that academics were *doing* decolonization. Where academics did comply, it was more likely to be superficial, in the form of tinkering with a reading list, or the addition of a localized topic, or the offering of tutorials in an African language. Such signalling of compliance was not immaterial; academics reported that their salary increases or promotions depended on affirmative responses to such institutional performance assessments.

In addition to summative decisions about individual performance, academics were also routinely asked to indicate whether they had decolonized their curricula in the course of the academic year. The University of Johannesburg was particularly energetic with such monitoring of curriculum behaviour; academics there, under pressure, would submit positive responses about mostly superficial changes, if any changes at all.

Other institutions, such as Stellenbosch University, included in their long checklists for the review and approval of new academic programmes an optional indication as to whether the curriculum being submitted showed any evidence of decolonization. This item was not required, nor was it critical to the approvals process. On the other hand, it could be referenced in management controls as indicating institutional responsiveness to the political pressure for the decolonization of the curriculum (see Chapter 3).

As the political demands for radical change started to subside, and as students returned to classes and academics to their teaching, pre-protest curriculum routines and regularities began to settle back into place. At the University of Pretoria, the teaching and learning reports once again spotlighted its longstanding focus on *educational innovation*,[1] with only a few lines signalling decolonizing efforts in one or another faculty.

---

[1] The designation of the University of Pretoria students as "the innovation generation" was a project initiated by its eleventh Rector, Calie Pistorius, at the start of his term in 2001.

At Wits University, deans continued to report on the nine-point transformation plan as before the protests, all duly recorded in meeting minutes. It was, to return to Sarah Ahmed's memorable phrase, "institutional-as-usual," except, of course, for curricula that threatened to disturb the epistemological peace.

8.2.4 Disciplining Intruder Knowledge

The break-out curricula on the margins of institutional life – or outside of them, as in the case of the decolonization of the ICT curriculum at Nelson Mandela University – could be contained, even celebrated, because they hardly constituted a threat to the institutional curriculum. One spanner in the works was the Cuban medical education curriculum, which, as recounted earlier, presented the most dramatic case yet of the disciplining of a radical idea within South African universities.

We use the word *disciplining* to refer to a particular mode of institutionalization, in which external (intruder) knowledge is made subject to the dominant and accepted disciplinary orientation towards specialist knowledge – in this example, medical education. The word discipline carries a useful double meaning in this context – both as the verb meaning "to bring under control," and, of course, the noun signifying the specialist knowledge of a field of study.

The South African medical students returning from training in Cuba were literally re-trained and re-oriented from a primary health care (PHC) orientation to make them fit into the medical education curriculum of their home universities. This was much more than a case of transitioning from a Spanish-language education to an English curriculum; rather, it was one of reorienting the very radical ideas (PHC) that had shaped their knowledge and skills towards the cure-based, first-world medical model of health care to which South African education still subscribes. A senior professor of medicine, and now Dean of Health Sciences at one of South Africa's top universities, described the institutionalization of the returning Cuba medical students this way:

For the Cubans, their health system is a profoundly decolonizing experience. The Cuban training project has brought out tensions for us, because for all of us, we've actually turned them into a local graduate. We're literally feeding them into our product, which is a problem because they're coming in the final year. So, they lose much of their sense of primary care. When you speak to them, they don't believe what just happened.

Part of the problem, as this medical science scholar explained, is that the institutional measures of accomplishment value the status quo:

We judge success by the number of specialists we produce, but actually the successful ones are those who have gone into [rural] primary care clinics, like Mbombela, where the guy who runs the clinic is a Cuban-trained graduate; the one who runs the Pomeroy healthcare clinic is also a Cuban-trained graduate.[2]

Yet even the mainstream students, in their classes during the final year of re-orientation, bought into distinctions between the "superior" Western-oriented model of medicine, in which they had been trained, and that of the returning Cuban-trained students:

That they have gone to these marginal places [in rural South Africa] is part of that re-gearing or re-engineering process. Yet they have always been marginalized in our classrooms. For our [traditional] students, the better they did, they less they wanted to be identified with those students on the Cuban program.

All of this put enormous pressure on the returning students:

The truth is their transition into our cure-based system is really hard. In Cuba, they never see a malnourished kid. They don't see TB in a regular ward because their system works to eradicate these things.

It was not simply the re-training of the Cuban-South African medical students that sought to induct them into a cure-based system; it was their very socialization in traditional medical schools, which "turned them inside out," with all the disorientation that followed. At the same time, how they were treated by regular students was a powerful social signifier as to what was acceptable knowledge in medical school education.

The senior officials in the government's Department of Health responsible for the Cuban programme were acutely aware of the institutionalization of the returning students, with their primary health care orientation:

That criticism is valid, indeed; we're aware of it. It's just a matter of trying to change old habits. Professionals and academics are very difficult to adapt to change.

---

[2] Mbombela is a city in the largely rural Mpumalanga province while Pomeroy is a small town in KwaZulu Natal province.

As the number of returning medical students increased from a small number of 50–60 to about 700 graduates, it was hoped that the sheer force of numbers would impact positively on the Western-oriented curriculum, but that did not happen, according to a senior health department appointee:

The colonized method of training doctors in South Africa was so intense that there is still the sense that the Cuban training is secondary or inferior. I do have a sense that not enough of that transformation is taking place as far as decolonizing the medical curriculum is concerned.

Another official remembered the strong criticism from one of the students that their training on return to South Africa "undermined what they had learned in Cuba," and that "the follow-through into the health system was not in line with transformation; it was curative rather than preventative." In the end, it had to be conceded that "the integration period of 18 months was intended to fit [the students] into the set-up of the South African health system."

If the institutionalization of radical ideas, such as decolonization, was one way of disciplining intruder knowledge, then much more routine mechanisms were in place to contain such proposals from being made in the first place. This is the elaborate apparatus for the regulation of new ideas.

8.2.5 *Regulating Radical Ideas*

It would be a mistake to read the processes of external and internal regulation of curriculum ideas on their own terms, that is, that regulation is merely about setting standards, assuring quality, or ensuring articulation. Regulation is, in the first instance, about control (see Blackmur 2007). It lodges the approval process within a central authority that sets the terms for what counts as acceptable knowledge within the curriculum. The immediate point of leverage for such control over knowledge might be located within national borders, but that power is given its legitimacy by international authorities in disciplines ranging from accounting to engineering (see Chapter 5).

The outer face of control might be lodged in rational, even reasonable, logics, such as curriculum standardization or international comparability. However, that façade of rationality comes apart when a radical proposal throws the proverbial spanner in the works, as seen in the case of the Cuban medical education curriculum. The radical idea needed to be institutionalized and disciplined for "those who are *out-of-procedure*" (Aparna and Kramsch 2018, 135). The way that regulators do this is to impose on institutions a particular mode of response that keeps them *in-procedure*, so to speak; as a former senior official from the CHE recalls, "Given the possible outcomes of accreditation (including 'no accreditation') ... institutions would in most cases [act in] compliance with the minimum standards [rather than through] critical engagement with the curriculum" (Lange 2017, 46).

However, the regulatory control over curriculum and qualifications never goes uncontested (Habib and Patel 2020). The long-simmering contests over who controls professional knowledge and its validation are, for example, a constant source of tension between the Council on Higher Education (CHE) and the accounting regulator (SAICE). It is in many ways an unresolvable conflict, because its resolution would require that one of the two parties gave up power, and therefore control, over professional knowledge in a particular industry.

Such contestation also involves the chief accrediting agency (CHE) and the universities themselves. In 2020, for example, the outspoken Vice-Chancellor of Wits University, and former chairperson of an association of university heads (Universities South Africa, or USAf), made a public case for the established research universities to be given the authority to approve their own curricula. The key argument was that the CHE was part of "a failing regulatory system" as one of the "moribund regulatory agencies" weighed down by "cumbersome administrative procedures and budgetary constraints" that slowed down the approval of online programmes as an urgent response to the pandemic lockdown (Habib and Patel 2020).

That did not sit well with the accrediting authority, which released an acid rebuke of the criticism – "we are not moribund" – even as it conceded that institutions could in the future "conduct their own external peer review process of new and existing qualifications and programmes." At the same time, the CHE would retain for itself the authority to "assess the rigour of the internal quality assurance mechanisms of the institutions" and "to recommend the accredited qualifications to the education department and qualifications authority for registration" (Mosia 2020). In other words, the CHE intended to keep regulatory control, even as it agreed to cede administrative functions to higher education institutions in the future.

What is one to make of these contestations among agencies tied up interminably by Gulliver's regulatory strings? Our thesis is that regulatory agencies are in fact doing their job; that regulation is, in essence, about slowing things down. As Gruenspecht and Lave (1989) explain, "Regulation might be thought of as imposing a vast amount of inertia" by requiring innovative projects to convince them of the need for change; this is even more the case, we would argue, for radical curriculum change endeavours.

Whether it is intended to or not, regulation creates complex processes of administrative review that stretch over several agencies, each with particular functions that require *compliance* with mandated standards. To complain that the regulatory authority is moribund, that its approval processes are cumbersome, that its administrative processes are complex, is to miss the point. Regulatory slowdown is a matter of conscious design, or, as Sarah Ahmed (2017) put it, "blockage is how the system works."

Therefore, when the regulator responds that "if only" it had more resources, more staff, or more time, then processes would be smoother or approvals delivered faster, the simple question to ask is: Why has that logical and reasonable expression of material need never been resolved?

With thousands of new programmes to approve – even before the pandemic-enforced lockdown of 2020 forced a shift to online learning – there is no guarantee that simply increasing funding would resolve the problem. The complex regulatory design could be fixed, such as by giving accreditation functions to an independent outside body or to the institutions themselves, but that would defeat the underlying purpose of regulation – *control*.

In the context of the political press for decolonization, as in the case of institutional demands for the urgent approval of online learning programmes, the regulatory apparatus is simply not geared for rapid decision-making.

This has three implications for *radical* change. First, that fundamental curriculum change, driven by the urgencies of the moment, will simply not be reviewed or approved quickly enough to satisfy political demands. Second, that if it requires regulatory approval, radical curriculum change will simply be deflated, given the passage of time required for approvals. And third, that the choice activists for a decolonized curriculum are therefore left with is either advancing less ambitious change *within* an already approved programme of study or pursuing radical ideas on an extracurricular basis.

It follows that understanding institutional behaviour is critical for the prospects of radical curriculum change. And yet, as demonstrated, institutions basically rode out the wave of radical protests, so that when the protests subsided, the interest and energy of the senior leadership of universities did too. In short, there was no longer any pressure for immediate change.

This study also revealed something crucial about the nature and work of regulatory agencies. Regulator logics are inherently at odds with activist logics when it comes to the project of radical curriculum change. Regulators demand compliance; activists require disruption. Agencies press for standardization; activists demand deviation from the established curriculum. The accreditation agencies seek their legitimation through benchmarking against international, mainly Western, norms; the curriculum activists seek the displacement of long-established and dominant norms in favour of African-centred epistemologies. Regulators define standards in relation to the conservation of professional norms; activists question the validity of those standards in the first place.

In view of this regulatory context, it is difficult to share the optimistic expectations of political activists as they sought to press home the quest for the decolonization of the curriculum. Unless, of course, radical curriculum ideas could be adopted, but kept in their place at the same time.

8.2.6 *Marginalizing Radical Initiatives*

Even as enclave curricula sit on the margins of institutional life, they reveal much about *how* institutions manage radical curriculum change, wherever they might sprout. Recall that enclave curricula have succeeded because they were introduced gradually into institutional life over long periods of time preceding the dramatic rupture of the 2015–2016 protest movement. In the inception years, there certainly was resistance from within and outside of the academic departments (think of the earlier case of archaeology at UP and the more recent one of psychology at Rhodes); but such enclave curricula were contained on the margins of institutional life.

We found that enclave curricula are invariably tied to the energy and idealism of individual scholars, some of whom attempt to recruit a broader group of academics behind ambitious projects, as in the case of philosophy at UP or the core curriculum for engineering at Wits.

Unless they are required courses in compulsory core curricula, radical offerings often fail to attract student numbers, as in the case of Shadreck Chirikure's inventive African archaeology programme at UCT (see Chapter 3); student numbers are low not because the subject is not riveting but because the institutional conditions for participation constrain enrolments for students outside of the department or the faculty concerned. Fewer students mean less funding, and less funding puts pressure on radical curricula, in terms of what institutions under "the managerial turn" in universities call *sustainability*.

Parenthetically, it is well-documented that radical programmes have a long history of marginalization within higher education institutions, both in South Africa and across the world (Marchbank 2009; Martin 2011; Byrne 2017). The most prominent examples of institutional marginalization are "centres" for African Studies, Gender Studies, or AIDS advocacy and research units. These centres typically struggle for financial survival because, unlike mainstream academic departments, their existence depends on raising external funding; their student numbers are typically small; and their staff exist precariously on contract positions. Given their marginal status, such radical or out-of-the-ordinary programmes can relatively easily be closed, stripped down, or simply incorporated within a traditional department. And while the leaders of such centres make constant appeals for the taking up of their curricula within the disciplines and departments, this seldom happens without the initiative of a supportive dean or head of department somewhere in the institution.

The marginal status of radical curricula merely underlines the fact that the institutional curriculum is solidly in place, while a radical disciplinary curriculum remains vulnerable to reversals, given the uncertainties about available expertise to teach inside the new vision. In fact, since most of the enclave curricula exist only because of the initiative and drive of certain *individual* academics, it is quite likely that they will be discontinued when key members of staff leave their institutions.

Enclave curricula stand out precisely because they are exceptional, rather than the norm within the curriculum establishment of universities. They are permitted to exist because they do not threaten the mainstream curriculum in, say, physics or media studies or occupational therapy. They might even enjoy a degree of institutional support for some time – yet, it has been correctly observed of institutions that they are

like a homeostatic system that responds to certain kinds of change with built-in mechanisms that restore certain parts of the status quo ... It allows for some hotter or cooler temperatures for a while, but after a time regresses automatically to where it was set. (Quoted in Soudien 2019, 148)

Radical enclaves exist, moreover, because of the liberal degrees of autonomy afforded to academics in South Africa to design and teach their own curricula, within limits, of course, as in the case of professional qualifications. Which raises the question: Why do more academics not take up the radical idea of decolonization within the autonomous spaces provided in higher education institutions?

8.2.7 Domesticating Radical Ideas

We found that most academics cannot, as a matter of *capacity*, and would not, as a matter of *ideology*, take up decolonization within their curricula. These dual factors hold direct consequences for what we call the domestication of decolonization, that is, the institutional taming of radical ideas to comport with the mainstream curriculum. How does the domestication of decolonization happen?

8.2.7.1 The Problem of Capacity

It was perhaps the single greatest flaw in the political strategy of the decolonization activists to believe that simply announcing the coming of a radical curriculum idea means that there is the capacity to take it up (see Jansen 2009; Vandeyar 2020). Modiri (2020, 158) writes of a large group of academics without "the training, the will or imagination to radically refigure the knowledge archive in a way that would initiate a conceptual decolonisation of the disciplines."

It certainly did not help that the press to decolonize the curriculum was often presented in the most abstract, arcane, and even alienating language of the high humanities. The primary articulators of the idea might well have done the critical readings and grasped the important concepts – but they confused most academics, who had never heard of concepts like *decoloniality* or *epistemicide*, and whose attempts to grapple with the often-abstruse writings of social theorists were even more bewildering.

This language of the high humanities, when applied to decolonization, was mostly furious, with ample references that alienated and intimidated in equal measure. Terms and phrases such as epistemic injustice, the ego-politics of knowledge, or disciplinary colonization were wielded as a superior language of analysis, for which the Latin American theorists of decolonization were the main culprits (see, for example, Grosfoguel 2012). Things could have been stated simply, with accessibility and education in mind; but these terms, as deployed on South African university campuses, at once created distance and instilled fear.

If academics in the mainstream humanities and social sciences were sometimes confounded by this pressing language of decolonization, those in the sciences, commerce, medicine, and engineering were left completely stranded inside a decolonial Tower of Babel. For many of these academics, alienated from a militant political discourse, as they experienced it, such language caused irritation and anger.

Even those with a sympathetic ear for the injustices experienced by, especially, black students could not understand what the appropriate *curricular* response might be, since they had no capacity within themselves to understand, and therefore address, such concerns *as a knowledge problem*. And so, academics did what they could under the pressurized circumstances – to make sense of the protestor complaints within the capacities which they *did* own, such as the ability to take remedial actions in the discipline.

As already described, academics' *interpretations* of decolonization aligned with their own professional needs and identities, which, in most cases, meant the depoliticization of a radical concept. Decolonization as remediation was already familiar from the academic development initiatives of South African universities, premised as they were on bridging the gap between the knowledge imparted by a poor school education and that required for success in an elite university.

This was something science and engineering academics could actually do – and thereby satisfy themselves that they were being responsive to the demands of decolonization. Such remedying interventions included the use of an African example; more connected teaching; better scheduling of examinations for off-campus or commuter students; fairer assessments; tutorships in local African languages; and accessible translations of key terms in second or third languages – good teaching, on the one hand, but also manageable demands on academics, on the other.

In the process, decolonization was tamed and lost its more radical ambitions: questioning knowledge itself, and its (western) origins, (white) authorship, (unequal) distribution, (derisive) content, and (disparate) outcomes. Thus, domestication meant that the fundamental concerns of decolonization as a radical idea – "a forensic understanding and critique of where, how, why and by whom 'legitimate' knowledge is produced" (Saini and Begum 2020) – was defanged. Instead of a politics of knowledge applied to the analysis of the curriculum, these remedial interpretations sustained a salvationist approach to students, in which the goal was their successful induction into academic knowledge as it already existed.

8.2.7.2 The Problem of Ideology

It was, however, not simply limited capacity that made it hard for academics to deal with the politics of decolonization but also a question of *ideology* – that deeper set of emotional attachments to, and political beliefs about, the knowledge that was being challenged. Capacity can be *expanded* through training; ideological commitments, on the other hand, do not simply give way in response to political dictation. Ideological commitments, often disguised as reasonableness, were expressed in two ways in the interviews conducted for this study.

On the one hand, challenges to deeply held beliefs about the nature of knowledge at its core evoked the ire of academic scientists. The investigatory questions of scientific inquiry, argued the famed mathematician George Ellis at UCT, are "hard questions with yes or no answers that are unaffected by political or social considerations," and "either we teach competent courses in these areas, and give the students a degree that makes them employable (and useful to the country), or we do not" (Ellis 2018). At stake were the universal laws of science, the scientific method, and the question of evidence. While Ellis' response was considered and laid out in extensive arguments for public debate, more common responses from academics were dismissive (like "an atom is an atom") or outrightly racist (as in comments about "returning to huts and caves").

The decolonization activists failed to engage these criticisms in a systematic manner. In the heat of battle, the ideological commitments of traditional scientists were either ignored or scorned. Those in the humanities and social sciences, often more familiar with critical discourses in their fields, made little effort towards dialogue and engagement with colleagues in science and engineering, with the result that ideological divisions about science, knowledge, and society became unbridgeable.

One reason for this lack of engagement might well have been the incompetence felt among progressive academics to engage scientists in fields about which they knew little; few South African academics are trained across disciplines in areas such as the social study of science (see, for example, Green 2020) or the medical humanities.[3] Another reason seemed to be the political arrogance of those schooled in the high humanities; their position seemed to be that "it is *your* problem if you do not understand the political cause." Of such attitudes, scholars of decolonization warn that "decolonisation approaches may be less generative when they lead to entrenched dogmatism or self-righteousness" (Stein et al. 2021, 63).

One attempt from our sample of enclave curricula to try to bridge this divide between academic scientists and political activists came from the polymer science research group at Stellenbosch University (see Chapter 7). Their starting point was that each side brings a valued perspective to the knowledge problem and that there were grounds for dialogue that could reconcile the social and the scientific, provided each group appreciated the insight and perspective of the other side. In creating such neutral ground for dialogic engagement between the scientific and the social, the polymer science group was able to create a safe space for difficult conversations.

However, in doing so, this approach yielded too much ground, from the perspective of those seeking a more radical curriculum change in the sciences. Such a conceptual model for understanding the science–society divide is very different from a radical politics of knowledge that demands that the curriculum deal decisively with the sticky issues of power, authority, identity, and inequality (see, for example, Harding 2011).

The problem, however, was not simply such standard beliefs about the nature of science. It was also ideological beliefs about one's place in

---

[3] Initiated by Catherine Burns, the Medical Humanities programme at the Wits Institute for Social and Economic Research (WISER) at the University of the Witwatersrand is the most prominent example of a concentrated research programme in this interdisciplinary area.

society – in this case, post-apartheid South Africa. By describing contemporary South African society as "colonial" by nature, and academic teachers as complicit in the colonial enterprise – one dean at Nelson Mandela University, a black woman scholar, struggled to deal with being called "a colonial administrator" – the activists were challenging the very identity of, especially, white academics. More than that, their right to teach was itself being questioned by the more radical advocates of decolonization for whom *whites* and *whiteness* were part of the problem.

The academic activist Joel Modiri (2020, 158) is not alone in arguing that "the call for decolonisation raises not only intellectual but also specific existential questions for white South African academics" and cautioning against "surrendering the struggle for intellectual sovereignty to beneficiaries of colonialism and apartheid."

Throughout our interviews with white academics, including those at the traditionally liberal universities, the question of their race and relevance were received with considerable discomfort. They seemed to wonder: Are they saying that I do not belong here? An existential angst brooded over the decolonization moment.

Such decentring of white authority was by no means a majority goal among activists, but it was there, chipping away at academic insecurities, and exposing vulnerabilities among white academics. Emotions ran high in these moments, especially in public forums. The anxiety felt among many white academics was real and deep, expressed in various places with responses that ranged from self-questioning to outrage. This is a composite sketch of those responses:

We are South Africans, all of us. We are not colonials; my ancestors (the Afrikaners) fought against the British, the real colonizers. I have taught you as my students for years and this never came up. I received rewards for my teaching and now I am told it is not good enough, that I do not belong here.

In this context, another take on decolonization found traction among disoriented academics, and that was to disfigure the radical idea into some form of indigeneity or indigenous knowledge. A prime example of such domestication is the edited collection *The Decolonization of the Curriculum Project: The Affordances of Indigenous Knowledge for Self-Directed Learning* (Bester, Bailey, and de Beer 2019). On its cover is the apartheid bushman, now known as the San. The volume's authors, mainly from the historically white Afrikaans universities, write with condescension and paternalism about indigenous actors and constantly draw firm distinctions between Western knowledge (the individualistic knowledge philosophy they attribute to North West University) and indigenous knowledge (the "relational ontology" they see in the San Code of Research Ethics [South African San Institute 2017]).

Indigeneity, in advanced fields such as ethnobotany or ethnomathematics, is a seductive interpretation of decolonization, given the obvious need to recognize, in a more emancipatory context, the suppression of prior knowledge. This, however, is something else – the *continuation* of an apartheid epistemology that lays emphasis on the "ethno" – the racial and ethnic *differences* in the cultural production of knowledge, as distinct from white knowledge. In these accounts, white knowledge is presented as advanced, and indigenous knowledge exists in primitive, unsophisticated forms.

Furthermore, there is no reference in these stories to the suppression of indigenous people (let alone earlier genocides) or to the exploitation of their knowledge (such as the San deployed by military intelligence under apartheid [Gordon 1982, 1987]) or the indigenous properties of white knowledge or the common bonds of knowledge that exist *across* racial and ethnic divides.

What you have, instead, is a gross romanticization of indigenous knowledge outside of critical readings of their racialized histories, politics, economics, and anthropologies that subjugated first peoples. For Choat (2021), "domesticating decolonisation" is what happens when guilt is relieved, complicity disavowed, and power relations remain unaddressed (see also Tuck and Yang 2012).

In summary, in tracking the course of a radical idea through institutional life, we found that *decolonization is interpreted*, rather than simply implemented (or not), an observation not unfamiliar to curriculum theory. What we additionally found, however, was that such interpretation takes various forms and directions depending on the capacities and ideologies of academic teachers.

This has significant implications for the politics of knowledge and for the project of radical curriculum change. In consequence, the limitations of capacity for radical change and the shaping influences of ideology domesticate the idea of decolonization to comport with settled understandings of knowledge – as in the revealing case of the institutional treatment of indigenous knowledge in accordance with its apartheid meanings.

8.3 Happens When Curriculum Theory Meets Institutional Theory?

It is our thesis that decolonization as a radical proposal for change has to come to terms with not only the behaviour of social actors within universities but also with the *institution* of higher education itself. After all, what the decolonization activists were demanding was not changes on the fringes of universities as organizations but deep changes in the very institutional fabric of higher education. "Fundamental change," observed the philosopher of organizations Leonard Waks (2007), "is for the most part situated at the institutional [rather than organizational] level." What does this mean? That the change being demanded required rethinking established curriculum ideas, norms, and values and the institutional processes (such as regulation) that kept them in place.

That is precisely where this book started, as a potentially productive intellectual meeting place between curriculum theory and institutional theory – two areas of affinity not adequately explored in the scholarship on the politics of knowledge (see Jónasson 2016). We know from curriculum theory that change is difficult, complex, and seldom achieved as intended; that curriculum change in practice is never a mirror image of official policy expectations; that an "ingredients approach" (simply add more, such as resources, personnel, time, etc.) to curriculum change is flawed; that curriculum change is invariably a political process, in which conflicting interests together shape curriculum outcomes; that curriculum ideals are *interpreted* by human actors rather than simply *implemented* in mechanical form; and that any curriculum change, even when it fails, leaves a mark in educational practice (Cuban 1998; Priestley 2011; Lange 2017; Nordin and Sundberg 2018).

What mainstream curriculum theory cannot adequately account for, however, is the behaviour of *institutions* as an explanation for curriculum stasis. Until now, there have been few studies that have focused systematically on how institutions deal with radical ideas for curriculum change. What does institutional theory help us understand about the path of decolonization through universities? More precisely, what did we learn about institutions and radical curriculum change?

We discovered the operations of *institutional intelligence*; that is, in responding to decolonization, institutions deployed a range of tactics to manage and diffuse a political crisis, namely, posturing, diluting, bureaucratizing, disciplining, regulating, marginalizing, and domesticating the radical curriculum idea. The net result of these institutional processes was to contain radical change that challenged established ideas, norms, and values that underpin and give expression to the institutional curriculum.

Institutions, we confirmed, punish deviance or disruption to the settled curriculum (see Crawford and Dacin 2020). The Cuban medical school curriculum, with its emphasis on primary health care, threatened to "transform the curriculum, decolonizing medical training in the country," according to the most senior government official in the Department of Health when we interviewed him. But this did not happen. Rather, the returning students were absorbed into medical schools and, according to one dean, "we kind of tried to turn them into a South African student." In terms of institutional theory, the students and their curriculum were mainstreamed (disciplined) and the external threat stabilized through the content taught and the assessments conducted during the reintegration period.

At the same time, institutions can simply ignore potential threats to the established curriculum, as happened with the *institutional* review of the LLB degree, the standard four-year training qualification for law students. An activist grouping within the peer review mechanism demanded that the curriculum be built around the radical concept of transformative constitutionalism. The stakes were high, since LLB accreditation might very well depend on compliance with the demand that the concept be "embedded in curricula" and "internalized by students." This was doctrinaire language.

In the end, the LLB review found that few institutions understood, let alone implemented, the required approach. Importantly, there were no consequences for non-compliance, for two related reasons. First, "transformative constitutionalism" was a decidedly partial, if not partisan, perspective on how to interpret the South African Constitution. Second, academic traditions in South Africa afford those who teach considerable autonomy in decisions about what and how to teach, even under managerial directive and emergency conditions (Czerniewicz, Trotter, and Haupt 2019, 13–14).

Beyond the responses of individual law faculties, how could such action be read from the perspective of institutional theory? Higher education institutions are endowed with academic autonomy. Unlike schools, which follow a government-mandated curriculum, universities in South Africa design and deliver their own curricula, within limits.

What this means is that when a radical curriculum idea (such as decolonization) threatens the settled curriculum, institutions respond by defanging the intruder curriculum in the ways already described.

Institutional autonomy is, however, a two-edged sword. On the one hand, autonomy can be invoked *to contain radical ideas*, as in the case of transformative constitutionalism and changes to the LLB curriculum. On the other hand, autonomy can be overridden in order *to entrench mainstream ideas*, as when academics sought the expansion of the health sciences curriculum to include, for example, oral health. In both cases, however, institutional autonomy works to sanction intruder knowledge and sustain the institutional curriculum across universities.

Our study shows that institutions are pliable, and therefore able to endure short-term political shocks. Institutions are more than willing to make short-term adjustments in response to the political pressure for radical curriculum change without fundamentally changing at all. This study was able to show through detailed curriculum analyses what "the latitude and the limits are that we confront if we attempted to change the existing institutional order" (Meyer and Rowan 2006, 4).

Institutions are also patient, capable of waiting out the high point of protests until things settle down. In accordance with the institutional theory literature, we confirmed that institutions are much more concerned about legitimacy than efficiency, and that this explains the extraordinary hold of the regulatory authorities and their conditions on what passes as acceptable or legitimate curriculum knowledge.

Regarding legitimacy, every African institution makes some claim to being "world class," regardless of their status and standing in their own country or in world rankings of universities. South Africa is no exception, and that it why the international validation of degrees matters to both universities and the broader public. Criteria such as the comparability of qualifications and the international recognition of professions matter much more than the political imperatives for curriculum change on demand. By trading on legitimacy, institutions can therefore wait out radical change, because the idea of the university *as it stands* remains both a treasured possession and pursuit of students and academics alike (Czerniewicz, Trotter, and Haupt 2019, 18–19; Long 2021, 93; see also Stein et al. 2021, 57).

Institutions, furthermore, are not all the same, even in the case of universities within one country. The press for decolonization found much more traction in historically white institutions, where the institutional cultures and complexes were experienced as alienating and where physical symbols of whiteness (like statues) provided ready opportunities for political spectacle. By contrast, decolonization found less purchase within historically black institutions, where material needs were primary and where concrete symbols from colonial times were less visible. The politics of knowledge, therefore, was much more evident in the curriculum wars on the former white campuses than at the younger black institutions created in the late 1950s under apartheid.

Institutions have short attention spans. As urgent as the demands for decolonization might have been in the 2015–2016 period, they were quickly displaced as the focus of attention in institutional policy by a return to earlier drivers of change (like educational innovation at University of Pretoria) or new agendas (like 4IR at University of Johannesburg). The student protests were successful in being able to demand, and indeed secure, the attention of institutional leaders, but they were not able to retain this attention as the energy and pressure of the decolonization moment faded into the background.

We also discovered how institutionally embedded actors make sense of radical curriculum change and, in the context of decolonization, "how people actively construct meaning within institutionalized settings through language" (Meyer and Rowan 2006, 6). In other words, radical change is not only what institutions require or demand from academic teachers; it is very much about how those teachers give it meaning within the limits of their capacities and ideologies. The ambiguity of meanings around decolonization provided the space for such divergent interpretations to emerge in the first place.

This study introduced a sustained political analysis of curriculum to institutional theories of education. We went beyond standard conceptual observations of equilibrium or isomorphism to look more closely at the circuitries of power that run through universities as institutions in order to understand curriculum stasis. Those powerful currents are not simply "man-made rules and procedures ... the building blocks of institutions" (Meyer and Rowan 2006, 6) but arrangements that exercise power to retain the settled curriculum, even if there is a tolerance level for enclave curricula on the margins of institutional life. In short, institutions are political agencies and not disembodied, neutral, or apolitical functions within university life.

Institutional norms, values, and interests, we found, are not necessarily disturbed by *structural* transformations in universities. For example, the transition from face-to-face teaching to online learning is a technological shift, not one that fundamentally challenges the politics of knowledge beneath any such change. In fact, more than one curriculum theorist would argue that the shift towards online learning under pandemic conditions entrenched institutional procedures of regulation and control through, for example, more rigid performance management metrics (Le Grange 2020).

In this context, it has been argued that much of the higher education reform undertaken after the end of apartheid was in fact "structural" in orientation – such as the elaborate structure of new qualifications through the National Qualifications Framework – and that it thereby eluded engagement with the politics of knowledge (Lange 2017). In the same vein, the mere expansion of new organizational forms, such as private higher education or homeschooling, hardly makes a crack in the epistemological bedrock of the institutional curriculum. Rather than signal seismic shifts in the politics of knowledge, these structural changes tend to reinforce existing knowledge arrangements and, in countries like South Africa, remain subject to regulatory approvals of the curriculum.

We do not, however, make the claim that nothing has changed in the curriculum as a result of the decolonization moment. There can be no doubt that academic teachers grappled with the meaning of decolonization and, in some cases, made changes to the content and methods of teaching, even if such alterations were often superficial or negligible in relation to the rock-solid institutional curriculum. Even the enclave curricula that represent radical change (see Chapters 6 and 7) were instances of gradual changes over time to the institutional curriculum.

Contrary to positions held by major institutional theories, the typical "exogenous shocks [decolonization, in this case] that bring about radical institutional configurations" (Mahoney and Thelen 2009, 2) were not evident in the historic student movement. With respect to the curriculum of South Africa's public universities, the evidence points, rather, to gradual institutional change reflecting "ongoing struggles within but also over prevailing institutional arrangements" (xi). These endogenous changes are more likely to appear in academic departments where individual academics, with or without allies, might be quietly forging ahead with more radical curriculum changes in the small spaces that institutional autonomy allows.

This gradualist approach to curriculum change is most evident in the case of the development of the core curriculum in engineering at Wits University. It took many years of negotiation across departments within engineering and across faculties in the university. Change stalled, and then took off again, and success was never guaranteed; at some points, the radical project seemed doomed. But with persistent leadership by the dean and other senior colleagues, the core curriculum was eventually adopted. The curriculum change was slow and steady; it stalled, but was eventually secured for implementation. Its origins, though, lay in the pre-2015 period and moved gradually ahead over time.

Based on our data, we would not describe "institutions as drivers of curriculum change" (Nordin and Sundberg 2018, 11). Institutions respond to pressures for change by acting to dilute, domesticate, or simply defy radical ideas, but they do not drive the process of change. Outside of the political pressure to change, institutions change slowly in the normal cycles of curriculum review, seldom confronting the foundations of its regnant epistemologies. The politics of knowledge is therefore left largely undisturbed. What we did find, however, is an extraordinary institutional agility in adapting to change in the face of external political pressures.

At the same time, institutions maintain a significant capacity for enforcing and securing *compliance* whenever there is the threat of curriculum deviance or disruption. We share the perspective that "compliance is built into the definition of the institution" (Mahoney and Thelen 2009, 10). When the political dust settled, radicals, like everyone else, acted compliantly and followed the rules. The costs of non-compliance with curriculum regulation serve as an effective disincentive for radical change – such as the loss of accreditation for a qualification or the loss of enrolments for subsidized funding. For the most part, students and academics play within the institutional rules when demands for radical curriculum change are presented.

An interesting paradox became evident: that even when there is extreme distress expressed about the university as an artefact of the colonial past, the institution itself is embraced. As one observer said of protesting students at UCT, "they can only attack the institutional order, despising it in public yet desiring it in secret" (Long 2021, 93). The same applies to academic teachers, for whom the institution, though mercilessly critiqued, is also a source of recognition and reward, as these advocates of radical reform explain:

Saying that we want something different does not necessarily equate to *wanting* to give up the securities and entitlements that are rooted in systems that maintain the status quo – particularly when those systems offer us the promises of affirmation, leadership, control, comfort, authority ... (Stein et al. 2021, 57)

In short, the possibilities for radical curriculum change are best evaluated through the lens of institutional theory. Institutions constrain radical ideas such as decolonization in the myriad ways we have described. Where radical change infiltrates the institutional curriculum, it is always on the margins and more likely to succeed through small, incremental transformations of knowledge. Even when there is a momentous shift in the external environment – as in the transition from apartheid to democracy – it does not mean that the foundations of curriculum knowledge also change in the process.

As demonstrated in the South African case, there was certainly change in the curriculum exoskeleton after apartheid; the founding of SAQA, the new qualifications authority regime, is a good example that led to thousands of new courses and degrees. But the curriculum endoskeleton, its soft tissue, hardly changed in the years since apartheid. To stretch the metaphor, it could be said that the institutional exoskeleton did its work – protecting inherited knowledge from political injury (Jansen 2009, 174).

What, then, is the contribution of this study to curriculum theory beyond the South African case? As a study in the micropolitics of knowledge, it demonstrates for the first time how radical curriculum change encounters *institutions* and with what consequences for the politics of knowledge.

8.4 What, Then, Are the Prospects for Radical Curriculum Change within Institutions?

In this study, we have made visible the institutional treatment of radical curriculum ideas in everyday academic life. It is not one or two of those responses to decolonization (such as regulation or domestication) that maintains the institutional curriculum; it is the combination of those varied responses that tempers radical change. For example, the immediate-term political management of a radical idea (through posturing, in this case) works in tandem with the longer-term institutional containment of that idea (through marginalization, for example) to maintain the sense of institutional-as-usual when it comes to the curriculum. It is a fair question at this point to ask: Is radical curriculum change even possible within higher education institutions?

More than one voice has raised concerns about the *possibility* of the de-institutionalization of the curriculum. Dalia Gebrial (2018, 41) was not the first to ask whether "the decolonial demand can ever be met within the institution." Others, such as Aparna and Kramsch (2018, 135), writing about the Asylum University experiment in the Netherlands, found that "speaking from the margins gives us power to call attention to the instability and uncertainty of bounded governing structures." The Asylum University is an open, independent, symbolic space that brings together refugees, activists, academics, and others to construct and engage knowledge outside the strictures of the conventional university.

Radical change is clearly possible when there is as yet no institution in place to govern the curriculum; put differently, when the very establishment of an institution is founded on radically different ideas, norms, and values, then fundamental change is within reach. This was the case, for example, with the establishment of the New School for Social Research (NSSR; now known simply as The New School) in 1919 by prominent academics who broke away from the establishment university, Columbia, to install a progressive model of education. The NSSR website records a history in which

... leading intellectuals helped transform the social sciences and philosophy in this country, presenting new theoretical and methodological approaches to their fields ... a school of free inquiry for students and faculty of different ethnicities, religions, and geographical origins who are willing to challenge academic orthodoxy, connect social theory to empirical observation, and take the intellectual and political risks necessary to improve social conditions. (New School for Social Research 2021)

No African university can claim such radical origins. South African universities are creatures of colonialism and apartheid (Mamdani

2019); not only do their institutional foundations rest on colonial origins, but those imperial legacies linger in curriculum traditions such as the predominance of the English language, and British culture and content across the disciplines.

We remain optimistic that change from within institutions is both challenging and possible at the same time. One reason that institutional change has been difficult is because, until know, there has not been a theory of change that starts with an analysis of institutions and how they maintain curriculum stasis.

If the problem is institutions, then clearly "very little change in content will be seen if inertial factors are not recognized" (Jónasson 2016). Our thesis therefore implies that radical change begins with an astute analysis of *institutions*, with the focus on what holds regnant knowledge in place. From this vantage point, we make ten concrete propositions.

First, radical curriculum change is only possible with a comprehensive and long-term *institutional plan* focused not simply on department- or faculty-level interventions but on the university as a whole. Institutions will outwait and outsmart spontaneous and sporadic acts of political protest. The political spectacle can demand attention, even instil fear, but it cannot begin to disrupt the strong currents of power that run along the circuits of established institutions. It will certainly not disrupt the settled curriculum.

Second, radical curriculum change will not happen without *university leadership* taking responsibility for institution-wide implementation. Left to deans and academics, as we have seen, the charge to take forward radical ideas often dissipates within departments and faculties. If there is not a serious investment in fundamental change at the senior levels of a university, the institutional uptake will be weak, uneven, and mostly non-existent. Whether it is the Vice-Chancellor of the UFS supporting a compulsory curriculum for all first years, or the Dean of Engineering at Wits implementing a core curriculum for all engineering students, or the HOD for Philosophy at UP creating a decolonial curriculum for all philosophy students, *the driver of change is leadership*. The leadership of an institution is the most important point of leverage for radical change.

Third, radical curriculum change across the disciplines requires *a patient, ongoing educational process* with academic teachers from the sciences and engineering to the humanities and social sciences.

Intellectual persuasion is more effective than political demands. The demonstration of curricular exemplars in the sciences or humanities builds conviction more than administrative compliance measures do. Starting with what learners (specialists in the disciplines, in this case) know is an abiding principle in learning – rather than the forceful presentation of abstract ideas from the high humanities.

Fourth, radical curriculum change that is *ideologically doctrinaire* will find itself dead in the institutional waters. Not only is such an approach partial and often preachy, but it also turns off academics, especially if they do not share those perspectives. Fundamental change requires much more than a shift in intellectual beliefs; it must grapple more deeply with the emotional attachments, disciplinary socialization, and professional standing of academics. The most successful curricula with decolonial attachments found in this study are not dogmatic but draw on a range of perspectives and methods, both African and Western, even as they make the case for a radical account of a field, whether it be media studies or polymer chemistry or archaeology.

Fifth, radical curriculum change must deal with students' unequal access to powerful knowledge across the disciplines. White and middle-class students enjoy much higher rates of academic success than poor, Black students; that is why the call from the historically black universities was not for decolonization but for access to the same knowledge as students in the more privileged universities. As one report put it, "For students at Turfloop [the University of Limpopo], decolonized education means getting good-quality education, like that taught at Wits" (Malabela 2017, 113; see also Vilakazi 2017).

This means that a radical approach to curriculum change has to figure out how to reconcile an abstract politics of knowledge (such as expressed in decoloniality) with the hard reality of an unequal distribution of knowledge by race, class, and gender. The proper response to this dilemma is decidedly not "academic development" as a salvationist, or "rescue the perishing," approach to knowledge. It should start with a set of conceptual arguments that recognize that access to powerful knowledge is itself a radical act and not simply a compensatory measure on the part of the institution. The hard intellectual labour on the tension between radical and remedial approaches has not yet been adequately done in the politics of curriculum. Contrast, for example, the intellectually vapid, self-congratulatory writings on the subject by Behari-Leak and Mokou (2019) with the more earnest *institutional* attempts to grapple with the complex subject of academic development in Jonker (2020).

Sixth, the most efficient way of advancing a radical curriculum in the face of institutional inertia is in the form of a compulsory core curriculum for every student. Such a curriculum offers the path of least resistance; it enables its leaders to draw on the best-equipped academic teachers without the need for too much reorientation or training; it can pool the best scholars offering *critical* perspectives on a range of pressing social questions, including decoloniality, ethics, politics, inequality, AI technologies, and climate science; and it involves academic teachers and planners from all the faculties, investing them in the change project. And such an intervention could be generative of new ideas, approaches, and methods within the different departments and faculties on critical studies of knowledge.

Seventh, the long-term basis for infusing radical ideas in the university curriculum is through strategic hires of new faculty. Filling vacancies with more traditional academics means missing the opportunity to bring in critical perspectives across the disciplines. An education faculty might hire an expert on Freierian pedagogy to teach educational foundations, or a science faculty might fill an "introduction to science" lecturer vacancy with an expert in critical studies in the history of science. A medical faculty could consciously introduce an interdisciplinary course in medicine by extending the search to someone from the medical humanities. Where there are ensconced teachers without a sense of "the critical" in such disciplines as, say, thermodynamics or clinical psychology or urban planning, it will be much easier to develop that sense of criticality through the strategic consideration of new hires.

Once again, such a strategic decision will require committed leadership at the level of deans and heads of departments to ensure that such opportunities for new academic appointments are fully realized. Otherwise, the reproduction of the same types of thinkers and the same ideas is likely to follow.

Eighth, radical curriculum change has to challenge the structures and strictures imposed by a convoluted regulatory system. The regulatory apparatus functions to slow things down, frustrate innovation, and sidestep the politics of knowledge, all under the guise of a technocratic neutrality. Regulation is not neutral; it imposes on the system, through measures of compliance, a particular view of knowledge that is technicist, outcomes-based, formulaic, narrowly administrative, and externally validated. There is nothing wrong with a strong technical basis for curriculum evaluation or with international validation for curriculum ideas. We argue, however, that such framing of curricular knowledge prohibits independent professional judgements of worthwhile knowledge that sits outside of official framing and, in the process, curtails radical initiatives that break with convention.

Ninth, radical curriculum change across institutions requires the steady production of Southern scholarship that is substantive and offers new intellectual departures for addressing the post-colonial condition. Much of the South African writing since the decolonization moment of 2015 has been rhetorical, repetitive, rehearsed, and remonstrative. The featured authors of the decolonization genre are mostly dead, important figures of the anti- and postcolonial eras. The living authors of, and works on, decoloniality are marked by anguished repetition, with few new departures for theory and even less for practice. Without African (or Asian, Latin American, etc.) scholars producing leading theoretical and empirical work on decolonization that advances beyond the politics of outrage, the struggle to change institutions will remain stranded on a self-important island of critique.

Finally, radical curriculum change requires critical self-reflection on decolonization's most treasured claims. The stridency of the position in favour of decolonization is not only anti-intellectual but, ironically, it also works against one of its own foundational assumptions – that what is needed is a multiplicity of perspectives on knowledge. This is precisely the kind of reflective analysis that Amy Allen (2016) does in her brilliant unthreading of critical theory, in particular the so-called Frankfurt School, for its silence on the post/colonial condition and its fetishization of European modernity. Unfortunately, when the primary impulse that steers decolonization is brute politics, the chances of an honest and deeper intellectual engagement with the subject are diminished – leaving a poor prognosis for radical change within staid institutions.

8.5 On the Future of Nostalgia, Institutions, and Radical Curriculum Change

South Africa does not represent the classical model of the colonial state. The Dutch and British settlers here became natives. With the formation of the Union in 1910, South Africa became a self-governing dominion with uneasy ties to the colonial authority, and in 1961 it declared itself an independent republic. Just before then, the principal liberation movement, the African National Congress, declared through its Freedom Charter (South African Congress Alliance 1955) that "South Africa belongs to all who live in it, black and white."

There was, of course, pushback against this flattening description of belonging in a country that denied citizenship to the majority of its population. How can one make sense of the South African state? From one perspective, South Africa was described as "colonialism of a special type" (CST), while another formulation held that apartheid was simply "a generic form of the colonial state in Africa" (Mamdani 2019). These analytic efforts notwithstanding, neither CST nor the "generic form" argument carried much weight in the broader public or political consciousness about South African identity.

As a result, in its long history of resistance politics South African activism never raised the language of decolonization. Protests were bannered as anti-apartheid, never anti-colonial. Education activism came with many resistance labels, from alternative education, to anti-apartheid education, education for liberation, and liberation before education. But not decolonization.

It came therefore as a complete surprise that in the 2015 protests *decolonization* was invoked as the language of resistance on campuses around South Africa. We suggest three reasons for this development.

First, decolonization was chosen as the antidote to *transformation*, which had, since the 1990s, become the post-apartheid government's language for change. Despite the promise of transformation, the country was mired in widespread corruption, deepening inequalities, and a very real struggle for affordable access to higher education. Transformation did not crack these problems, and so decolonization became the *language of replacement*.

Second, decolonization, at least in its Latin American iteration as decoloniality, gave activists an undiluted *language of lament*. The world was divided into the evil and the good: the colonizer and the colonized; the Global North and the Global South; the West and the rest of us. Nothing better characterizes this literature than its rehearsal of old laments. Nevertheless, it did provide a hard and uncompromising line of distinctions that served the political cause of the student protest movement. It was as if the lament spoke for itself, "a way of thinking that attributes creative power to mere negation" (Long 2021, 90).

Third, decolonization invoked a *language of nostalgia*, from times when the threat was more tangible (i.e., the colonial government) and the solutions much simpler (i.e., eject the foreign language), as in the 1960s and 1970s. It was not surprising, therefore, that the writings of choice among activist students were those of anti-colonial fighters such as Frantz Fanon, on Algeria, and decolonization activists such as Ngũgĩ wa Thiong'o, from Kenya. That emotional connection to a nostalgic past had to be sustained:

> To maintain fidelity to the great ideals of the anti-colonial wars of resistance and the revolutionary political and intellectual traditions of anti-colonialism and anti-racism ... we must hold to the aporetic promises of decolonisation in its most combative and most capacious imaginings. (Modiri 2020, 172)

What future does nostalgia hold for the goal of radical curriculum change? We argue that the radical project requires a reframing of curriculum change from the limiting language of decolonization to a broadly critical approach to change. In this view, the hard distinctions of North/South or European/African must be regarded as anachronistic for describing cross-border knowledge relationships in the twenty-first century (Jansen 2019).

In addition, the resuscitation of a 1960s dependency-framework view of knowledge and power has two principal limitations. First, it places Africans in the position of perpetual victims. And it misrecognizes the many ways in which research statuses in cross-border collaborations have changed, as detailed elsewhere (Jansen 2019). A reorientation from such a view demands a *decolonization of the mind* by Europeans as much as by Africans. We need to see each other differently, compose our problems collaboratively, and assume authority for research leadership jointly. The fact that money comes primarily from the North (a hard economic reality) should not mean the intellectual subjugation of research or researchers from the South.

This means that African (or Asian, or Latin American) scholars must be much more assertive in this new era and not subject themselves to self-inflicted wounds by using the language of victimhood from a bygone era or the self-defeating language of lament of the decoloniality writers. It requires, as mentioned before, a substantive theoretical and empirical scholarship that emerges from Africa, through the inventive work of African scholars. Remaining in the position of perpetual critics without a foundation of new scholarship across the disciplines locks African academics inside a language of critique – since that is all we have. In the absence of a new and original African scholarship across the disciplines, our students resort to magical thinking in place of science, as in the case of the #ScienceMustFall incident at UCT,[4] and our academics call on widely discredited individuals to debunk the foundations of mathematics, like the Hindu nationalist C. K. Raju (GroundUp 2017a).

But the future of nostalgia also requires a completely different take on the use of misplaced conceptual language. In the heat of political struggle, decolonization in the hands of activists became the proverbial hammer that saw every institutional problem as a colonial nail. Not every problem within institutional life is a simple and lingering legacy of colonial rule. One example must suffice.

Authoritarian pedagogic relationships have their origins in the pre-colonial societies of chiefs and elders, and the status of children as learners. Furthermore, the curriculum in South Africa has been shaped by successive knowledge regimes, including that of the democratic state; it cannot, therefore, be read as nothing more than a reflexive hangover of the imperial order. Such a reading of curriculum change absolves successor regimes of all agency (and responsibility) for both curriculum change and continuity, and that, quite simply, is disingenuous (Jansen 2019).

Another self-defeating move among decolonization activists was its failure to sense the dangerous two-step dance that moved from a radical critique of knowledge to an essentialist understanding of the racial African. On this score, the critical psychologist and keen observer of the decolonization moment Wahbie Long (2021, 21) is worth quoting in full:

The clamour for decolonisation is a necessary attempt at centering the lived experiences of the dispossessed in university curricula, but it threatens also to parochialize higher education with its nativist, anti-humanist and anti-universalist message – at the same time that fascist movements are encouraging an identical mentality in an increasingly polarized world.

---

[4] In October 2017, a UCT student in a panel discussion argued that science was a product of Western modernity and that "Decolonising the science would mean doing away with it entirely and starting all over again to deal with how we respond to the environment and how we understand it." (UCT Scientist 2016)

It is therefore a sad commentary on South African scholars that there was little sustained critical engagement with decolonization as a social science concept when it emerged on the political scene. Such a silent, uncritical disposition might well have been the result of fear, for there was enormous pressure on academics to conform to the new orthodoxy. And that is precisely where the danger lies, for, as Jonathan Rauch (2018) warns in this timely reflection on "The Constitution of Knowledge,"

if universities are rackets, merely imposing some opinions on everyone else or pursuing someone's political agenda, then the constitution of knowledge is a racket, too. If universities foster cultures of conformity rather than of criticism, if they traffic in politicized orthodoxies and secular religions, then the winner is not social justice but trolling. Which is all downside.

Nostalgia has its place in institutional analysis (Foster and Voronov 2015). There is, without doubt, a restorative nostalgia among settled scholars who long for the idealized institutions of their memories as they existed under apartheid. So too, there is a "postcolonial nostalgia," which has caught the attention of recent scholarly analysis about longings for empire, whether in cinematic productions or in the "great again" imagination of Trumpism.

Yet, we seldom give attention to liberation nostalgia, those longings for struggle that emerge from a deep dissatisfaction with contemporary institutions – in this case, institutions of higher education in the post-apartheid period.

It is possible, of course, for a new generation of activists to also long for a struggle they were never a part of, but whose forceful, strident, and history-making wars against colonial rule resonate in the present in the face of obdurate institutions. Glorifying a distant past is, of course, a tricky business, as Jacob Dlamini (2009) explores in his *Native Nostalgia*. And yet, nostalgia can be summoned, even weaponized, as it was when student activists interpreted Fanon as sanctioning violence against institutions. This was a dangerous moment, whose logics were played out in the massive destruction meted out against university properties. Fanonists rushed to explain that this position was a misinterpretation of Fanon on violence (Pithouse 2016), but it was too late. Such was the felt anger against institutions of the democratic state that students believed had failed them.

Emerging from the smoke of the intense student decolonization struggles, ironically, is an expression of faith in institutions, even as

they are attacked. Institutions can and should deliver on the democratic promise; student activists did not abandon them but returned to
them as places of hope.

However, for universities to deliver on the curriculum change
project, a new radicalism is required that takes institutional analysis
seriously as a point of departure for the decolonization of knowledge.
Otherwise, radical curriculum change will fail to deliver on its elevated
political promises.

In South Africa, at least, decolonization of the curriculum did not
fail to be taken up in institutions because it was too radical. The
problem was that it was not radical enough.

References

Abdelnour, Samer, Hans Hasselbladh, and Jannis Kallinikos. 2017. "Agency and Institutions in Organization Studies." *Organization Studies* 38 (12): 1775–1792. https://doi.org/10.1177/0170840617708007.

Achebe, Chinua. 1976. *Morning Yet on Creation Day: Essays*. Garden City, NY: Anchor Press.

Adebisi, Foluke. 2020. "Decolonisation Is not About Ticking a Box: It Must Disrupt." *University World News*, 29 February 2020. www.university worldnews.com/post.php?story=20200227143845107#:~:text=Thus%2C 2C%20decolonisation%20continues%20to%20be,not%20know%20 what%20decolonisation%20means%3F.

Adendorff, Hanelie and Margaret A. L. Blackie. 2020. "Decolonizing the Science Curriculum: When Good Intentions Are Not Enough." In *Building Knowledge in Higher Education: Enhancing Teaching and Learning with Legitimation Code Theory*, edited by Christine Winberg, Sioux McKenna, and Kirstin Wilmot, 237–254. London: Routledge.

Ahmed, Sara. 2012. *On Being Included: Racism and Diversity in Institutional Life*. Durham, NC: Duke University Press.

2017. "The Institutional As Usual: Diversity Work as Data Collection." *feministkilljoys* (blog), 24 October 2017. https://feministkilljoys.com/2017/10/24/institutional-as-usual/.

Allais, Stephanie Matseleng. 2003. "The National Qualifications Framework in South Africa: A Democratic Project Trapped in a Neo-Liberal Paradigm?" Paper presented at RAU Sociology in Development Studies Seminar 2003/6, Rand Afrikaans University, 14 March 2003. https://ccs.ukzn.ac.za/files/allais.pdf.

Allen, Amy. 2016. *The End of Progress: Decolonizing the Normative Foundations of Critical Theory*. New York: Columbia University Press.

Anderson, Deborah A. 2018. "Inflated Accounts: Institutional Posturing by Legitimacy-Constrained Regulators." *Academy of Management Proceedings* 2018 (1). https://doi.org/10.5465/AMBPP.2018.36.

Andrews, Matt, Michael Woolcock, and Lant Pritchett. 2017. *Building State Capability: Evidence, Analysis, Action*. Oxford: Oxford University Press.

Aparna, Kolar and Oliver T. Kramsch. 2018. "Asylum University: Re-situating Knowledge-Exchange Along Cross-border Positionalities." In *Decolonising the University*, edited by Gurminder K. Bhambra, Dalia Gebrial, and Kerem Nisancıolu, 93–107. London: Pluto Press.

Apple, Michael W. 2000. *Official Knowledge: Democratic Education in a Conservative Age*. London: Routledge.

Apple, Michael W. and Linda Christian-Smith. 1991. *The Politics of the Textbook*. New York: Routledge.

Bank, Leslie John. 2019. *City of Broken Dreams: Myth-Making, Nationalism and the University in an African Motor City*. Cape Town: HSRC Press.

Behari-Leak, Kasturi and Goitsione Mokou. 2019. "Disrupting Metaphors of Coloniality to Mediate Social Inclusion in the Global South." *The International Journal for Academic Development* 24 (2): 135–147. https://doi.org/10.1080/1360144X.2019.1594236.

Benavot, Aaron. 2012. "Neo-Institutionalism in Education: An Emergent Paradigm and Its Critics." Presentation delivered at the Center for the Study of International Cooperation in Education, Hiroshima University, 23 February 2012. https://cice.hiroshima-u.ac.jp/wp-content/uploads/2014/06/147-handout.pdf.

Bester, Susan, Roxanne Bailey, and Josef de Beer. 2019. *The Decolonisation of the Curriculum Project: The Affordances of Indigenous Knowledge for Self-Directed Learning*. Cape Town: AOSIS.

Bettini, Yvette, Rebekah R. Brown, and Fjalar J. de Haan. 2015. "Exploring Institutional Adaptive Capacity in Practice: Examining Water Governance Adaptation in Australia." *Ecology and Society* 20 (1): 47. https://doi.org/10.5751/ES-07291-200147.

Bhabha, Homi. 1990. "The Third Space: An Interview with Homi Bhabha." In *Identity: Community, Culture, Difference*, edited by Jonathan Rutherford, 207–221. London: Lawrence & Wishart.

Blackmur, Douglas. 2007. "The Public Regulation of Higher Education Qualities: Rationale, Processes, and Outcomes." In *Quality Assurance in Higher Education: Trends in Regulation, Translation and Transformation*, edited by Don F. Westerheijden, Bjorn Stensaker, and Maria João Rosa, 15–45. Dordrecht: Springer.

Booysen, Susan. 2016. *Fees Must Fall: Student Revolt, Decolonisation and Governance in South Africa*. Johannesburg: Wits University Press.

Byrne, Deirdre. 2017. "Teaching and Researching Women's and Gender Studies in Post-apartheid South Africa." *Gender a Výzkum* 18 (1): 113–129. https://doi.org/10.13060/25706578.2017.18.1.352.

Cai, Yuzhuo and Yohannes Mehari. 2015. "The Use of Institutional Theory in Higher Education Research." In *Theory and Method in Higher*

Education Research, edited by Jeroen Husman and Malcolm Tight, 1–25. Bingley: Emerald Group Publishing Limited. https://doi.org/10.1108/S2056–375220150000001001.

Central University of Technology. 2018. "Decolonisation of Curriculum Continues at the 4th Annual SoTL Conference." www.cut.ac.za/news/decolonisation-of-curriculum-continues-at-the.

Centre for Community Technologies. 2019. "Communities Engaging in Smart Technology and Industry 4.0." Port Elizabeth: Nelson Mandela University.

CHE (Council on Higher Education). 2017a. "Decolonising the Curriculum: Stimulating Debate." Briefly Speaking, no. 3. 1 November 2017. www.che.ac.za/#/docview.

2017b. "Quality Enhancement Project Phase 2: Focus Area Curriculum." Pretoria: Council on Higher Education.

2018. "The State of the Provision of the Bachelor of Laws (LLB) Qualification in South Africa: Report." Pretoria: Council on Higher Education.

Cherrington, Avivit M., Marisa Botha, and André Keet. 2018. "Editorial: 'Decolonising' Education Transformation." *South African Journal of Education* 38 (4): 1–4. https://doi.org/10.15700/saje.v38n4editorial.

Chiang, Mina. 2017. "Decolonisation of Higher Education in South Africa: Case of Rhodes University." Institute for Development Studies, 6 December 2017. www.ids.ac.uk/opinions/decolonisation-of-higher-education-in-south-africa-case-of-rhodes-university/.

Chick, Kristen and Ryan Lenora Brown. 2019. "Art of the Steal: European Museums Wrestle with Returning African Art." *Christian Science Monitor*, 30 April 2019. www.csmonitor.com/World/Africa/2019/0430/Art-of-the-steal-European-museums-wrestle-with-returning-African-art.

Chiumbu, Sarah and Mehita Iqani. 2019. *Media Studies: Critical African and Decolonial Approaches*. Cape Town: Oxford University Press.

Choat, Simon. 2021. "Decolonising the Political Theory Curriculum." *Politics* 41 (3): 279–295. https://doi.org/10.1177/0263395720957543.

Chowdhury, Sunetra. 2018. "Comments from the UgTLC Members on the Discussion Document on a Curriculum Change Framework Which Was Released by the Curriculum Change Working Group (CCWG) on 28 June via the VC Desk." www.news.uct.ac.za/images/userfiles/downloads/media/2018-09-13_CurriculumChangeFramework_Engineering.pdf.

Combrink, Herkulaas M. v. E. and Lauren L. Oosthuizen. 2020. "First-Year Student Transition at the University of the Free State during Covid-19: Challenges and Insights." *Journal of Student Affairs in Africa* 8 (2): 31–44.

Commission of Inquiry into Higher Education and Training. 2017. *Report of the Commission of Enquiry into Higher Education and Training to the President of the Republic of South Africa*. Pretoria: The Presidency, Republic of South Africa.

Connell, Raewyn. 2016. "Decolonising Knowledge, Democratising Curriculum." Paper for the University of Johannesburg Discussions on Decolonisation of Knowledge, March 2016. www.uj.ac.za/faculties/humanities/sociology/PublishingImages/Pages/Seminars/Raewyn%20Connell's%20Paper%20on%20Decolonisation%20of%20Knowledge.pdf.

Conradie, Stephane, Elmarie Costandius, Sophia Sanan, Gera De Villiers, and Neeske Alexander. 2018. "Decolonising Spaces: Engaging with Visual Redress at Stellenbosch University." Paper presented at the South African Visual Arts Historians Conference Troubling Legacies, Stellenbosch, 4–6 July 2018.

Contraband Cape Town. 2015. "Luister." YouTube, 20 August 2015. www.youtube.com/watch?v=sF3rTBQTQk4.

Costandius, Elmarie. 2015a. "Exploring the Potential of Visual Art in Negotiating Social Transformation at Stellenbosch University." Presentation delivered at Stellenbosch University, 22 September 2015. www.slideshare.net/jakobp78/exploring-the-potential-of-visual-art-in-negotiating-social-transformation-at-stellenbosch-university.

———. 2015b. "Socially Just Pedagogy and Community Interaction: A Reflection on Practice." Paper presented at the Scholarship of Teaching and Learning Conference, University of Johannesburg, 27 August 2015.

———. 2019a. "Engaging with Visual Redress at Stellenbosch University: Decolonise Spaces." Presentation delivered at the Fourteenth International Conference on the Arts in Society, Polytechnic Institute of Lisbon, Lisbon, Portugal, 19–21 June 2019.

———. 2019b. "Exploring the Socio-political History of the Arts in Stellenbosch: A Contribution to Decolonise the Art Curriculum." Paper presented at the Fourteenth International Conference on The Arts in Society, Polytechnic Institute of Lisbon, Lisbon, Portugal, 19–21 June 2019.

Costandius, Elmarie and Eli Bitzer. 2015. "Engaging Curricula through Critical Citizenship Education: A Student Learning Perspective." In *Engaging Higher Education Curricula: A Critical Citizenship Perspective*, edited by Elmarie Costandius and Eli Bitzer, 55–72. Stellenbosch: African Sun Media.

Crawford, Brett and M. Tina Dacin. 2020. "Punishment and Institutions: A Macrofoundations Perspective." In *Macrofoundations: Exploring the Situated Nature of Activity*, edited by Christopher W. J. Steele, Timothy R. Hannigan, Vern L. Glaser, Madeline Toubiana, and Joel Gehman, 97–119. Bingley: Emerald Publishing Limited.

Crossan, Mary M., Henry W. Lane, Roderick E. White, and Lisa Djurfeldt. 1995. "Organizational Learning: Dimensions for a Theory." *International Journal of Organizational Analysis* 3 (4): 337–360. https://doi.org/10.1108/eb028835.

Cuban, Larry. 1998. "How Schools Change Reforms: Redefining Reform Success and Failure." *Teachers College Record* 99 (3): 453–477.

——— 1999. *How Scholars Trumped Teachers: Change without Reform in University Curriculum, Teaching, and Research, 1890–1990*. New York: Teachers College Press.

Curriculum Change Working Group. 2018. *Curriculum Change Framework*. Cape Town: University of Cape Town.

Czerniewicz, Laura, Henry Trotter, and Genevieve Haupt. 2019. "Online Teaching in Response to Student Protests and Campus Shutdowns: Academics' Perspectives." *International Journal of Educational Technology in Higher Education* 16 (1): 1–22. https://doi.org/10.1186/s41239-019-0170-1.

Davis, Dennis M. and Karl Klare. 2010. "Transformative Constitutionalism and the Common and Customary Law." *South African Journal on Human Rights* 26 (3): 403–509. https://doi.org/10.1080/19962126.2010.11864997.

Deever, Bryan. 1996. "If not Now, When? Radical Theory and Systemic Curriculum Reform." *Journal of Curriculum Studies* 28 (2): 171–191. https://doi.org/10.1080/0022027980280204.

Department of Archaeology, University of Cape Town. 2021. "AGE3011F: Roots of Black Identity." www.archaeology.uct.ac.za/age/courses/undergraduate.

DHET (Department of Higher Education and Training). 2015. "Higher Education on the Second Higher Education Summit." www.gov.za/speeches/2015-durban-statement-transformation-higher-education-17-oct-2015-0000#.

——— 2016. *Guidelines for Applications for PQM Clearance of New or Changed Academic Qualifications*. Pretoria: Department of Higher Education and Training.

Dlamini, Jacob. 2009. *Native Nostalgia*. Auckland Park: Jacana Media.

Douglas, Mary. 1986. *How Institutions Think*. Syracuse, NY: Syracuse University Press.

Eizadirad, Ardavan. 2019. "Decolonizing Educational Assessment Models." In *Decolonizing Educational Assessment: Ontario Elementary Students and the EQAO*, edited by Ardavan Eizadirad, 203–228. Cham: Palgrave Macmillan.

Ellis, George. 2018. "Comment on UCT Curriculum Change Framework," 10 October 2018. www.news.uct.ac.za/downloads/reports/ccwg/2018-10-10_CCF_Comment_EProfGeorgeEllis.pdf.

Etheridge, Jenna. 2018. "Decolonising Education: How One SA University Is Getting It Done." *News24*, 7 May 2018. www.news24.com/news24/ Analysis/decolonising-education-how-one-sa-university-is-getting-it-done-20180507.

Fatyela, Awethu and Darelle Van Greunen. 2017. "Decolonizing ICT: Can Technology Aid Fundamental Socio-Economic Transformation and Social Justice?" Paper presented at the Strategic Narratives Of Technology And Africa Conference, Madeira Interactive Technologies Institute, Funchal, Portugal, 1–2 September 2017. https://snta.m-iti.org/ index.php/snta/snta/paper/view/43.

Foster, William M. and Maxim Voronov. 2015. "Nostalgia and Subjectivity in Institutional Analysis." *Academy of Management Proceedings* 2015 (1): 12187. https://doi.org/10.5465/ambpp.2015.12187abstract.

Freire, Paulo. 1970. *Pedagogy of the Oppressed*. New York: Herder & Herder.

Galea, Sandro, Linda P. Fried, Julia R. Walker, Sasha Rudenstine, Jim W. Glover, and Melissa D. Begg. 2015. "Developing the New Columbia Core Curriculum: A Case Study in Managing Radical Curriculum Change." *American Journal of Public Health* 105 (S1): S17–S21. https://doi.org/10.2105/AJPH.2014.302470.

Gebrial, Dalia. 2018. "Rhodes Must Fall: Oxford and Movements for Change." In *Decolonizing the University*, edited by Gurminder K. Bhambra, Kerem Nişancıoğlu, and Dalia Gebrial, 19–36. London: Pluto Press.

Georgiades, William. 1980. "Curriculum Change: What Are the Ingredients?" *NASSP Bulletin* 64 (434): 70–75. https://doi.org/10 .1177/019263658006443414.

Gerber, Melissa. 2017. "Seeing Venus: 'Enfreakment' and Spectacle in Hendrik Hofmeyr's Saartjie." Paper presented at the 11th Annual South African Society for Research in Music Conference, School of Music and Conservatory, North-West University, Potchefstroom, 31 August–2 September 2017. www.academia.edu/40896249/Seeing_Venus_ Enfreakment_and_Spectacle_in_Hendrik_Hofmeyrs_Saartjie_2009.

Gerwel, Jakes. 1987. "Inaugural Address as Rector and Vice-Chancellor of the University of the Western Cape," Belville, 7 June 1987.

Goedgedacht Forum. 2018. "Decolonising Higher Education: The Lived Experience of Stellenbosch & Rhodes Pointing a Way to the Future." Forum, Cape Town, 26 April 2018.

Gordon, Lewis R. 2014. "Disciplinary Decadence and the Decolonisation of Knowledge." *Africa Development* 39 (1): 81–92.

Gordon, Robert. 1987. "Anthropology and Apartheid: The Rise of Military Ethnology in South Africa." *Cultural Survival Quarterly* 11 (4): 58.

Gordon, Robert J. 1982. "South Africa's Pact with the Bushmen." *Anthropology Resource Center Newsletter* 6 (1): 6.

Green, Lesley. 2020. *Rock | Water | Life: Ecology and Humanities for a Decolonial South Africa*. Durham, NC: Duke University Press.

Grosfoguel, Ramon. 2012. "The Dilemmas of Ethnic Studies in the United States: Between Liberal Multiculturalism, Identity Politics, Disciplinary Colonization, and Decolonial Epistemologies." *Human Architecture* 10 (1): 81.

GroundUp. 2017a. "UCT Invites 'Conspiracy Theorist' to Talk about Decolonisation of Science." *GroundUp*, 28 September 2017. www .groundup.org.za/article/uct-invites-conspiracy-theorist-talk-about-decolonisation-science/.

2017b. "UCT Trashed as Fee Protests Escalate." *GroundUp*, 2 November 2017. www.groundup.org.za/article/uct-trashed-fees-protests-escalate/.

Gruenspecht, Howard K. and Lester B. Lave. 1989. "The Economics of Health, Safety, and Environmental Regulation." In *Handbook of Industrial Organization*, edited by Richard Schmalensee, Robert D. Willig, Mark Armstrong, and Robert H. Porter, 1507–1550. Amsterdam: North-Holland.

Grundlingh, Albert. n.d. "The Battle of Andringa Street." Department of History, University of Stellenbosch. www.sun.ac.za/english/Documents/ Unsorted/The%20Battle%20of%20Andringa%20Street.pdf.

Habib, Adam. 2016. "The Politics of Spectacle – Reflections on the 2016 Student Protests." *Daily Maverick*, 5 December 2016. www .dailymaverick.co.za/article/2016-12-05-op-ed-the-politics-of-spectacle-reflections-on-the-2016-student-protests/.

2019. *Rebels and Rage: Reflecting on #FeesMustFall*. La Vergne: Jonathan Ball Publishers.

Habib, Adam and Shirona Patel. 2020. "Moribund Council on Higher Education Is Immobilising Academic Agility." *Daily Maverick*, 4 November 2020. www.dailymaverick.co.za/article/2020-11-04-mori bund-council-on-higher-education-is-immobilising-academic-agility/.

Hall, Richard, Lucy Ansley, Paris Connolly, Sumeya Loonat, Kaushika Patel, and Ben Whitham. 2021. "Struggling for the Anti-racist University: Learning from an Institution-Wide Response to Curriculum Decolonisation." *Teaching in Higher Education*: 1–18. https://doi.org/ 10.1080/13562517.2021.1911987.

Harding, Sandra. 2011. *The Postcolonial Science and Technology Studies Reader*. Durham, NC: Duke University Press.

Harrison, Faye V. 1992. "Decolonizing Anthropology: Moving Further toward an Anthropology for Liberation." *Anthropology News* 33 (3): 24–24. https://doi.org/10.1111/an.1992.33.3.24.

Harvey, Arlene and Gabrielle Russell-Mundine. 2019. "Decolonising the Curriculum: Using Graduate Qualities to Embed Indigenous Knowledges at the Academic Cultural Interface." *Teaching in Higher Education* 24 (6): 789–808. https://doi.org/10.1080/13562517.2018.1508131.

Hendricks, Cheryl. 2018. "Decolonising Universities in South Africa: Rigged Spaces?" *International Journal of African Renaissance Studies* 13 (1): 16–38. https://doi.org/10.1080/18186874.2018.1474990.

Howard, Gary R. 2016. *We Can't Teach What We Don't Know: White Teachers, Multiracial Schools*. New York: Teachers College Press.

Howard, Winant and Omi Michael. 2014. *Racial Formation in the United States*. London: Taylor & Francis.

HPCSA (Health Professions Council of South Africa). 1999. "Education and Training of Doctors in South Africa: Undergraduate Medical Education and Training." Pretoria: HPCSA.

2009. "Regulations Relating to the Registration of Students, Undergraduate Curricula and Professional Examinations in Medicine." Pretoria: HPCSA.

2015. "Questionnaire for Self-Assessment of Faculties/Schools for Undergraduate Education and Training of Medical Doctors, Dentists, And Clinical Associates." Pretoria: HPCSA.

Institute for Creative Arts, University of Cape Town. 2017. "The Second 3rd Space Symposium: Decolonising Art Institutions: Papers, Disruptions, Performances, Interventions." Cape Town, 24–26 August 2017.

Institutional Transformation Committee. 2017. "Transformation Plan of Stellenbosch University." Stellenbosch: Stellenbosch University.

Isaac, A. Kamola. 2011. "Pursuing Excellence in a 'World-Class African University': The Mamdani Affair and the Politics of Global Higher Education." *Journal of Higher Education in Africa* 9 (1–2): 147–168.

Jablonski, Nina G., ed. 2020. *Persistence of Race*. Stellenbosch: African Sun Media.

James, Frances. 2020. "Why We Need to Talk About the Decolonization of Higher Education." *QS Quacquarelli Symonds* (blog). 19 January 2020. www.qs.com/why-we-need-to-talk-about-the-decolonization-of-higher-education/.

Jansen, Jonathan D. 2002. "Political Symbolism as Policy Craft: Explaining Non-reform in South African Education after Apartheid." *Journal of Education Policy* 17 (2): 199–215. https://doi.org/10.1080/02680930110116534.

2009. *Knowledge in the Blood: Confronting Race and the Apartheid Past*. Stanford, CA: Stanford University Press.

2016. *Leading for Change: Race, Intimacy and Leadership on Divided University Campuses*. Abingdon: Routledge.

2017. *As by Fire: The End of the South African University*. Cape Town: Tafelberg.

2019. *Decolonisation in Universities: The Politics of Knowledge*. Johannesburg: Witwatersrand University Press.

Jansen, Jonathan and Samantha Kriger. 2020. *Who Gets in and Why: Race, Class and Aspiration in South Africa's Elite Schools*. Cape Town: UCT Press.

Jansen, Jonathan D. and Cyrill Walters, eds. 2020a. *Fault Lines: A Primer on Race, Science and Society*. Stellenbosch: African Sun Media.

2020b. "A Century of Misery Research on Coloured People." In *Fault Lines: A Primer on Race, Science and Society*, Jonathan D. Jansen and Cyrill Walters, 73–91. Stellenbosch: African Sun Media.

Jippes, Mariëlle, Erik W. Driessen, Nick J. Broers, Gerard D. Majoor, Wim H. Gijselaers, and Cees PM van der Vleuten. 2015. "Culture Matters in Successful Curriculum Change: An International Study of the Influence of National and Organizational Culture Tested with Multilevel Structural Equation Modeling." *Academic Medicine* 90 (7): 921–929. https://doi.org/10.1097/ACM.0000000000000687.

Johansson, Stefan and Rolf Strietholt. 2019. "Globalised Student Achievement? A Longitudinal and Cross-Country Analysis of Convergence in Mathematics Performance." *Comparative Education* 55 (4): 536–556. https://doi.org/10.1080/03050068.2019.1657711.

Jónasson, Jón Torfi. 2016. "Educational Change, Inertia and Potential Futures: Why Is it Difficult to Change the Content of Education?" *European Journal of Futures Research* 4 (1): 1–14. https://doi.org/10.1007/s40309-016-0087-z.

Jonker, Anita. 2020. "Unlearning Race: The 'Introduction to the Humanities' Curriculum at Stellenbosch University." In *Fault Lines: A Primer on Race, Science and Society*, edited by Jonathan D. Jansen and Cyrill Walters, 237–249. Stellenbosch: African Sun Media.

Joseph, Pamela Bolotin. 2012. *Cultures of Curriculum*. New York: Routledge.

Kabir, Ananya Jahanara and Elina Djebbari. 2019. "Dance and Decolonisation in Africa: Introduction." *Journal of African Cultural Studies* 31 (3): 314–317. https://doi.org/10.1080/13696815.2019.1632173.

Kasoma, Francis P. 1996. "The Foundations of African Ethics (Afriethics) and the Professional Practice of Journalism: The Case for Society-Centred Media Morality." *Africa Media Review* 10: 93–116.

Keet, André. 2014. "Epistemic Othering and the Decolonisation of Knowledge." *Africa Insight* 44 (1): 23–37.

Khasnabish, Alex and Max Haiven. 2014. "Why Social Movements Need the Radical Imagination." *Open Democracy*, 22 July 2014. www .opendemocracy.net/en/transformation/why-social-movements-need-radical-imagination/.

Kister, Ulrike. 2021. "Funda-mentalities: Pedagogic Twists and Turns in South African Philosophy (of Education)." In *Decolonisation as Democratization: Global Insights into the South African Experience*, edited by Siseko Khumalo. Pretoria: HSRC Press.

Klare, Karl E. 1998. "Legal Culture and Transformative Constitutionalism." *South African Journal on Human Rights* 14 (1): 146–188. https://doi .org/10.1080/02587203.1998.11834974.

Krige, Nadia. 2019. "Unpacking the Achievement Gap." *UCT News*, 2 October 2019. www.news.uct.ac.za/article/-2019-10-02-unpacking-the-achievement-gap.

Kruger, Nicklaus. 2018. "Science Deans Forum: Decolonising Science, Determining Knowledge and Developing Graduates." University of the Western Cape. www.uwc.ac.za/news-and-announcements/news/science-deans-forum-decolonising-science-determining-knowledge-and-develop ing-graduates-508.

Kuhn, Thomas. (1962) 2012. *The Structure of Scientific Revolutions*. Chicago: University of Chicago Press.

Kulundu, Injairu, Dylan Kenneth McGarry, and Heila Lotz-Sisitka. 2020. "Think Piece: Learning, Living and Leading into Transgression: A reflection on Decolonial Praxis in a Neoliberal World." *Southern African Journal of Environmental Education* 36 (2020): 111–130. https://doi.org/10.4314/sajee.v36i1.14.

Lalu, Premesh and Noëleen Murray. 2012. *Becoming UWC: Reflections, Pathways and Unmaking Apartheid's Legacy*. Bellville: Centre for Humanities Research, University of the Western Cape.

Lambert, John. 2004. "'Munition Factories … Turning out a Constant Supply of Living Material': White South African Elite Boys' Schools and the First World War." *South African Historical Journal* 51 (1): 67–86. https://doi.org/10.1080/02582470409464830.

Langa, Malose. 2017. *#Hashtag: An Analysis of the #FeesMustFall Movement at South African Universities*. Johannesburg: Centre for the Study of Violence and Reconciliation.

Lange, Lis. 2017. "20 Years of higher education curriculum policy in South Africa." *Journal of Education* 68: 31–57.

Le Grange, Lesley. 2020. "Could the Covid-19 Pandemic Accelerate the Uberfication of the University?" *South African Journal of Higher Education* 34 (4): 1–10. https://doi.org/10.20853/34-4-4071.

Le Grange, Lesley, Petro Du Preez, Labby Ramrathan, and Sylvan Blignaut. 2020. "Decolonising the University Curriculum or Decolonial-Washing? A Multiple Case Study." *Journal of Education* (80): 25–48. http://dx.doi.org/10.17159/2520-9868/i80a02.

Lerch, Julia, Patricia Bromley, Francisco O. Ramirez, and John W. Meyer. 2017. "The Rise of Individual Agency in Conceptions of Society: Textbooks Worldwide, 1950–2011." *International Sociology* 32 (1): 38–60. https://doi.org/10.1177/0268580916675525.

Lilley, Andrew. 2018. "Comment on CCWG Document: South African College of Music (SACM) Jazz." www.news.uct.ac.za/downloads/reports/ccwg/Comment_CCWG_AndrewLilley.pdf.

Liyanage, Mia. 2020. "Miseducation: Decolonising Curricula, Culture And Pedagogy in UK Universities." HEPI Debate paper 23. Oxford: Higher Education Policy Institute.

Long, Wahbie. 2021. *Nation on the Couch: Inside the Mind of South Africa.* Cape Town: MF Books.

Mahoney, James and Kathleen Thelen. 2009. *Explaining Institutional Change: Ambiguity, Agency, and Power.* New York: Cambridge University Press.

Malabela, Musawenkosi. 2017. "We Are Already Enjoying Free Education: Protests at the University of Limpopo (Turfloop)." In *#Hashtag: An analysis of the #FeesMustFall Movement at South African Universities,* edited by Malose Langa, 108–120. Johannesburg: Centre for the Study of Violence and Reconciliation

Mamdani, Mahmood. 2019. "Decolonising Universities." In *Decolonisation in Universities: The Politics of Knowledge,* edited by Jonathan D. Jansen, 15–28. Johannesburg: Witwatersrand University Press.

March, James G. and Johan P. Olsen. 1983. "The New Institutionalism: Organizational Factors in Political Life." *The American Political Science Review* 78 (3): 734–749. https://doi.org/10.2307/1961840.

——— 2010. *Rediscovering Institutions: The Organizational Basis of Politics.* New York: Simon and Schuster.

Marchbank, Jen. 2009. "'Ding, Dong, the Witch Is Dead, the Wicked Witch Is Dead': The Reported Demise of Women's Studies in the United Kingdom." *Feminist Studies* 35 (1): 194.

Martin, William G. 2011. "The Rise of African Studies (USA) and the Transnational Study of Africa." *African Studies Review* 54 (1): 59–83. https://doi.org/10.1353/arw.2011.0003.

Mather, Ruth. 2015. "Teaching on a Moving Train: Curriculum Bias & Radical Curriculum Change." *History Workshop Online,* 22 June 2015. www.historyworkshop.org.uk/teaching-on-a-moving-train-curriculum-bias-radical-curriculum-change/.

Maton, Karl. 2014. *Knowledge and Knowers: Towards a Realist Sociology of Education*. Abingdon: Routledge.

Matthews, Sally. 2018. "Confronting the Colonial Library: Teaching Political Studies Amidst Calls for a Decolonised Curriculum." *Politikon* 45 (1): 48–65. https://doi.org/10.1080/02589346.2018.1418204.

Mayaba, Nokhanyo Nomakhwezi, Monwabisi K. Ralarala, and Pineteh Angu. 2018. "Student Voice: Perspectives on Language and Critical Pedagogy in South African Higher Education." *Educational Research for Social Change* 7 (1): 1–12. https://doi.org/10.17159/2221-4070/2018/v7i1a1.

Mbembe, Achille Joseph. 2016. "Decolonizing the University: New Directions." *Arts and Humanities in Higher Education* 15 (1): 29–45. https://doi.org/10.1177/1474022215618513.

Meyer, Heinz-Dieter and Brian Rowan. 2006. "Institutional Analysis and the Study of Education." In *The New Institutionalism in Education*, edited by Heinz-Dieter Meyer and Brian Rowan, 1–13. Albany, NY: SUNY Press.

Meyer, John W. and Brian Rowan. 1977. "Institutionalized Organizations: Formal Structure as Myth and Ceremony." *The American Journal of Sociology* 83 (2): 340–363. https://doi.org/10.1086/226550.

Miles, Matthew B., M. Ekholm, and Roland Vandenberghe. 1987. *Lasting School Improvement: Exploring the Process of Institutionalization*. Paris: Organisation for Economic Co-operation and Development.

Mill, David. 1987. "SADF's Bushmen: Desert Nomads on SWAPO's Track." *Soldier of Fortune*, January 1987, 32–37.

Mkhumbuzi, Busisiwe. 2016. "Email to Professor David Benatar." Facebook, 13 April 2016.

Mlamla, Sisonke. 2020. "Stellenbosch University Forges Ahead with Its Decolonisation Drive." *Cape Argus*, 20 February 2020. www.iol.co.za/capeargus/news/stellenbosch-university-forges-ahead-with-its-decolonisation-drive-43055870.

Modiri, Joel. 2020. "The Aporias of 'Decolonisation' in the South African Academy." In *From Ivory Towers to Ebony Towers: Transforming Humanities Curricula in South Africa and African-American Studies*, edited by Oluwaseun Tella and Shireen Motala, 157–173. Auckland Park: Fanele.

Moeke-Pickering, Taima Materangatira. 2010. "Decolonisation as a Social Change Framework and Its Impact on the Development of Indigenous-Based Curricula for Helping Professionals in Mainstream Tertiary Education Organisations. PhD diss., University of Waikato."

Moore, Kate-Lyn. 2017. "The Art of Decolonisation." *UCT News* 24 August 2017. www.news.uct.ac.za/article/-2017-08-24-the-art-of-decolonisation.

Morreira, Shannon and Kathy Luckett. 2018. "Questions Academics Can Ask to Decolonise Their Classrooms." *The Conversation* 17 October 2018. https://theconversation.com/questions-academics-can-ask-to-decolonise-their-classrooms-103251.

Morreira, Shannon, Kathy Luckett, Siseko H. Kumalo, and Manjeet Ramgotra. 2020. "Confronting the Complexities of Decolonising Curricula and Pedagogy in Higher Education." *Third World Thematics* 5 (1–2): 1–18. https://doi.org/10.1080/23802014.2020.1798278.

Mosia, N. Themba. 2020. "'We Are Not Moribund' – Council on Higher Education Responds to Adam Habib and Shirona Patel." *Daily Maverick*, 12 November 2020. www.dailymaverick.co.za/article/2020-11-12-we-are-not-moribund-council-on-higher-education-responds-to-adam-habib-and-shirona-patel/.

Muldoon, James. 2019. "Academics: It's Time to Get Behind Decolonising the Curriculum." *The Guardian*, 20 March 2019. www.theguardian.com/education/2019/mar/20/academics-its-time-to-get-behind-decolonising-the-curriculum.

Myburgh, James. 2020. "The Fallist and the Professor." *Politicsweb*, 30 April 2020. www.politicsweb.co.za/opinion/the-fallist-and-the-professor.

National Government of South Africa. 2021. "Council on Higher Education (CHE)." https://nationalgovernment.co.za/units/view/90/council-on-higher-education-che.

Ndelu, Sandile. 2017. "'Liberation Is a Falsehood': Fallism at the University of Cape Town." In *#Hashtag: An Analysis of the# FeesMustFall Movement at South African Universities*, edited by Malose Langa, 58–82. Johannesburg: Centre for the Study of Violence and Reconciliation.

Ndlovu-Gatsheni, Sabelo J. 2018. *Meanings and Implications of Decolonization for Higher Education in South Africa.* Pretoria: University of South Africa Press.

Nelson Mandela University. 2017. *Toward a Curriculum Framework Workshop 2.* Port Elizabeth: Nelson Mandela University.

2018. *Curriculum Principles Workshop 3: Drafting the Curriculum Statements.* Port Elizabeth: Nelson Mandela University.

New School for Social Research. 2021. "Our History." www.newschool.edu/nssr/history/.

Noah, Trevor. 2019. *Born a Crime.* Johannesburg: Pan Macmillan.

Nordin, Andreas and Daniel Sundberg. 2016. "Travelling Concepts in National Curriculum Policy-Making: The Example of Competencies." *European Educational Research Journal* 15 (3): 314–328. https://doi.org/10.1177/1474904116641697.

2018. "Exploring Curriculum Change Using Discursive Institutionalism: A Conceptual Framework." *Journal of Curriculum Studies* 50 (6): 820–835. https://doi.org/10.1080/00220272.2018.1482961.

Nzimande, Blade. 2015. Speech by Minister Blade Nzimande at the Higher Education Summit Held at the Inkosi Albert Luthuli ICC, Durban, 15 October 2015.

O'Malley, Katie. 2020. "The 'Decolonise The Curriculum' Movement Goes from Strength to Strength, in the Hands of UK's Youth." *Elle*, 21 October 2020.

O'Neill, Paul, Lucy Steeds, and Mick Wilson. 2017. *How Institutions Think: Between Contemporary Art and Curatorial Discourse*. Feldmeilen, Switzerland: LUMA Foundation.

Peters, Michael Adrian. 2018. "Why Is My Curriculum White? A Brief Genealogy of Resistance." In *Dismantling Race in Higher Education: Racism, Whiteness and Decolonising the Academy*, edited by Jason Arday and Heidi Safia Mirza, 253–270. Cham: Springer.

Pikirayi, Innocent. 2017. "Listening to Great Zimbabwe's Local Histories and Its Toponyms." *SAA Archaeological Record* 17 (4): 33–34. http://onlinedigeditions.com/publication/?m=16146&i=440506&view=articleBrowser&article_id=2888941.

Pinar, William F., William M. Reynolds, Patrick Slattery, and Peter M. Taubman. 1995. "Understanding Curriculum as Institutionalized Text." In *Understanding Curriculum: An Introduction to the Study of Historical and Contemporary Curriculum Discourses*, edited by William F. Pinar, 661–791. New York: Peter Lang.

Pithouse, Richard. 2016. "Violence: What Fanon really said." *Mail & Guardian*, 7 April 2016. https://mg.co.za/article/2016-04-07-violence-what-fanon-really-said/.

Powell, Walter W. and Paul DiMaggio. 1991. *The New Institutionalism in Organizational Analysis*. Chicago: University of Chicago Press.

Praeg, Leonhard. 2016. "Just teaching: A proposal for engaged decoloniality." Presentation at the Department of Philosophy, University of Pretoria Lekgotla, Pretoria, 12–13 July 2016.

2017. "Just Thinking." A Modified Version of Keynote Address to the University of Pretoria's 2017 Humanities Faculty Postgraduate Conference, Pretoria.

Pressley, Nelson. 2016. "Notes on Political Theater: The Perils of Spectacle." *Washington Post*, 18 November 2016. www.washingtonpost.com/entertainment/theater_dance/notes-on-political-theater-the-perils-of-spectacle/2016/11/18/1c48c088-aa92-11e6-977a-1030f822fc35_story.html.

Priestley, Mark. 2011. "Whatever Happened to Curriculum Theory? Critical Realism and Curriculum Change." *Pedagogy, Culture & Society* 19 (2): 221–237. https://doi.org/10.1080/14681366.2011.582258.

Progress SA. 2019. "Please Don't Introduce a Colour Bar for Teaching at UCT: An Open Letter to VC Phakeng on the Curriculum Change Framework." *Politicsweb*, 20 February 2019. www.politicsweb.co.za/comment/please-dont-introduce-a-colour-bar-for-teaching-at.

Rauch, Jonathan. 2018. "The Constitution of Knowledge." *National Affairs*, no. 37. www.nationalaffairs.com/publications/detail/the-constitution-of-knowledge.

Rauch van der Merwe, Tania. 2019. "The Political Construction of Occupational Therapy in South Africa: Critical Analysis of a Curriculum as Discourse." PhD diss., University of the Free State, 2019.

Reid, William A. 1999. *Curriculum as Institution and Practice: Essays in the Deliberative Tradition.* Mahwah, NJ: Erlbaum.

Republic of South Africa. 2008. "National Qualifications Framework Act No. 67 of 2008". Pretoria: Republic of South Africa.

2016. "Proclamation no. 1 of 2016 by the President of the Republic of South Africa: Establishment of a Commission of Inquiry into Higher Education and Training." www.justice.gov.za/commissions/FeesHET/docs/20160122-gg39608-Proc01-CommHighEducTraining.pdf.

Rhodes University. 2016a. "A Proposal for a Curriculum Review at Rhodes University." A proposal presented by Chrisie Boughey, DVC Academic and Student Affairs. Grahamstown: Rhodes University.

2016b. "Curriculum in the context of transformation: Reframing traditional understanding and practices." Grahamstown: Rhodes University.

2017. "Rhodes University Transformation Summit: Envisioning an Institutional Transformed." Grahamstown: Rhodes University.

Richards, Howard. 2011. "Human Development and the Transformation of the Academy." *Journal of Developing Societies* 27 (2): 201–206. https://doi.org/10.1177/0169796X1102700205.

Rosenberg, Eureta and Lesley Le Grange. 2020. "Attitudinal Difference Surveys Perpetuate Harmful Tropes: A Comment on Nattrass." *South African Journal of Science* 116 (art.8469): 1–7. https://doi.org/10.17159/sajs.2020/8469.

Roux, Theunis. 2009. "Transformative Constitutionalism and the Best Interpretation of the South African Constitution: Distinction Without a Difference?" *Stellenbosch Law Review* 20 (2): 258–285.

Saini, Rima and Neema Begum. 2020. "Demarcation and Definition: Explicating the Meaning and Scope of 'Decolonisation' in the Social and Political Sciences." *The Political Quarterly* 91 (1): 217–221. https://doi.org/10.1111/1467-923X.12797.

Sandmeier, Rebekka. 2018. "Letter to DVC: Transformation, Prof Loretta Feris, and DVC: Teaching and Learning, A/Prof Lis Lange." 31 July 2018. www.news.uct.ac.za/images/userfiles/downloads/media/2018-07-31_CurriculumChangeFramework_SACM.pdf.

SAQA (South African Qualifications Authority). 2013. "Policy and Criteria for the Registration of Qualifications and Part Qualifications on the National Qualifications Framework." Pretoria: SAQA.

———. 2014. "NQF Implementation Framework 2015-2020." Pretoria: Pretoria: SAQA.

———. 2015. "NQF Implementation Framework 2015-2020." Pretoria: SAQA

———. 2017. "Summary of Conceptualisation and Debates on Decolonization, v.1." Pretoria: SAQA.

———. 2018a. "SAQA Colloquium 'Decolonisation and the NQF: Way Forward': Report." Pretoria: SAQA.

———. 2018b. "SAQA's Position on Decolonisation: SAQA Statement." Pretoria: SAQA.

———. 2018c. "SAQA's Research Agenda." Pretoria: SAQA.

———. 2018d. "Towards Understanding Africanisation: Notes from SAQA's Colloquium on Decolonisation, February 13, 2018." Pretoria: SAQA.

———. 2020. "Policy and Criteria for Recognising a Professional Body and Registering a Professional Designation for the Purposes of the National Qualifications Framework Act, Act 67 of 2008 (As Amended, 2020)." Pretoria: SAQA.

Schiebinger, Londa and Claudia Swan. 2007. *Colonial Botany: Science, Commerce, and Politics in the Early Modern World*. Philadelphia: University of Pennsylvania Press.

Schmahmann, Brenda. 2019. "Public Art and/as Curricula: Seeking a New Role for Monuments Associated with Oppression." In *Decolonisation in Universities: The Politics of Knowledge*, edited by Jonathan Jansen, 182–201. Johannesburg: Wits University Press.

Senne, Busang. 2017. "Why Are Women Getting Naked In The #Feesmustfall Protests?" *Cosmopolitan*.

Shay, Suellen. 2016. "Decolonising the Curriculum: It's Time for a Strategy." *The Conversation*, 13 June 2016. https://theconversation.com/decolonising-the-curriculum-its-time-for-a-strategy-60598.

Soudien, Crain. 2019. "Testing Transgressive Thinking: The 'Learning through Enlargement' Initiative at UNISA." In *Decolonisation in Universities: The Politics of Knowledge*, edited by Jonathan Jansen, 136–154. Johannesburg: Wits University Press.

South African Congress Alliance. 1955. "The Freedom Charter." www .sahistory.org.za/archive/freedom-charter-original-document-scan.

South African San Institute. 2017. "San Code of Research Ethics." www .globalcodeofconduct.org/wp-content/uploads/2018/04/San-Code-of-RESEARCH-Ethics-Booklet_English.pdf.

Stein, Sharon, Vanessa Andreotti, Dallas Hunt, and Cash Ahenakew. 2021. "Complexities and Challenges of Decolonising Higher Education: Lessons from Africa." In *Decolonisation as Democratisation: Global Insights into the South African Experience*, edited by Siseko H. Kumalo, 48–65. Pretoria: HSRC Press.

Stellenbosch University. 2017a. "In Search of Parameters for the Imperative of the Decolonisation of the Curriculum." Stellenbosch: Stellenbosch University.

———. 2017b. "Recommendations of the Task Team for the Decolonisation of the Stellenbosch University Curriculum." Stellenbosch: Stellenbosch University.

———. 2020a. "Contributions to the Rector's Management Report to Senate & Council (2020)." Stellenbosch: Stellenbosch University.

———. 2020b. "Submission of a New Programme: Form A – Programme Information." Stellenbosch: Stellenbosch University. www.sun.ac.za/english/learning-teaching/ctl/Documents/FORM%20A_Submission%20of%20a%20new%20programme%202017.doc.

Stoler, Ann Laura. 2016. *Duress: Imperial Durabilities in Our Times.* Durham, NC: Duke University Press.

Strauss, Helene. 2014. "Spectacles of Promise and Disappointment: Political Emotion and Quotidian Aesthetics in Video Installations by Berni Searle and Zanele Muholi." *Safundi* 15 (4): 471–495. https://doi.org/10.1080/17533171.2014.926196.

Swartz, Leslie, Cheryl De la Rey, Norman Duncan, Loraine Townsend, and Vivien O'Neill. 2016. *Psychology: An Introduction.* 4th ed. Cape Town: Oxford University Press.

Tabata, Isaac Bangani. 1960. *Education for Barbarism: Bantu Education in South Africa.* London: Pall Mall Press.

Thakur, Vineet and Peter C. J. Vale. 2020. *South Africa, Race and the Making of International Relations.* London: Rowman & Littlefield International.

Tomaselli, Keyan G. 2015. "Hacking through Academementia: Autoethnography, Data and Social Change." *Educational Research for Social Change* 4 (2): 61.

Tuck, Eve and K. Wayne Yang. 2012. "Decolonization Is not a Metaphor." *Decolonization: Indigeneity, Education & Society* 1 (1): 1–40. https://jps.library.utoronto.ca/index.php/des/article/view/18630/15554.

UCT Scientist. 2016. "Science Must Fall?" YouTube, 16 October 2016. www.youtube.com/watch/C9SiRNibD14.

University of Cape Town. 2010. "Social Responsiveness Report 2010." Cape Town: University of Cape Town.

——— 2017. "Curriculum Change Review, Science Faculty Curriculum Transformation Discussion." Cape Town: University of Cape Town.

University of Johannesburg. 2016. "Guidelines for Curriculum Transformation." In *Report on Decolonisation*, 16–18. Johannesburg: University of Johannesburg.

——— 2017. "Charter on Decolonisation: Purpose, Principles and Practice." Johannesburg: University of Johannesburg.

University of KwaZulu-Natal. 2019. "Center of Study and Investigation for Decolonial, Course Description and Programme." Durban, 21–26 January 2019. Durban: UKZN.

University of Pretoria. 2016a. "Draft Framework Document: Reimagining Curricula for a Just University in a Vibrant Democracy." Pretoria: University of Pretoria.

——— 2016b. "Unsettling Paradigms: The Decolonial Turn in the Humanities Curriculum at Universities in South Africa." Pretoria: University of Pretoria. www.up.ac.za/unsettlingparadigms.

——— 2018. "Teaching and Learning Review 2018." Pretoria: University of Pretoria.

University of the Western Cape. 2016. "Response to the List of Student Demands." Bellville: University of the Western Cape.

UWCFeesWillFall. 2016. A Memorandum of Demands to the University of the Western Cape, 27 September 2016.

Van Marle, Karin. 2009. "Transformative Constitutionalism as/and Critique." *Stellenbosch Law Review* 20 (2): 286–301.

Van Staden, Martin. 2019. "The dangers of 'transformative constitutionalism'." *Politicsweb*, 19 June 2019. www.politicsweb.co.za/opinion/the-dangers-of-transformative-constitutionalism.

Vandeyar, Saloshna. 2020. "Why Decolonising the South African University Curriculum Will Fail." *Teaching in Higher Education* 25 (7): 783–796. https://doi.org/10.1080/13562517.2019.1592149.

Vilakazi, Marcia. 2017. "Tshwane University of Technology: Soshanguve Campus Protests Cannot Be Reduced to #FeesMustFall." In *#Hashtag: An Analysis of the #FeesMustFall Movement at South African Universities*, edited by Malose Langa, 49–57. Johannesburg: Centre for the Study of Violence and Reconciliation.

Vorster, Jo-Anne. 2016. *Curriculum in the Context of Transformation: Reframing Traditional Understanding and Practices*. Grahamstown:

Centre for Higher Education Research, Teaching and Learning, Rhodes University.

Waks, Leonard J. 2007. "The Concept of Fundamental Educational Change." *Educational Theory* 57 (3): 277–295. https://doi.org/10.1111/j.1741-5446.2007.00257.x.

Walters, Shirley. 2018. "Working the 'In-Between-Spaces' for Transformation within the Academy." *South African Journal of Education* 38 (4): 1–9. https://doi.org/10.15700/saje.v38n4a1700.

Wiseman, Alexander W., M. Fernanda Astiz, and David P. Baker. 2014. "Comparative Education Research Framed by Neo-Institutional Theory: A Review of Diverse Approaches and Conflicting Assumptions." *Compare* 44 (5): 688–709. https://doi.org/10.1080/03057925.2013.800783.

World Café. 2021. "Method." www.theworldcafe.com/key-concepts-resources/world-cafe-method/.

Zawada, Britta. 2020. "Invisible Statues of Colonisation: Regulatory Curriculum Requirements in South African Higher Education." *Africa Education Review* 17 (3): 142–157. https://doi.org/10.1080/18146627.2019.1683457.

Index

Made in the USA
Las Vegas, NV
26 July 2022

52174533R00153